D1649139

INTOLERANCE
AND THE
GOSPEL

INTOLERANCE
AND THE
GOSPEL

SELECTED TEXTS FROM THE
NEW TESTAMENT

GERD LÜDEMANN
Assisted by Tom Hall

 Prometheus Books
59 John Glenn Drive
Amherst, New York 14228–2197

Published 2007 by Prometheus Books

Inquiries should be addressed to
Prometheus Books
59 John Glenn Drive
Amherst, New York 14228–2197
VOICE: 716–691–0133, ext. 207
FAX: 716–564–2711
WWW.PROMETHEUSBOOKS.COM

11 10 09 08 07   5 4 3 2 1

Library of Congress Cataloging-in-Publication Data

Lüdemann, Gerd.
    Intolerance and the Gospel : selected texts from the New Testament / Gerd Lüdemann.
        p. cm.
    Includes bibliographical references and index.
    ISBN-13: 978-1-59102-468-2 (hardcover: alk. paper)
    ISBN-10: 1-59102-468-4 (hardcover: alk. paper)
    Religious tolerance—Biblical teaching. 2 Bible. N.T.—Criticism, interpretation, etc. 3. Religious tolerance—Christianity—History of doctrines. I. Title.

BS2545.R45L8313 2006
261.2—dc22   2006022896

Printed in the United States of America on acid-free paper

CONTENTS

PREFACE

A little over 125 years ago, Friedrich Nietzsche offered a scathing assessment of Christianity, one that has of late become increasingly recognized for its essential validity:

> *Christianity as antiquity.* When we hear the ancient bells growling on a Sunday morning we ask ourselves: is it really possible! this for a Jew, crucified two thousand years ago, who said he was God's son. The proof of such a claim is lacking. Certainly the Christian religion is an antiquity projected into our times from remote prehistory; and the fact that the claim is believed—whereas one is otherwise so strict in examining pretensions—is perhaps the most ancient piece of this heritage. A god who begets children with a mortal woman; a sage who bids men to work no more, have no more courts, but look for the signs of the impending end of the world; a justice that accepts the innocent as a vicarious sacrifice; someone who orders his disciples to drink his blood; prayers for miraculous interventions; sins perpetrated against a god, atoned for by a god; fear of a beyond to which death is the portal; the form of the cross as a symbol in a time that no longer knows the function and the ignominy of the cross—how ghoulishly all this touches us, as if from the tomb of a primeval past! Can one believe that such things are still believed?[1]

This book is the English edition of my *Die Intoleranz des Evangeliums. Erläutert an ausgewählten Schriften des Neuen Testaments* (Springe: zu Klampen, 2004). It represents a thorough reworking of that text with some new ideas. I have also omitted elements specifically related to the German situation of church and theology and added details related to theological discussions in North America. Unless otherwise indicated, the translations are my own. I have employed underlines, italics, boldface, and capitals to stress repetitions of keywords and ideas in an attempt to foster a close and discerning reading of the text.

The present study is rooted in the best traditions of freethought and Protestant theology and for that reason seeks to offer to the concerned and literate public a clear and plausible presentation of its results and

7

mode of procedure. For such methodological details see the introduction. Chapter I deals with the idea of intolerance and the nature of intolerance in both the Old Testament and Jewish spheres of influence, and the Greco-Roman world. Chapters II–V comment on selected New Testament writings. I have written every chapter in such a way that it can stand on its own as well as constituting a part of the argument as a whole. The epilogue lays out the consequences of my study for the Christian churches and our society. Appendices 1–4 deepen the train of thought of the book in specific ways. Appendix 5 is the English version of an essay ("The Intolerant Gospel") that originally appeared in a German newspaper. I recommend it as an introduction to the overall topic addressed by this book and as a summary of my arguments.

Apart from the aforementioned points, let me spell out two main goals of the book: my intent is to introduce selected New Testament texts in such a way as to lay bare their ancient purposes and meanings. To this end I had not only to wrench the various texts loose from their assumed context in the past, but also to deal with them apart from the canon of Holy Scripture, which assigned them to the exalted sphere of an eternal rule for the church. For I wish to explain them to interested contemporaries, and thus further contribute to the unveiling of Primitive Christianity. Needless to say, in the course of a thorough historical analysis the human relevance of these texts should also become transparent.

This book therefore aims to demonstrate the high degree of relevance of these ancient writings for the present day. Indeed, it was because of a rigid intolerance rooted in theological assumptions that the various writings of the New Testament willy-nilly produced many of the dogmatic and ideological problems that plague contemporary Christian churches. On the one hand the pastors of most churches are more or less obliged to base their preaching on the Bible and such equally exclusivist doctrinal formulas as the Apostles' Creed. And yet the churches claim to make an important contribution to democracy and to be reliable partners in the defense of modern political institutions which are based on human rights and religious freedom—that is, they must at least espouse tolerance. From this at least implicit conflict arises the troubling question of whether the intolerance of Bible and creed can be harmonized with life in the necessarily pluralistic modern state.

The staff of Vanderbilt Divinity School library made every possible effort to get me the books that I needed. I am grateful to Frank Schleritt, Walter Höfig, and Alf Özen for helping me at various stages of the preparation of the manuscript. My good friend Tom Hall has seen the project through from beginning to end.

Gerd Lüdemann
Göttingen, Germany
July 5, 2006

NOTE

1. Friedrich Nietzsche, *Human, All-Too Human*, sec. 113, in *The Portable Nietzsche*, ed. Walter Kaufmann (New York: Viking Press, 1954), pp. 52–53.

INTRODUCTION

Method and Purpose

One disagreeable aspect of my lifelong concern for the truth is having discussions with theologians come to a stop at crucial points: they suddenly fall silent, make meaningless replies, change the subject, interject a priori assertions, or reply affably but without responding to what one has just said—and indeed seeming to have no real interest in it. This results not only from the chilling certitude of their concept of truth, but from a sense that it is not worth their trouble to be bothered with us stubborn people. But true dialogue requires attention and relevant answers; it cannot accept silence or elusiveness; above all, it demands that all faith statements—which after all are couched in human language, directed at objects, and intended to elucidate the world—must be open to examination and re-examination, not only factually but also inferentially. Those who consider themselves to have unassailable possession of the truth are unable to talk meaningfully with others; they have already sacrificed communication on the altar of dogmatic belief.[1]

—Karl Jaspers

TOLERANCE AND THE GOD OF THE BIBLE— A CONTRADICTION

To teach our children tolerance—the ability to "allow (something that you dislike or disagree with) to exist or to occur without interference"[2]—is one of the chief goals of education. Indeed, tolerance is one of the basic values of our society. "ISSUES OF TOLERANCE AND TOLERATION are surely high on anyone's agenda for thinking about politics and history today."[3] No religious group will ever be accepted as an integral

11

part thereof without seeming to uphold it. Indeed, the mainline churches are active partners with government in actively propagating tolerance and opposing those who by means of hate, propaganda, or even use of force seek to undermine democracy. Yet seldom does anyone ask whether the Holy Scriptures that are the basic document of the Christian churches underwrite the concepts of tolerance and religious freedom—or, for that matter, the inherent dignity of the individual human being. Even a cursory look at any of a number of biblical documents shows that their ultimate concern is not human beings and their individual rights and freedoms, but rather the Deity and its plans for the elect people. Moreover, the God therein portrayed, far from being subject to any vote or popular show of acceptance, is an autonomous and indeed autocratic monarch who never shrinks at the necessity of enforcing his will.

HISTORICAL CRITICISM AS LIBERATION

My purpose in the following book is to expand on these observations and take up ideas that have interested me since my early student days at the University of Göttingen. As a beginning student I was exposed to historical criticism.[4] I learned that the biblical account of the history of Israel has little to do with the actual events. Indeed, biblical and historical Israel must be separated much as the historical Jesus and the Christ of faith must be distinguished. In the former case only few sayings and actions of the Galilean teacher remain. The space of a postcard would be sufficient—our teachers told us with a sly look—to list the authentic words and deeds of the historical Jesus. Christians, most of them known only by aliases, fabricated large portions of the gospel narratives and of Acts. Seeing themselves as spokesmen of the risen Christ, they did this to answer burning problems that arose in their congregations as well as to defend the church against nonbelieving Jews and the officials of the Roman Empire.

Historical criticism of this sort provided a great liberation from the burden of tradition. Proceeding empirically, critically, and with great enthusiasm, I followed the history of Israel and the rise of the Christian church without recourse to the fictions of an authoritarian faith that resorted to miracles instead of offering natural explanations. I am especially grateful to my teachers for enabling me to recognize that in the final analysis the central doctrine of Christianity, Jesus' resurrection from the dead, was an *interpretation* of Jesus' death. For thus it was that I overcame any lingering anxieties about eternal punishments: the mythological worldview that included resurrection, Second Coming, and final judgment collapsed once and for all. Perhaps the key advantage of a critical view of the Bible is that one can easily communicate its meaning to almost any reasonable person, whereas an interpretive scheme that relies on revelation can for the most part be mediated only to people who have already adopted a supernaturalist view of reality.

HISTORICAL-CRITICAL INTERPRETATION OF THE BIBLE AND THE INTOLERANCE OF THE GOSPEL IN THE WRITINGS OF RUDOLF BULTMANN

To my considerable surprise, the same teachers who opened my eyes to the origins of the Jesus traditions considered theology to be chiefly an exercise in interpretation of Scripture,[5] and saw their own work as service devoted to the church.[6] Accordingly, they found it necessary to place restrictions on the historical approach. In the final analysis, they argued, it is illegitimate to deal with the history behind the New Testament as an independent topic, for any reconstruction of the situations and events behind the texts is legitimate only insofar as it remains subordinate to and supportive of the New Testament proclamation. A New Testament theologian must face unflinchingly the eschatological claim of the various texts and thereby avoid the mistake of liberal exegetes who betray theology to history.

Rather than further document the above recollections, I shall turn to the great model of my New Testament teachers, Rudolf Bultmann (1884–1976), who dealt at great length with the issues at hand and whose historical and theological approach to Scripture continues to be in considerable vogue.

In an article from 1924, "Liberal Theology and the Latest Theological Movement,"[7] Bultmann accounts for his departure from liberal theology. He asserts that although the object of theology is God, liberal theology "has dealt not with God but with man."[8] He mentions two main deficiencies of liberal theology:

(1) Hoping to liberate the picture of Jesus from the burden of dogmatics and to gain an accurate historical picture of Jesus on
which to base faith, liberal theologians have overlooked the
fact that any historical result has only a relative validity.
Indeed, they have overlooked that "the world which faith wills
to grasp is absolutely unattainable by means of scientific
research."[9]

(2) The historical results of liberal theology "are only relative entities, *entities which exist only within an immense inter-related com-
plex.* Nothing which stands within this inter-relationship can
claim absolute value."[10] Besides, "*Christianity* is understood as
a phenomenon of this world, subject to the laws of social psychology.
It is equally clear that such a conception runs exactly counter
to the Christian view."[11]

Bultmann's article from 1925, "The Problem of a Theological Exegesis of the New Testament,"[12] sheds light on another aspect of his
protest against liberal theology. According to Bultmann the decisive
question in exegesis is whether we want to encounter the text "neu-
trally" so as to discover its historical content, or whether, in pursuit of
truth, we decide to let the subject matter contained in the text speak to
us. For "the possibility of an 'objective' exegesis is guaranteed solely by
the capacity of history itself for the subject at hand. And this is given
expression only where the exegete is ready to allow the text to speak
with authority."[13] The first option, the demand of impartial exegesis,
Bultmann considers naive; the second he sees as the proper Christian
attitude. For this latter viewpoint, he insists, reflects "recognition of the
uncertainty of our existence . . . an attitude toward history which
acknowledges it as authoritative and thus sees it not with the detach-
ment of the spectator but in the light of present decision."[14] In short, he
argues that Christian exegesis disavows the validity of a neutral perspective.

Bultmann's work on the New Testament is guided by his fundamental interest in interpretation, a goal he clearly distinguishes from
the reconstruction of past history.

Neither exists, of course, without the other, and they stand constantly
in a reciprocal relation to each other. But the question is: which of the
two stands in the service of the other? Either the writings of the New
Testament can be interrogated as the "sources" which the historian

interprets in order to reconstruct a picture of primitive Christianity as a phenomenon of the historical past, or the reconstruction stands in the service of the interpretation of the New Testament writings under the presupposition that they have something to say to the present.[15]

Bultmann's approach had especially important consequences for his research on Paul. In an article from 1920, "Ethical and Mystical Religion in Primitive Christianity," following the lead of his liberal teachers, he could still write, "[T]he conversion of Paul . . . is the ecstatic experience of a Hellenistic Jew, which drew him under the sway of the Kyrios cult of the Hellenistic congregation."[16] Yet after his theological detour Bultmann is hesitant to use objective, neutral language in speaking of Paul's conversion. As he writes in 1930, "Paul himself had no interest in his personal development, but only in the theological meaning of his conversion; and it is solely the latter that we are in a position to know."[17]

From now on he finds in the Apostle's transformation a new insight that includes a message to the interpreter. He writes:

> For just this is what his conversion meant: In it he surrendered his previous understanding of himself. . . . [I]t was obedient submission to the judgment of God, made known in the cross of Christ, upon all human accomplishment and boasting. It is as such that his conversion is reflected in his theology.[18]

But how is Bultmann going to write history after so radically deobjectifying it? In the introduction to his *Primitive Christianity: In Its Contemporary Setting*[19] Bultmann assures his readers that he does "not seek to prove that Christianity is true, nor even that it is the climax of the religious evolution of antiquity."[20] Besides, he does not "intend to explain the reasons why Christianity finally triumphed over its competitors, thus assuming its superiority over them."[21] That is heartening news indeed, for several generations of Christian scholars had spent their energy on employing Hegelian philosophy to demonstrate that Christianity is superior both to Paganism and Judaism. That is not what Bultmann as a historian intends. Indeed, such motives are alien to him. The reasons are simple.

> The truth of Christianity, like that of any other religion or philosophy, is always a matter of personal decision, and the historian has no right

to deprive any man of that responsibility. Nor, as is often asserted, is it his business to end up by assessing the value of what he has been describing. He can certainly clarify the issues involved in the decision. For it is his task to interpret the movements of history as possible ways of understanding human existence, thus demonstrating their relevance today. By bringing the past to life again, he should drive home the fact that here *tua res agitur*: this is your business.[22]

The aim, then, of Bultmann's book on Primitive Christianity is this:

> It is not an original piece of historical research. It does not claim to offer any new material for the study of comparative religion or fresh combinations of facts already known. It takes such research for granted. Its purpose is rather that of *interpretation*. We shall ask what understanding of human existence is enshrined in primitive Christianity, what new philosophy of life. Or, to put it more cautiously, is there such an understanding, and if so, how far does it go?[23]

Yet, despite Bultmann's stated intention to abstain from value judgments, his description of Judaism amounts to a caricature written from a Christian perspective. The very hermeneutics of *tua res agitur* seem to lead Bultmann to false historical judgments. For one thing, he describes Jewish piety as based on a formal obedience,[24] for another, he attributes to Jesus' contemporaries an uncertainty about salvation[25] and claims that Judaism thinks of God's relationship to his people only in legalistic terms. Indeed, Bultmann opines, "Jesus must have had good reasons for saying what he did about straining at the gnat and swallowing the camel (Matt. 23:24). The ritual commandments having lost their original meaning, man's relation to God was inevitably conceived in legalistic terms."[26] However, these and other statements derive from a Christian dogmatic perspective that, purposely but unconsciously blind to its own existence, has the sole aim of glorifying the doctrine of Christian salvation against the dark foil of Judaism.[27]

In other discourses on Judaism, Bultmann emphasizes that the negative remarks of the apostle Paul have a theological aim. For example, when Paul assails the Jews because, "being ignorant of the righteousness that comes from God, and seeking to establish their own, they have not submitted to God's righteousness. Christ is the end of the law . . ."[28]—or when he declaims that "the law brings wrath . . . "[29]—he is not making factual or empirical judgments but theological statements based on faith; for "Paul regards *man's existence* prior to *faith* in the transparency it has gained to the eye of faith."[30] As the foregoing examples demonstrate, Bultmann obviously regarded Paul's theological approach as theologically normative. This does not, however, persuade me to accept assertions that historical research has once and for all refuted.

I therefore remain skeptical of approaches that rely on hermeneutics to rescue the historical validity of Paul's statements about the law. The Zurich New Testament professor Hans Weder is an example. In an article titled "Law and Sin: Reflections on a Qualitative Leap in Paul's Thought"[31] he writes: "The question of whether the historical Paul has accurately construed historical Judaism and its understanding of the law is of secondary importance. . . . Arguments based on the law—whether Jewish or Christian law—necessarily lead us to conclude that Paul has misunderstood the law."[32] The reason is that "Paul's criticism of the law reveals a situation that cannot on the basis of the law—Jewish or Christian—be made plausible."[33] The situation alluded to is the leap of faith, carelessly referred to as revelation, by which Paul—and Weder, and indeed Bultmann—come to see the death of Jesus as a source of atoning grace that frees humans from the petty strictures of an outmoded legal code. The trouble is, of course, that a priori claims like grace and divinely arranged salvation belong to a realm of discourse quite apart from legal codes and logical demonstration. However grand it may seem to trump mere rational plausibility by playing the revelation card, such a maneuver cannot pass muster in the forum of scholarly demonstration.

Bultmann's statements about the relationship between reconstruction and interpretation are based in his conviction that the biblical text is both a call for decision and a valid historical record. For that reason he does not pay enough attention to the history that a properly critical theology should try to reconstruct. In those cases where interpretation and reconstruction conflict, Bultmann too often turns to a reconstruction that is amenable to a theologically determined interpretation. Indeed, he seems to employ two different notions of history: factual history, and existential history of the *tua res agitur* variety.[34] He writes: "But the decisive question is whether we confront history in such a way that we acknowledge its claim upon us, its claim to say something new to us. When we give up a neutral attitude toward the text, the question of truth can dominate the exegesis."[35]

Thus Bultmann thinks it hopeless "to justify theology as science before the forum of an unbelieving culture."[36] Indeed, he judges any attempt in that direction as a "self-surrender of theology,"[37] for the "object of theology is visible only to faith, and this faith itself belongs to its object—in fact, it *is* its object in the sense that in faith itself God's act, the eschatological occurrence, takes place in itself."[38] In other words, theology becomes an intellectual rationalization of a religious certitude of faith. As such it can be an academic discipline only on the condition that a specific revelation constitutes the decisive event of grace. Such a claim, however, is clearly unscientific. For one thing, its basis is an irrational call for faith; for another, it subordinates factual history to existential history. According to Bultmann, then, theology properly understood "cannot dispense with the categories of right teaching and heresy,"[39] for a dogmatism of the old style remains its basis.

It is therefore not surprising that Bultmann the exegete not only finds the gospel intolerant, but also considers it his real theological task to attest to the intolerance of the revelation. In connection with his exegesis of the Good Shepherd speech in the Gospel of John,[40] he writes:

> There are not various possible answers to man's quest for salvation, but only one. A decision must be made. This is the basis for the *intolerance of the revelation*.
>
> *Tolerance*, i.e. the recognition of every honest intention as of equal right, is demanded in that sphere of man's activity where the goal is left to man's intention and ability. . . . Thus outside the revelation man is always a seeker, so that it is pointless for man to pass judgment on others; what is required is tolerance. . . .
>
> Yet man's search ends when he is confronted with the revelation which opens up to every man the true understanding of himself. Here absolute recognition is demanded. Here there can be no tolerance. But of course it is the *revelation* which is intolerant; *men* can only be tolerant of each other. . . .

> Yet the believer does not commit himself to the revelation in order to champion its cause, but only in order to listen to it, to recognise its victory. His intolerance is not a denial of the sincerity and seriousness of the non-believer's commitment. . . . His intolerance consists in refusing to make concessions in gaining a hearing for the revelation, for the claim of that power which has made all human commitment obsolete and illusory. It consists in upholding the "truth" that all human commitment and endeavour, through which man seeks to find

his true being, is bound to fail; that the revelation demands that man abandon his attempt to find himself by giving himself up to this or that cause, because God in his revelation has already given up himself for men; that Jesus has come to give life and fullness.[41]

Yet Bultmann obviously plays old Harry with history. From the texts of the New Testament he filters the absolute claim of truth—the intolerance of the gospel—and keeps the demand of intolerance. But this seems to involve a contradiction, for the truth claim was part of a worldview that included imminent expectation of the end-time—a notion that has come to grief because Christians kept dying and Jesus did not return. This is to say nothing of the gospel proclamation's absolute reliance on the ancient view of a three-tiered universe—another myth that collapsed a long while ago.

Although fully aware of the failure of the imminent expectation, Bultmann sought to validate the truth claims of the essential biblical texts. Yet it is completely unjustified to ascribe to those texts absolute authority over the truth claims of other religions. Indeed, absolute truth claims are part of most religions. Whether we look at Jesus, his disciples, Paul, Mohammed, Joseph Smith, or more recent prophets, we see that each has laid claim to absolute truth derived from revelation and on that basis demanded total obedience. In short, history itself has put into question any and all claims to absolute truth. One gets nowhere by arguing that only through obedience can one understand the truth claim of the Christian revelation. That is precisely the game that other religions play, and the truth claim of any religion is vitiated by the conflicting truth claims of the many religions. Besides, as a free human being I must reject the arbitrary and presumptuous proposal that I must assent to a religion's truth claims before I can understand them. The objection of Arthur Schopenhauer holds for every revelation-based religion:

Of the many hard and deplorable things in the fate of man, not the least is that we exist without knowing whence, whither, and to what purpose. Whoever has grasped and seen through the sense of this evil and is thoroughly imbued with it, will hardly be able to resist a feeling of irritation towards those who pretend to have special information about this matter, which they wish to convey to us under the name of revelations. I would like to advise these revelation-gentlemen not to talk so much at the present time about revelation, otherwise one of these days it might easily be revealed to them what revelation really is.[42]

It is at best incongruous that Bultmann the great demythologizer should have joined the dogmatists. Yet it is clear that in his system the ancient dogma of inspiration remains implicitly valid; for according to his formulations something is held to be true not because it is true, but because it is part of the biblical revelation, the preaching of the cross and resurrection of Jesus Christ.

TRUTH CLAIMS OF THE CHURCH AND PRIVILEGES OF KNOWLEDGE VERSUS FUNDAMENTAL PLURALISM

The above argument may surprise many a reader because Bultmann is widely perceived as a radical critic owing to his program of demythologizing the Bible. But appearances are deceptive. Rather than let the facts speak clearly, Bultmann and his pupils replace factual history with existential history and thereby promote both a truth claim and a command of obedience to the Christian faith. In doing so, unfortunately, they have made factual history nearly unrecognizable.

Down through the ages Christian theologians and church officials have presupposed that truth can be precisely known and that through the revelation of the gospel they have a privileged access to it. Such a claim to truth is on its face questionable for the simple reason that anything "perfect" tends not to be so in its earlier stages.[43] An exclusive faith in revelation is even more questionable, because it excludes the mutually exclusive rival claims of other religions. Last but not least, the exclusive truth claim of the Christian religion has been made a mockery of by the tens of millions of atrocities it has fomented over twenty centuries.

Whoever wants to be religious in a free society must adopt a tolerant attitude toward other religious viewpoints and retain a degree of modesty with respect to his or her own religion. For the undeniable fact of pluralism establishes the relativism of religious truth claims. Since more than one path to enlightenment exists, no religion can ever again justify an absolute claim to truth. In his play *Nathan the Wise*, Gotthold Ephraim Lessing implicitly pronounced a ban on any search for religious truth that claims to have found the final answer. According to him, the worth of any religion depends on the degree to which it fosters our common humanity. This must be applied to any worldview, including atheism. At the same time, Lessing's insight implies the obsolescence of any absolute religion of the old style and marks out a future for an enlightened humanism, religious or nonreligious, that leaves dogmatism, irrationalism, and fundamentalism behind.

HISTORICAL OBSERVATIONS ON THE RISE OF CHRISTIANITY AND ITS DESCRIPTION FROM THE ASPECT OF RELIGIOUS INTOLERANCE

Since Edward Gibbon (1737–1794)[44] the following insights have emerged as a consensus among historians of Primitive Christianity:

(a) The Christian religion spread in the first two centuries almost without any suppression by the Roman state and benefited from the empire's tolerant policies in matters of religion.

(b) Christians introduced religious intolerance into Greco-Roman culture. This intolerance, derived in no small part from the First Commandment, ultimately led to persecution by the Romans.

(c) The intensity and scale of Roman persecution of Christians in the first three centuries was far exceeded by Christian persecution of pagans in the fourth and fifth centuries, and fifteen hundred years of ecclesiastical attacks on Jews and "nonorthodox" Christians confirm the normalcy of the earlier pattern.

(d) Rival religious groups that vied with the early church were doomed, if only by their own religious tolerance.

Now it is time to follow up these insights in order to understand the success of Christianity. In the following I shall deal with this *one* aspect of the rise of Primitive Christianity—its religious intolerance.

Chapter I of this book deals in its *first section* with the rise of monotheism in Israel and its relation to the doctrine of election and thus to intolerance. It is no wonder that all three were so commingled in the birth pangs of Christianity that a bitter controversy ensued as to whether the church or the synagogue was the heir of Israel. A *second section* examines the concept and indeed the ideal of tolerance in the Greco-Roman world. It is hardly surprising that the church and the

Roman state came to blows when Christians refused to pay fealty to the emperor cult. In a *third section* I examine this side of Christian intolerance.

Chapters II and III offer a running commentary that analyzes eight New Testament writings. I seek to determine the purposes of these texts, and to uncover the fundamental beliefs of their authors as well as those of the other Christians whom they vigorously attack. This analysis is aimed at portraying the conflict that had arisen because one Christian community—its representatives are the authors of the aforementioned eight New Testament documents—denied the correctness of another's beliefs. All eight writings belong to a time when Christian leaders labeled other Christians as heretics and strove to eliminate any further dialogue with them. The fates had their little jest, however, inasmuch as all attacking parties became official representatives of the church when their writings were included in the New Testament, which shortly afterward became a well-defined entity. By later establishing the canonicity of both the Old and New Testament, the "church catholic" delivered to following generations a normative document of faith on the basis of which orthodox bishops excommunicated many heretics. Indeed, many of the texts on which I comment in the following pages paved the way for the future maltreatment of dissenting Christian voices. They demonstrate how proto-orthodox authors slandered other Christians because of differences in doctrine, and thereby sought to eliminate them as rivals. And what they did spiritually, later bishops did physically. Since major elements of the Primitive Christian movement were led by their absolutist notion of God to preach absolute spiritual separation from all those of a different persuasion, the eight writings examined in these chapters serve as exemplars of the essentially intolerant spirit of the New Testament. (This, of course, makes it all the more ironic that the translation of "gospel" is "good news.") Here the truth of Ludwig Feuerbach's insight becomes especially evident: "Faith is essentially intolerant; essentially, because with faith is always associated the illusion that its case is the case of God, its honour his honour."[45]

In tracing the train of thought of the various New Testament writings, it is my special concern to bring to life both the authors and their opponents, and thus to show both a scholarly interest in and an appropriate respect for all the parties involved. I deliberately include the whole text in my analysis (and not only the intolerant portions) because only in this way does a proper degree of impartiality seem possible. I stress the need for impartiality, because nowadays too many exegetes not only side with the New Testament writers against their "opponents" but worse yet take the charges of the proto-orthodox authors at face value.[46] The reproach of libertinism is but one such accusation that is widely accepted[47] even though research has shown that "Gnostic libertinism" is a sham and must be refuted on the basis of newly discovered texts.[48] In addition, the concentration in many contemporary theological schools on the writings of the New Testament without giving dissenting voices a chance to be heard can hardly be imagined to represent the last word. The pursuit of truth, not an apologetic proclamation of the Holy Scriptures, ought to be the chief goal of academic theology. We must also show more inclusiveness in biblical studies by striving to understand the so-called heretics and lending them the benefit of our voices.

Be that as it may, for me the final goal of all history writing is to serve present society. Therefore, since the eight selected texts are an integral part of the New Testament that undergirds the faith of contemporary Christians, I have included a final chapter that focuses on the concept of tolerance and compares the teaching of the present churches with the doctrines that underlie the New Testament writings. Here we must face the fact that some of these texts are documents of religious intolerance, all the more so since their notion of God excludes other paths to faith and their message has thwarted religious tolerance more than it has fostered it.[49] Given the intolerant character of the scriptures and creeds on which Christian churches are founded, one is entitled to question what role they can properly play in a pluralistic society. If they are not to die, must they not undergo a change that will totally transform their biblical foundation?

ANSWERS TO OBJECTIONS

One may charge me with anachronism for measuring the biblical message against the modern ideals of tolerance and diversity.[50] Yet I fear that such an objection ultimately leads to nihilism, because it tends to see all evils as excusable. Try as we may to understand or rationalize it, the mass slaughter of Canaanites approved by the Old Testament—like genocides of any kind in any age—will always be a crime. Besides, whenever we think of tolerance the following facts must be kept in mind:

(a) Both tolerant and intolerant conduct and thought existed before the rise of the idea of tolerance and intolerance. Thus the history of tolerance is not the same as the history of the idea of tolerance.

(b) Long before the beginnings of Christianity, tolerance had often been both enjoined and acted upon.[51] Thus one may reasonably ask whether and how the God portrayed in the Christian scriptures showed tolerance—as well as why on numerous occasions he chose to be intolerant.

(c) Leaders of the church from antiquity to modern times have faced demands for tolerance. Yet in most, if not all, cases they refused to be tolerant and justified their actions on the basis of *what the Bible teaches.* Thus tolerance and intolerance in the church were essentially elements of biblical interpretation. That means, of course, that the biblical texts deserve a closer look, and it once again justifies the right to demand of any biblical text a fair indication of its tolerance and intolerance.

NOTES

1. Karl Jaspers, *Der philosophische Glaube* (Munich: R. Piper & Co. Verlag, 1948), p. 61.

2. *The Oxford Compact English Dictionary* (Oxford: University Press, 2000), p. 1211. "Tolerance" comes from the Latin *tolerare,* to endure.

3. John Christian Laursen and Cary J. Nederman, "General Introduction: Political and History Myths in the Toleration Literature," in *Beyond the Persecuting Society: Religious Toleration before the Enlightenment,* ed. John Christian Laursen and Cary J. Nederman (Philadelphia: University of Pennsylvania Press, 1998), p. 1.

4. My New Testament teachers were Georg Strecker (1929–1994) and Hans Conzelmann (1915–1989), my Old Testament teacher was Walther Zimmerli (1907–1984).

5. See Hans Conzelmann, *Theologie als Schriftauslegung* (Munich: Christian Kaiser, 1974). In English the title of this book is "*Theology as Interpretation of Scripture.*"

6. See the statement in Georg Strecker's preface to his *The Johannine Let-*

ters: A Commentary on 1, 2, and 3 John (Minneapolis: Fortress Press, 1996), p. xiii: "It is true of this commentary on the Johannine Letters . . . that its proper goal is not scholarly discussion, but the unity of theory and praxis in service of the church's preaching." Indeed, from the outset this conviction permeates Strecker's exegetical work.

7. Rudolf Bultmann, *Faith and Understanding* I, ed. with an introduction by Robert W. Funk (New York: Harper & Row, 1969), pp. 28–52.

8. Ibid., p. 29.

9. Ibid., p. 31.

10. Ibid.

11. Ibid., p. 32.

12. In *The Beginnings of Dialectical Theology*, vol. 1, ed. James M. Robinson (Richmond, VA: John Knox Press, 1968), pp. 236–56.

13. Ibid., p. 245.

14. Ibid., p. 249.

15. Rudolf Bultmann, *Theology of the New Testament*, 2 vols. (New York: Charles Scribner's Sons, 1951–55), 2:251.

16. In *The Beginnings of Dialectical Theology*, vol. 1, pp. 224–25 (221–35).

17. Rudolf Bultmann, *Existence and Faith* (New York: Meridian Books, Living Age Books, 1960), p. 114.

18. Bultmann, *Theology of the New Testament*, 1:188.

19. Rudolf Bultmann, *Primitive Christianity: In Its Contemporary Setting* (New York: Meridian Books, Living Age Books, 1956). The German original is *Das Urchristentum im Rahmen der antiken Religionen* (Zürich: Artemis, 1949).

20. Ibid., p. 11.

21. Ibid.

22. Ibid., pp. 11–12.

23. Ibid., p. 12.

24. See his judgment, ibid., p. 68: "Radical obedience would have involved a personal assent to the divine command, whereas in Judaism so many of the precepts were trivial or unintelligible that the kind of obedience produced was formal rather than radical."

25. Ibid., p. 70: "A further consequence of the legalistic conception of obedience was that the prospect of salvation became highly uncertain."

26. Ibid., pp. 67–68.

27. See E. P. Sanders, *Paul and Palestinian Judaism: A Comparison of Patterns of Religion* (Philadelphia: Fortress Press, 1977).

28. Rom. 10:3–4.

29. Rom. 4:15a.

30. Bultmann, *Theology of the New Testament*, 1:270.

31. Hans Weder, "Gesetz und Sünde. Gedanken zu einem qualitativen Sprung im Denken des Paulus," *New Testament Studies* 31 (1985): 357–76.

32. Ibid., pp. 369–70.

33. Ibid., p. 359.

34. See on this aspect of Bultmann's thought Robert W. Funk, *Language, Hermeneutic, and Word of God: The Problem of Language in the New Testament and Contemporary Theology* (New York: Harper & Row, 1966), pp. 110–11 (reporting on Heinrich Ott's objections to Bultmann).

35. Rudolf Bultmann, "The Problem of a Theological Exegesis of the New Testament," in *The Beginnings of Dialectical Theology*, vol. 1, p. 239.

36. Rudolf Bultmann, "Theology as a Science," in id., *The New Testament and Mythology and Other Basic Writings*, selected, edited, and translated by Schubert M. Ogden (Philadelphia: Fortress Press, 1984), p. 66 (45–67).

37. Ibid.

38. Ibid.

39. Ibid., p. 65.

40. Rudolf Bultmann, *The Gospel of John: A Commentary* (Oxford: Basil Blackwell, 1971). My quote is taken from the section, "The exclusiveness and the absoluteness of the Revelation: 10.7–10," pp. 375–80. The first German edition of this most influential commentary appeared in 1941.

41. Ibid., pp. 378–81.

42. Arthur Schopenhauer, *Parerga and Paralipomena: Short Philosophical Essays*, vol. 2 (Oxford: Oxford University Press, 1974), p. 361.

43. "In the beginning the gods did not at all reveal all things clearly to mortals. Yet by searching, they find them out better in the course of time" (Xenophanes, fifth century BCE).

44. Edward Gibbon, *On Christianity* (Amherst, NY: Prometheus Books, 1991).

45. Ludwig Feuerbach, *The Essence of Christianity* (Amherst, NY: Prometheus Books, 1989), p. 255.

46. Note, on the contrary, the enlightened comment on the "heretics" by the sixteenth-century theologian Sebastian Franck (1499–1542): "I very much wish that we had the copies and true originals of the works of the heretics. . . . Those first heretics, in the days of the apostles, must have presented a plausible case. . . . Many of their sayings were distorted, and many things were falsely attributed to them. The good was omitted, the bad accentuated or increased" (Roland H. Bainton, ed., *Concerning Heretics: Whether they are to be persecuted and How they are to be treated: A Collection of the opinions of learned men Both ancient and modern: An anonymous work attributed to Sebastian Castellio* [New York: Columbia University Press, 1935], pp. 188–89).

47. See only Duane F. Watson, "The Second Letter of Peter," in *The New Interpreter's Bible*, vol. 12 (Nashville, TN: Abingdon Press, 1998), p. 325.

48. See Michael Allen Williams, *Rethinking "Gnosticism": An Argument for Dismantling a Dubious Category* (Princeton, NJ: Princeton University Press, 1996), pp. 163–88.

49. On Sebastian Castellio and Sebastian Franck, who have derived religious tolerance from the Bible, see below, pp. 211–12 nn18–21.

50. Thus Stephen C. Barton, "Paul and the Limits of Tolerance," *Tolerance and Intolerance in Early Judaism and Christianity*, ed. Graham N. Stanton and Guy G. Stroumsa (Cambridge: Cambridge University Press, 1998), pp. 121–23.

51. See Bernhard Kötting, *Religionsfreiheit und Toleranz im Altertum* (Opladen: Westdeutscher Verlag, 1977); Wolfgang Speyer, "Toleranz und Intoleranz in der alten Kirche," in *Christentum und Toleranz*, ed. Ingo Broer and Richard Schlüter (Darmstadt: Wissenschaftliche Buchgesellschaft, 1996), pp. 58–59; Alan Levine, "Introduction: The Prehistory of Toleration and Varieties of Skepticism," in *Early Modern Skepticism and the Origins of Toleration*, ed. Alan Levine (Lanham, MD: Lexington Books, 1999), pp. 6–10; Cyrus Masroori, "Cyrus II and the Political Utility of Toleration," in *Religious Toleration: "The Variety of Rites" from Cyrus to Defoe*, ed. John Christian Laursen (New York: St. Martin's Press, 1999), pp. 13–36.

Chapter I

Tolerance in the Old Testament, Judaism, and the Greco-Roman World at the Time of the New Testament Writings

The Jewish religion was the only religion in the East and in the Hellenistic world in which the worship of foreign gods was fundamentally regarded as apostasy and could be punished with death.[1]

—Martin Hengel

1. TOLERANCE IN THE OLD TESTAMENT AND IN JUDAISM

The earliest Christians were Jews who regarded the Hebrew Bible and its Greek translation, the Septuagint, as Holy Scripture and the God of Israel as the father of Jesus Christ. He was also their father, and had repudiated Judaism and consecrated the church by electing its members to be his new chosen people.[2] The soon-to-be-founded Gentile Christian congregations did not change that. For even though Gentiles brought their own culture into the church, it soon took on a distinctly Jewish coloration in matters of theology. And although by New Testament times Jewish culture had been largely assimilated by the Greco-Roman world, it nevertheless clung jealously to the doctrine that Yahweh had elected Israel, a nation that therefore had an identity of its own and was an entity in itself. Whoever wants to understand "tolerance" or "intolerance" in the writings of the New Testament must try to discover both the origins and evolution of these concepts within the Old Testament and how they were understood in the Jewish world of the first century CE.

The First Commandment and Monotheism in the Old Testament[3]

The first commandment, with its requirement to worship Yahweh[4] alone and not to serve other gods—along with the threat of severe punishment for disobedience—dominates large parts of the Old Testament as we now have it.

Exodus 20:2–3

(2) I am Yahweh your God, who brought you out of the land of Egypt, out of the house of bondage. (3) You shall have no other gods besides me. (RSV)

Joshua 23:16

(16) If you transgress the covenant of Yahweh your God, which he enjoined on you, and go and serve other gods and bow down to them, then the anger of Yahweh will be kindled against you, and you shall perish quickly from the good land which he has given to you. (NRSV)

2 Kings 17:5–7

(5) Then the king of Assyria invaded all the land and came to Samaria; for three years he besieged it. (6) In the ninth year of Hoshea the king of Assyria captured Samaria; he carried the Israelites away to Assyria. . . . (7) This occurred because the people of Israel had sinned against Yahweh their God, who had brought them up out of the land of Egypt from under the hand of Pharaoh king of Egypt. They had worshipped other gods. (RSV/NRSV)

Jeremiah 11:9–11

(9) Again Yahweh said to me, "There is revolt among the men of Judah and the inhabitants of Jerusalem. (10) They have turned back to the iniquities of their forefathers, who refused to hear my words; they have gone after other gods to serve them; the house of Israel and the house of Judah have broken my covenant which I made with their fathers. (11) Therefore, thus says Yahweh, Look, I am bringing evil upon them which they cannot escape; though they cry to me, I will not listen to them." (RSV)

Apart from these passages, a number of statements not only underscore the sole worship of Yahweh but also express a rigid monotheism that negates the very existence of other gods. Let a single example stand for many:

Deuteronomy 4:39

Know therefore this day, and lay it to your heart, that Yahweh is God in heaven above and on the earth beneath; there is no other. (RSV)

Various Manifestations of Yahweh

Now I shall sketch the historical development that led to Yahweh's claim[5] of exclusiveness and eventually to monotheism by distinguishing the several stages of this evolution.

At the time of the two monarchies of Israel and Judah, Yahweh resembled other deities in that he appeared under different names: he was hailed not only as Yahweh of Samaria or Yahweh of Teman[6] but also as Yahweh of Jerusalem. Thus, "it was not unusual for Israelites and Judahites to wage war against each other or enter into coalitions in his name."[7] An even more difficult theological dilemma arose when in 722 BCE Assyria conquered Samaria, annihilated the kingdom of Israel,[8] and thereby overcame its god Yahweh—but failed to subdue the kingdom of Judah, which acknowledged the same deity. Challenged to explain why Yahweh had allowed this defeat, the prophets answered that Yahweh himself had ordered the liquidation of Israel as punishment for its sins.[9] To quote Reinhard Gregor Kratz,

The prophetic intimation of the catastrophe became the announce-
ment of a total judgment brought by Yhwh, and the complaint about
the chaotic conditions became an accusation and the reason for the
judgment which had already taken place in Israel and was still imminent in Judah. Under the impact of the downfall of Israel, and in the
face of the Assyrian expansion southwards, in this way there emerged
among the prophets for the first time, or at any rate for the first time
explicitly, a notion of the unity of Yhwh and his people transcending
the oppositions between Israel and Judah.[10]

The Unity of Yahweh: One God, One Nation, One Cult

The priests who composed the earliest version of Deuteronomy (Ur-
Deuteronomy) about 621 BCE took other important steps toward the
establishment of the monotheistic concept;[11] the most important of
these were the restriction of cult ceremonies to specified locations and
the vesting of considerable authority in levitical priests supported by
the community.[12] This institutionalization of the unity of the cult and
Yahweh, especially when reinforced for several centuries by the presence of king and Temple in Jerusalem, enabled a monotheistic Judaism
to survive the loss of king, Temple, and holy city in 587 BCE. Along
with his priestly supporters, Yahweh could not only survive in a new
selected place, but could also return to Jerusalem. Only fifty years after
the disaster of 587, the altar of sacrifice was restored, and two decades
later the Temple once again proclaimed the oneness of Yahweh and his
sacred cult.

Because the composers of Deuteronomy and its later editors
regarded themselves as both spokesmen and wardens of Yahweh, they
demanded cultic purity and strict separation from other nations. Since
Israel is a holy people elected by Yahweh, it must avoid any contact with
other nations. Political neutrality and religious tolerance are out of the
question. Deuteronomy's isolationist and exclusivist program is the
heart of its theology, and not a pragmatic addendum or an arbitrary
aberration. The aim of establishing the myth of Israel's special existence
and protecting it against foreign influences almost inevitably produced
an ideology of war and revived, among other things, the ancient practice of ban—the devotion to destruction of all human beings and animals—which, though, assigned the fruits of victory such as gold, and
the like to Yahweh[13]—or in practice to the Temple apparatus.

Connected with the idea of the unity and purity of the cult is the doctrine of election. The other side of this coin, however, is the rejection and indeed the disapprobation of all things foreign, a rebuff that at times takes the form of a ritually based hate of everything that does not belong to Israel. The ideology of separation increased during the Exile (587–539 BCE) and was afterward further deployed to cover everything not intrinsic to the pure cultic community. We see this animus reflected in the call for the total annihilation of the Canaanites and the Amalekites, and to it belongs a psalm composed during the Babylonian Exile and crying for revenge:

Psalms 137:1, 8–9

(1) By the waters of Babylon, there we sat down and wept, when we remembered Zion. . . . (8) O daughter of Babylon, you devastator! Happy shall he be who requites you with what you have done to us! (9) Happy shall he be who takes your little ones and dashes them against the rock! (RSV)

This separation from the hostile outside world corresponds to the close attachment to Yahweh.

Deuteronomy 6:4–5

(4) Hear, O Israel: Yahweh is our God, Yahweh is one; (5) and you shall love Yahweh your God with all your heart, and with all your soul, and with all your might.

On the basis of this theological standard, priestly chroniclers composed the annals of Israel and Judah found in the so-called deuteronomistic history that extends from 1 Samuel 1 to 2 Kings 25. Its writers ascribe any success or failure of the kings of Israel and Judah to the degree these rulers had championed or rejected Yahweh's demand for the centralization of his cult. And all the while, no doubt, these theological narrators "hoped for a renewal of the Davidic monarchy according to the criteria of Ur-Deuteronomy."[14]

Yahweh's Exclusivity and the Monotheistic Faith

Since the renewal of the Davidic kingdom was impossible under either the Babylonians (612–539 BCE) or the Persians (539–333 BCE), Jewish theologians[15] "grounded the existence of 'Israel' wholly in the relationship with God."[16] Into the existing exodus narrative they incorporated the Decalogue,[17] headed by the exclusionary injunctions of its first two articles. "From now on no longer the centralization of the cult but the First Commandment is the criterion by which the people of God, 'Israel,' made up of Israel and Judah, has to allow itself to be measured."[18]

It was not long before the monolatric demand to worship Yahweh alone developed into the claim that aside from Yahweh no other gods existed. This development first becomes visible in Deutero-Isaiah.

Isaiah 44:6–8

(6) Thus says Yahweh, the King of Israel and his Redeemer, Yahweh of hosts: "I am the first and I am the last; besides me there is no god. (7) Who is like me? Let him proclaim it, let him declare and set it forth before me. Who has announced from of old the things to come? Let them tell us what is yet to be. (8) Fear not, nor be afraid; have I not told you from of old and declared it? And you are my witnesses! Is there a God besides me? There is no Rock; I know not any." (RSV)

Isaiah 45:5–7

(5) "I am Yahweh, and there is no other, besides me there is no God; I gird you, though you do not know me, (6) that people may know, from the rising of the sun to its setting, that there is none besides me. I am Yahweh, and there is no other. (7) I form light and create darkness, I make weal and create woe, I am Yahweh, who does all these things."

Isaiah 45:20–22

(20) "Assemble yourselves and come, draw near together, you sur-

vivors of the nations! They have no knowledge who carry about their wooden idols, and keep on praying to a god that cannot save. (21) Declare and present your case; let them take counsel together! Who told this long ago? Who declared it of old? Was it not I, Yahweh? And there is no other god besides me, a righteous God and a Savior; there is none besides me. (22) Turn to me and be saved, all the ends of the earth! For I am God, and there is no other." (RSV)

The sense of Yahweh's distance from his people during the Babylonian Exile—or in some minds his absence and his supposed powerlessness—abruptly changed with Cyrus's edict in 538 BCE:[19] now it appeared that the God so recently despaired of was indeed king of the whole world, ruling over Babylonians and Persians and all other nations. Thus Yahweh became the only God, with no rival god beside him, and this claim was soon added to the prophetic books and the works of history.

The priestly writers of the sixth century also reflect a strict monotheistic viewpoint; it is strikingly clear in the very first verse of their contribution to the scriptural tradition: "In the beginning God created the heavens and the earth."[20] The next verse shows that the priestly author has reworked ancient mythological material that presupposed a dualism between God and matter,[21] but in the following one God's divine fiat puts everything in order: "God said, 'Let there be light,' and there was light."[22]

Israel's Belief in God during the Hellenistic Age

The empire that Alexander the Great (356–323 BCE) created in the East was held together not only by central government but also by the unity of language, customs, and culture.[23] His overthrow of the Persian Empire made Palestine a part of the Hellenistic world and ushered in a dark yet fascinating period of Israelite-Jewish history. To this era belong the roughly 165 years between Alexander's move to the East in 334 BCE and the Hellenistic reform in Jerusalem that—inspired by Jewish circles—the Seleucid Antiochus IV Epiphanes (who became king in 175 BCE) carried out.[24] Central to this reform was the introduction of gymnasium education.[25]

The process began when one Jesus—he preferred to call himself by his Greek name Jason[26]—a member of the priestly family of the Oniads, approached the king not long after his installment and offered him a large sum of money in return for being made high priest in Jerusalem.[27] Along with this he asked the king for permission to build in Jerusalem a gymnasium following the Greek model, and to introduce a curriculum for the education and training of young men (the ephebate).[28] "The 'gymnasium,' i.e., the sports-stadium, during the Hellenistic period formed the symbol and basis for the Greek way of life. Physical education was something alien to the Oriental, but a natural thing for the Greeks. Wherever Greeks came together, or people who wanted to be counted as Greeks, they started athletic exercises."[29] Related to it was the ephebate, which included musical and literary subjects.[30]

The Hellenism that Jason and his associates wanted to introduce to Jerusalem was not intended to involve apostasy from Judaism.[31] Neither the rites of the Temple cult nor observance of Mosaic Law were directly affected, for both remained valid largely as elements of popular custom; but the legal foundations of the priestly theocracy were radically undermined. Civil order and governmental policy would no longer be the province of priests and the wise; in the future, governance would be vested in the demos, that is, the citizenry acting through the *gerousia* (council of elders) and the officials it appointed.The result, of course, would be to demote the priestly nobility, and it is indicative of their willingness to adopt Greek customs that this consequence was clearly understood. At any rate, Antiochus reacted favorably to Jason's proposed reforms, appointed him as high priest, and when he visited Jerusalem in 172 BCE was "welcomed magnificently by Jason and the city, and ushered in by a blaze of torches and with shouts."[32]

Convinced of the popular indifference about which name should be used to invoke divinity, the reform Jews around Jason fostered the idea of a supranational deity. In other words, if the several Greek and Oriental gods—even when addressed by their indigenous names—ultimately derive from the One God, they are simply different expressions of monotheism. In the light of Hellenistic enlightenment, Jason and his friends identified the Greek supranational idea of deity with their own universalistic notion of the one God of Israel. "The ideal of the educated, which became common property as a result of the Stoa, was not segregation in a national religion with separatist customs, but world citizenship."[33] The Palestinian philosopher Meleager of Gadara (b. 140 BCE) expressed the mainstream view of his educated contemporaries and those before them by exclaiming, "Stranger, we dwell in one country, the world."[34] The supranational Greek idea of one deity living at many places seems to have transformed polytheism into an encompassing monotheism of Stoic provenance. It is clear that the Jewish "Letter of Aristeas to Philocrates," which in the first century BCE tells of the origin of the translation of the Hebrew Bible into Greek, was influenced by this Stoic monotheism.

In this letter—a pseudepigraphic document describing the Jews to King Ptolemaeus II—one statement about them by the supposed author, "Aristeas," is particularly eye-catching: (16) "These people worship God the overseer and creator of all, whom all men worship including ourselves, O King, except that we have a different name. Their name for him is Zeus and Dis. The primitive men, consistently with this, demonstrated that the one by whom all live[35] and are created is master and Lord of all."[36] To be sure, the identification of Yahweh, Zeus, and Dis is made by the Greek Aristeas and not by a Jew. Yet, since the "Letter of Aristeas"—like other Hellenistic-Jewish writings that employ Greek rather than biblical persons as their supposed authors—is directed at a Jewish audience, the identification of Zeus and Yahweh seems to reflect the opinion of the anonymous Jewish author.[37] The view he held on this issue was clearly not idiosyncratic, but reflected a relatively widespread attitude. Indeed, "at about the time when Yahweh was identified with Olympian Zeus in Jerusalem, in Greek-educated circles of Jews in Alexandria there were reflections on the problem of the relationship between the God of Israel and the 'Zeus' of the philosophers."[38]

The course of events of this decisive period in the history of Judaism is difficult to reconstruct, for legends and interpretations have distorted the actual happenings.[39] 1 Macc. 1:41–42 reports a decree of Antiochus "to his whole kingdom that all should be one people, and that all should give up their particular customs." Verse 43 reports that "even many from Israel gladly accepted his religion," and verses 44–49 list the traditional Jewish rites and practices that were forbidden. Verse 50 concludes the decree with the warning that "whoever does not obey the command of the king shall die." While it is true that the author of 1 Maccabees may have exaggerated, he probably preserved the gist of the king's measures. They culminated in a royal decree to dedicate the Jewish Temple to Zeus Olympios[40]—an event of far-reaching importance reflected in biblical writings as the "abomination of desolation."[41]

The first passive resistance in 165 BCE soon developed into a full-blown revolution. Its leaders were Mattathias, the head of the family of the Maccabees, and his son Judas the Maccabean, with whom the Jewish group known as the "assembly of the pious" joined forces to fight for the survival of Judaism.[42] This struggle proved successful, but only because Antiochus's draconian efforts to abolish Jewish worship and introduce Greek rites triggered an overpowering reaction. To the Maccabees and the pious Jews who lived in rural areas this was a perversion of Israel's faith, for they took it to signify that a nongod had taken the place of the true and only God. They saw no other option but to resort to war. And indeed, after more than a quarter of a century of bitter fighting they achieved political independence.[43] This in turn led to brutal measures against nonbelievers, apostates, and Gentiles who lived in the Holy Land. Deuteronomy served as a legal basis. As the great ancient historian Eduard Meyer observed, "What happened in the second century BCE in the narrow region of Palestine repeated itself many times on the world stage at a much larger level. The religious wars and the persecutions of heretics undertaken by Christianity, Calvinism, and Islam were ultimately caused by the commands of Deuteronomy."[44]

In 63 BCE Pompey put an end to the interim rule of the Maccabees. To be sure, their kingdom had lasted barely a century, but we must not forget that if the Hellenizing "process had been allowed to continue peacefully, presumably Judaism in Palestine would in time have become barely recognisable."[45] Be that as it may, the Hellenistic crisis and the way it was solved produced a watershed in the history of Judaism. As Martin Hengel aptly remarks,

> This deep crisis, which led to the attempt—which was undertaken primarily by Jewish forces themselves—decisively altered the religious and spiritual face of Palestinian Judaism. The ground was laid for that polemical and legalistic accentuation of Jewish piety which characterizes it in the New Testament period.[46]

Monotheism in the New Testament

The exclusive Jewish monotheism that I have delineated above—a mixture of monolatry and theoretical monotheism—must be recognized as the seedbed from which all early Christian writings sprang. That is especially true for the letters of Paul, but it characterizes the rest of the New

Testament as well, since all of it proclaims the message of the one and true God whose exclusivity had been sharpened by the Hellenistic crisis of the second century BCE.

The content of such a message was indeed a tall order for the Gentile Christians, for the worship of the one and only God entailed the command to regard all the other gods as idols. There can be no doubt that for the Corinthians and other Gentile Christians this was a real difficulty. Up to the time of their conversion they were able to worship several deities at the same time, because no priest of the individual cults would object, nor did he or she claim the absolute truth for his or her specific religion.[47] Paul's message, however, stands in stark contrast to the tolerance of the Hellenistic religions. He addresses the new converts in Thessalonica thus: "You have turned away from the idols to God, in order to serve the living and true God."[48] At another place he writes about his exclusive monotheistic faith: "For if it is true that there are so-called gods in heaven or on earth—even as there are many gods and many lords—yet for us there is one God, the Father from whom are all things and for whom we exist."[49]

The Jewish mother religion handed on to its Christian offshoot not only its intolerant monotheism but also the notion of having been elected. This led to the tragic consequence that the church understood itself to be the new Israel, a conceit that necessarily resulted in its self-proclaimed replacement of the old Israel. The logic of this supercessionist theology ran as follows: Now at the end of time God has put the church in the place of Israel because the latter failed to acknowledge his son, Jesus, as the Messiah and thereby rejected his mercy.[50] Yet what the Christians regarded as substitution, educated Gentiles considered apostasy. In the second century CE the critic Celsus wrote about the Christians: "I will ask them where they have come from, and who is the author of their traditional laws. Nobody, they will say. In fact, they themselves originated from Judaism, and they cannot name any other source for their teacher and chorus-leader. Nevertheless they rebelled against the Jews."[51] Call it substitution or apostasy—in either case there can be no doubt of the underlying similarity between Israel's understanding of God and that displayed by the church.

2. TOLERANCE IN THE GRECO-ROMAN WORLD[52]

In the summer of 384 CE Symmachus, a senator and the prefect of the city of Rome, addressed his famous Third Relatio to the young emperor Valentinian II, who resided in Milan, requesting that the altar of Victory be once again erected in the assembly hall of the Roman senate.[53] It had been the custom to offer incense on the altar of Victory before each session of the senate. This sacrifice and the image of Victory supposedly helped to propitiate the gods who had made Rome strong. Symmachus argued his case with passionate words and rhetorical artistry:

> Let us imagine that Rome herself stands in your presence and pleads with you thus, "Best of emperors, fathers of the country, respect my length of years won for me by the dutiful observance of rite, let me continue to practise my ancient ceremonies, for I do not regret them. Let me live in my own way, for I am free."[54]

In petitioning the emperor's tolerance Symmachus puts these words into Roma's mouth:

> It is reasonable that whatever each of us worships is really to be considered one and the same. We gaze up at the same stars, the sky covers us all, the same universe compasses us. What does it matter what practical system we adopt in our search for the truth? Not by one avenue only can we arrive at so tremendous a secret.[55]

But Bishop Ambrose of Milan, whose status gave him direct access to the emperor, intervened without hesitation. Adducing the gospel's exclusive and final authority, he rebutted the prefect as follows:

> According to Symmachus "not by one avenue only can we arrive at so tremendous a secret." Yet, we Christians have heard from the mouth of God things that are unknown to you. That which you claim to know by an obscure hunch we have as a reliable possession from the wisdom and truth of God.[56]

This same claim inspired Ambrose in his intolerance toward heretics, Gentiles, and Jews. Ambrose's great pupil, Augustine of Hippo Regius, followed the same pattern. He agreed to the emperor's suppression of the pagan cult places as well as the sacrifices and temples that supported them—and cited Deuteronomy as his authority![57] And this sort of intolerance remained operative until modern times.

On the Cultural Background of the Third Relation of Symmachus

Symmachus's relativizing of different faiths—each of them the reflection of a mysterious power—has similarities with both Roman thought and Hellenistic religiosity. Indeed, the Roman point of view was amenable to the coexistence of divergent ideas of the divine essence in a religiously based state.

In his influential work *City of God*, Augustine cited the passages from Varro's *Antiquities of the Human and Divine Affairs* (116–27 BCE) that defined the official Roman policy toward religions in general. According to Augustine, Varro—basing himself on precursors[58]—makes a tripartite division of theology: the mythical, the physical, and the civil. Augustine quotes Varro's explanation in

City of God 6.5

The name "mythical" applies to the theology used chiefly by the poets, "physical" to that of the philosophers, "civil" to that of the general public. The **first type** [i.e., mythical theology] **contains** a great deal of fiction that is in conflict with the dignity and nature of the immortals. It is in this category that we find one god born from the head, another from the thigh, a third from the drops of blood. We find stories about thefts and adulteries committed by gods, and gods enslaved to human beings. In fact we find attributed to gods not only the accidents that happen to humanity in general, but even those that can befall the most contemptible of human beings.[59]

The **second type** [physical theology] that I have pointed out is one on which the philosophers have left a number of works, in which they discuss who the gods are, where they are, of what kind and of what character they are: whether they came into being at a certain time, or have always existed. Whether they derive their being from fire, the belief of Heraclitus, or from numbers, as Pythagoras thought, or from atoms as Epicurus alleges. And there are other like questions all of which people's ears can more readily tolerate within the walls of a lecture-room than in the market place outside.[60]

The **third type** [civil theology] is that which the citizens in the towns, and especially the priests, ought to know and to practice. It contains information about the gods which should be worshipped officially and the rites and sacrifices which should be offered to each of them.[61]

In summary Varro remarks:

> The first type of theology is particularly suited for the theatre; the second is particularly concerned with the world; the special relevance of the third is to the city.[62]

Augustine adds to the excerpt from Varro's tripartite theology this remark: "It is easy to see to which he gives the highest value. Obviously it is the second type, the theology, as he said earlier, of the philosophers."[63] But this seems only partly correct. To be sure, Varro assigns the "mythical theology" to the theater, where it became the target of ridicule by the Gentile and later the Christian audience.[64] Yet he clearly considered "civil theology" a subject of some importance because it dealt with sacrifices and other aspects of civil religion that both ensured the favor of the state gods and preserved the traditions of the elders. "Physical theology" he essentially dismissed, since it dealt with nothing more important than fanciful discussions about gods whom Varro had totally depersonalized and defined pantheistically as part of the world.[65] Swayed, perhaps, by his own nonpersonal, entirely intellectual concept of deity, he even suggested that for 170 years after the founding of the city, Roman veneration of the gods was practiced without the use of images. Note that Varro's relationship to religion was totally enlightened and free of any superstition or anything we would call faith or belief.[66]

This attitude was shared by many a Roman skeptic, and stood in stark contrast to the Christian religion with its claim to have been divinely granted the sole truth. Distancing himself from Varro's tripartite theology, the church father Tertullian opined as follows:

> Where should one find absolute truth? . . . The theses of the philosophers are uncertain, because they vary from one another, the poets

produce nothing but indecency that is moreover unmoral, and among the civilian authorities everything is arbitrary because it is determined at pleasure.[67]

As enlightened intellectuals, the representatives of physical theology had an indifferent attitude to the question of absolute truth, and therefore simply indulged the uneducated masses in their apparently childlike need for myths. They recognized, however, that the religious rites of civil theology remained important for the state even if their truth claims did not stand up to critical examination. For the wise, in short, religion meant praxis and not belief. Not only was it simply a matter of pragmatic wisdom to keep civil religion in close relationship to the state, but as an image of an eternal powerful order, the national cult took on divine features. After all, its chief representative was the emperor, whose "godly" role and power enabled him to unify the nations and resolve differences of opinion. The religious bond of civil theology was thus the cult of the emperor, which initially, at least, required the participation of only such elite persons as high political authorities and senior military personnel. Moreover, the cult of the emperor did not require belief or faith, but only political loyalty.[68]

3. THE PERSECUTION OF CHRISTIANS BY THE ROMANS AS A TEST CASE OF TOLERANCE AND INTOLERANCE

Roman toleration of the Christian church was a crucial factor in the expansion of the new movement. Roman authorities interfered in religious matters only in those rare cases when the general order seemed to be threatened.[69] For the state, and later for the emperor, the fundamental aim of religious politics was to promote social stability and public order. Paul profited at least indirectly from official toleration in his large-scale missionary work. Indeed, the first hostile reactions he faced came from the citizenry and not from the Roman government. On that score, the Acts of the Apostles has depicted the course of events correctly.[70]

In considerable contrast to the liberal attitude of its Gentile neighbors, Christianity's exclusionist monotheism inhibited contact with them. These worshippers of Greek and oriental deities saw no difficulty in combining respect for the official gods of Rome with adherence to their own religions. Most Christians were unwilling to do so because they regarded the Father of Jesus Christ as the only true God. Herein they displayed a zeal reminiscent of that shown by the Maccabees, who two hundred years earlier had proclaimed Yahweh as the God of Israel and as the only Lord of the world; and like those God-possessed rebels, they tended to see everything apart from God as demonic and to be avoided. Christians further alienated themselves from society in three obvious ways: they refused to patronize Gentile butchers lest they eat meat sacrificed to idols;[71] they avoided the theater because many plays dramatized stories of pagan deities; and they abstained from festivities in honor of the local civic gods. Furthermore, since their converts came primarily from the lower classes, Christian missionaries by and large shunned debate with educated Gentiles and called for unquestioning acceptance of their message on the grounds that faith alone is the key to salvation. A Gentile observer from the second century quotes the following exhortations of Christian missionaries: "Do not ask questions; just believe! Your faith will save you! The wisdom in the world is an evil, and foolishness a good thing!"[72] Gentile neighbors could hardly help noticing that Christians had intentionally erected a high fence between themselves and the rest of the world.[73]

To be sure, the command to avoid Gentiles was not always observed. After all, Corinthian Christians sued each other before Gentile judges,[74] and at first Paul openly joined the "strong" community members there[75] in eating meat that had been offered to idols[76]—even though he afterward disavowed the practice for the sake of the "weak" brothers and expected every "strong" Christian to do the same.[77] (After Paul's time eating meat sacrificed to idols was confined to "heretical" Gnostic groups.)[78] And in hopes of Christian offspring, mixed marriages were tolerated,[79] even though they involved close relations with the outside world.

Still, the walls that surrounded the Christian congregations remained quite high, and consequently many anti-Christian rumors spread. They focused on such closed rites as baptism and, above all, the Eucharist. Consider the following catalogue of Gentile suspicions reported by Minucius Felix, a defender of Christianity at the end of the second century CE. These rumors had probably originated more than a century earlier, as we can infer from the fact that Pliny, a governor at the beginning of the second century, reported to Emperor Trajan that these meals of the Christians were harmless.[80]

Minucius Felix Octavius 9:5–6[81]

(5) Now the story about the initiation of new members is as abhorrent as it is well known. A child covered with dough to deceive the unwary is placed before the one to be initiated. The novice kills this child with wounds which completely escape the eye; he himself mistakenly thinks that the thrusts through the covering of dough are harmless. They greedily lick up the blood of the child—what a sacrilege!—truly competing over its dismemberment. By this sacrifice they become brothers. With this complicity in such a crime they guarantee one another mutual silence. . . .

(6) Their feastings are also well known. People speak of them everywhere. . . . On a solemn day they assemble for their feast with all their children, sisters, mothers, and people of every gender and age. When the company is warmed by a rich meal and the fervor of impure lust is made hot by drunkenness, a dog that has been tied to the lampstand is provoked to spring forward vigorously, by being thrown pieces of meat that fall beyond the length of the cord by which it is tied. Thus the treacherous light is overturned. Now the bonds of unspeakable passion entangle them in a darkness that encourages shamelessness, as chance disposes.

Even when Gentiles were correctly informed about Christian teachings and practices, they were not likely inclined to sympathize with the new religion. After all, Christians possessed no images and even prayed to a god who had suffered the death of a slave on the cross.[82] The reproach of atheism was not long in coming. Besides, people soon attributed to Christians what they had previously attributed to Jews: a general hostility toward the rest of the human race.[83]

Specific Persecutions

The persecution under Nero represented the cruelty of an individual who blamed Christians for the great fire in Rome in order to make them the target of widespread disaffection and unrest. This short-lived persecution did not set a precedent for future dealings with Christians,[84] for it was recognized as the tyrannical action of an individual.[85] Yet its result was that the public became aware of the difference between the Christians and the Jews.

Domitian, who reigned as emperor from 81 to 96 CE, is commonly identified as the second significant persecutor of Christians.[86] Although such a designation may exaggerate his actions, the Revelation of John and the First Letter of Peter attest to the fact that during his rule the oppression of Christians amounted to more than local molestations.

For example, the book of Revelation depicts in chapters 13, 17, and 18 the ferocious actions of a wild beast—obviously an image of the Roman Empire—and Rev. 2–3 indicate the historical setting: the churches of Ephesus, Smyrna, Pergamon, Thyatira, Sardis, Philadelphia, and Laodicea. These congregations are suffering affliction,[87] individual members have been cast into prison,[88] and the Christian Antipas has suffered martyrdom in Pergamon,[89] where the throne of Satan is located.[90] And Christ's servant John, who has been driven into exile on the island of Patmos, reports all this.[91]

1 Peter stems from about the same time as Revelation and is addressed to "the elect strangers in the world, scattered throughout Pontus, Galatia, Cappadocia, Asia, and Bithynia."[92] Its pseudonymous author speaks to the Christian diaspora, advising the faithful to accept the present persecution as the last brief trial before the end-time,[93] and urging Christians to endure with patience the slanders and calumnies of their Gentile contemporaries.[94] It is especially noteworthy in the present context that "Peter" is reacting to a sharp ratcheting up of persecution. His description of the opposition between church and world reaches a climax at the end of the letter: "Let none of you suffer as a murderer, a thief, a criminal, or even as a mischief maker; yet if any of you suffers as a Christian, do not consider it as a disgrace, but glorify God because you bear his name."[95] Clearly this reflects both specific and widely occurring circumstances, especially since the author later includes the faithful throughout the Roman Empire in his description of Christian suffering.[96]

Twenty years later we come across what may well be a yet intensified degree of persecution in the same geographical area. It was in the fall of 112 CE that Pliny sent his questions concerning the Christians to Emperor Trajan from one of the coastal cities of North Pontus.[97] Some time earlier—apparently shortly after Pliny's arrival—local butchers had complained that Christians were responsible for a serious loss of income.[98] By instituting extraordinary proceedings[99] that required Christians to repudiate their faith or be executed, Pliny managed to stem the growth of Christianity and reinvigorate Roman state religion. I print the whole correspondence so that the reader may better be able to follow my historical reconstruction and subsequent argument.

Pliny, Letters 10.96[100]

Pliny to the Emperor Trajan

(1) It is my custom to refer all my difficulties to you, Sir, for no one is better able to resolve my doubts and to inform my ignorance.

I have never been present at an examination of Christians. Consequently, I do not know the nature or the extent of the punishments usually meted out to them, (2) nor the grounds for starting an investigation and how far it should be pressed. Nor am I at all sure whether any distinction should be made between them on the grounds of age, or if young people and adults should be treated alike; whether a pardon ought to be granted to anyone retracting his beliefs, or if he has once professed Christianity, he shall gain nothing by renouncing it; and whether it is the mere name of Christian which is punishable, even if innocent of crime, or rather the crimes associated with the name.

For the moment this is the line I have taken with all persons brought before me on the charge of being Christians. (3) I have asked them in person if they are Christians, and if they admit it, I repeat the question a second and a third time, with a warning of the punishment awaiting them. If they persist, I order them to be led away for execution; for, whatever the nature of their admission, I am convinced that their stubbornness and unshakeable obstinacy should not go unpunished. (4) There have been others similarly fanatical who are Roman citizens. I have entered them on the list of persons to be sent to Rome for trial.

Now that I have begun to deal with this problem, as so often happens, the charges are becoming more widespread and increasing in variety. (5) An anonymous pamphlet has been circulated which contains the names of a number of accused persons. Among these I considered that I should dismiss any who denied that they were or ever had been Christians when they had repeated after me a formula of invocation to the gods and had made offerings of wine and incense to your statue—which I had ordered to be brought into court for this purpose along with the images of the gods—, and furthermore had reviled the name of Christ: none of which things, I understand, any genuine Christians can be induced to do.

(6) Others, whose names were given to me by an informer, first admitted the charge and then denied it. They said that they had ceased to be Christians two or more years previously and some of them even twenty years ago. They all did reverence to your statue and the images of the gods in the same way as the others, and reviled the name of Christ. (7) They also declared that the sum total of their guilt or error amounted to no more than this: they had met regularly before dawn on a fixed day to chant verses alternately among themselves in honor of Christ as if to a god, and also to bind themselves by oath, not for any criminal purpose, but to abstain from theft, robbery, and adultery, to commit no breach of trust, and not to deny a deposit when called upon to restore it. After this ceremony it had been their custom to disperse and reassemble later to take food of an ordinary, harmless kind; but they had in fact given up this practice since my edict, issued on your instructions, which banned all political societies. (8) This made me decide that it was all the more necessary to extract the truth from two slave-women, whom they call deaconesses. I found nothing but a degenerate sort of cult carried to extravagant lengths.

(9) I have therefore postponed any further examination and hastened to consult you. The question seems to be worthy of your consideration, especially in view of the number of persons endangered. For a great many individuals of every age and class, both men and women, are being brought to trial, and this is likely to continue. It is not only the towns, but villages and rural districts too, which are infected through contact with this wretched cult. I think, though, that it is still possible for it to be checked and directed to better ends. (10) For there is no doubt that people have begun to throng the temples which had been almost entirely deserted for a long time. The sacred rites which had been allowed to lapse are being performed again, and flesh of sacrificial victims is on sale everywhere, though up till recently scarcely anyone could be found

to buy it. It is easy to infer from this that a great many people could be reformed if they were given an opportunity to repent.

Pliny, Letters 10.97

Trajan to Pliny the Younger

You have followed the right course of procedure, my dear Pliny, in your examination of the cases of persons charged with being Christians, for it is impossible to lay down a general rule to a fixed formula. These people must not be hunted out. If they are brought before you and the charge against them is proved, they must be punished, but in the case of anyone who denies that he is a Christian, and makes it clear that he is not by offering prayers to our gods, he is to be pardoned as a result of his repentance however suspect his past conduct may be. But pamphlets circulated anonymously must play no part in any accusation. They create the worst sort of precedent and are quite out of keeping with the spirit of our age.

COMMENT

From Pliny's letter, written at the beginning of the second century, we get a clear picture of how deeply the Christian religion had penetrated wide parts of the Roman province of Pontus-Bithynia—the home of the Christian communities to which 1 Peter had been addressed two decades earlier. The Roman response to this encroachment was not long in coming. Indeed, executions were the standard expedient whenever the local government sensed a threat to public order. The situation closely resembled that seen in 1 Peter, where the label "Christian" was sufficient reason for the Romans to intervene and Christians were anonymously accused. Pliny's note that some individuals had given up their Christian faith twenty years ago—presumably during a persecution—strongly suggests a probable date for the writing of both Revelation and 1 Peter. Two other points deserve to be underlined. First, Pliny punished those who refused to renounce Christianity not for their Christian faith but for their obstinacy, which was considered disdain of state power. Second, Pliny's letter makes it evident that no standard procedure for dealing with Christians had been established.

The provisions included in Trajan's answering letter became legally binding:

(a) Put an end to government-sponsored searches for Christians.
(b) Reported Christians are to be tried; confessed Christians must be punished.
(c) Any accused who sacrifice to the Roman gods will go unpunished.[101]
(d) Anonymous accusations are not permitted.[102]

Trajan's letter contained a new provision for Rome's future dealings with the church: hereafter, Christianity itself would be a punishable offense. On the other hand, not only did it narrow the legal basis for attacking Christians, but also the accusing party faced an increased risk. For now, by offering a sacrifice, the accused could clear himself or herself of guilt and at the same time establish grounds to sue the accuser for being malicious prosecution. Above all, Christians could now speak in public about the church without automatically incurring legal consequences. The result was a notably contradictory Roman policy toward Christians. For one thing, persons were subject to execution for being Christians, but might not be actively searched out. For another, a person who simply offered a public denial of his or her Christianity was automatically acquitted of a capital crime. Thus from a legal standpoint, Trajan's rescript was a disaster.

Possibly for that very reason many governors sought to avoid condemning those brought to trial; some simply sent the accused away. In the next-to-the-last decade of the second century, near the end of the emperor Commodus's reign, the Roman governor of an Asian province was taken aback when, in the midst of his regular judicial duties, he was faced with an excited crowd of people who had pushed their way into his courtroom. To his considerable consternation, they all voluntarily and vociferously announced that they were Christians, by which declaration they implicitly indicated their unwillingness to sacrifice to the Roman emperor, for this was the litmus test commonly used to identify Christians. Indeed, the enthusiastic throng exhorted the governor to carry out his office by summarily handing them all over to be executed. Since they had forced his hand, he straightaway ordered a few of them to their death. At this, however, the rest importuned him ever more vigorously to be granted the same privilege. He cried out to them in rage and frustration, "You wretches, if you want to die, you have cliffs to leap from and ropes to hang yourselves with!"[103] Clearly this official was not confronting his first Christians; he showed himself quite aware of their desire for martyrdom at the hands of Rome. All in all, Roman administrators spent more time and energy avoiding legal actions against Christians than they did prosecuting them.[104]

Result

In the foregoing we have examined persecutions of Christians as test cases of tolerance and intolerance. The result is sobering and clear: During the first two centuries the Roman government generally displayed a high degree of tolerance toward Christians. To be sure, governors sometimes strayed from the ancient principle of tolerance in forcing Christians to sacrifice or be killed. On the other hand, this practice arose largely because Christians had introduced religious intolerance into the Greco-Roman world, and had thereby led the Romans to view Christian intolerance as constituting a political threat. In the third century the situation grew increasingly polarized. For one thing, the spiritual climate of Rome responded to growing social instability by showing in many places a politically motivated religious zeal that replaced the relative indifference of the first two centuries. For another, the empire was threatened on its borders, and its survival depended as never before on civic allegiance and morale. In such a situation, Christians who exhibited divided loyalties or who refused to serve in the army alarmed the government, and accordingly the test of offering sacrifice for the emperor was increasingly relied on to identify those whose patriotism might be in question. It is an instructive paradox of world history that the emperor cult, which involved a very low degree of religious intensity and rituals of an entirely civil nature, should have become a test case for political loyalty, especially since it called for an offer of allegiance that few Christians had previously refused.

NOTES

1. Martin Hengel, *Judaism and Hellenism: Studies in Their Encounter in Palestine during the Early Hellenistic Period*, 2 vols. (Philadelphia: Fortress Press, 1974), 1:287.

2. In Greek, *laos*. See on this and related questions my *Paul: The Founder of Christianity* (Amherst, NY: Prometheus Books, 2002), pp. 138–65.

3. For the following see Bernhard Lang, *Monotheism and the Prophetic Minority: An Essay in Biblical History and Sociology* (Sheffield: Almond Press, 1983), pp. 13–59; Reinhard Gregor Kratz, *The Composition of the Narrative Books of the Old Testament* (London: T & T Clark, 2005).

4. Although most translations of the Bible render the Hebrew for the purported name of God as "the Lord," I shall in most cases use what was probably the original form: "Yahweh." To be sure, since the written form of ancient Hebrew did not utilize explicit vowels, only the consonants YHWH, the so-called tetragrammaton, are certain. Therefore we cannot assert with total certainty the original pronunciation of this name. A reasonably probable rendition, however, can be derived from the shorter form *Yah* (e.g., in Hallelu-yah—"praise Yahweh") and from old Greek texts. The reason for the uncertainty is that early forms of Judaism forbade the use of the divine appellative in order to preclude violation of the second commandment (Exod. 20:7; Deut. 5:11). (Even today many Jews omit the vowel when writing the divine title [G-d] for much the same reason.) In Jesus' days the holy name was pronounced only in the Temple—in the course of priestly blessings and penitential prayers of the high priest in the innermost forecourt of the Temple—lest the sacred name be profaned by Gentile ears. In synagogue worship the name YHWH was replaced by the title "*adonay*" (Lord), and the Greek translation of the Hebrew Bible (the Septuagint, or LXX) replaces YHWH with *kyrios* (again, Lord). So scrupulous was avoidance of the divine name that probably the customary pronunciation of the tetragrammaton was forgotten within a few years of the destruction of the Temple in 70 CE. Thereafter the divine name existed no longer as a spoken word, but only as a written symbol. The Jewish scholars who in later years added vowel indicators to the Hebrew text assigned to the otherwise unpronounceable element YHWH the vowels of the Hebrew word for Lord (*adonay*, but with the initial *a* abbreviated to *e*). A subsequent misunderstanding resulted in the artificial word *Jehovah*, first used by Calvin and the Calvinist branch of Christianity. In recent years, however, the use of Yahweh has become all but universal in both textual and oral usage.

5. When I say "Yahweh's claim" I always mean "the claims of the party that venerated Yahweh." For the sake of brevity I will simply write "Yahweh's claim" etc. and speak of him as a person.

6. Amos 1:12.

7. Kratz, *Composition of the Narrative Books*, p. 313.

8. 2 Kings 17.

9. Cf. Amos 8:2: "The end has come upon my people Israel. I will never again pass them by." Another passage in the book of the prophet explains the destruction as punishment for sin, Amos 2:6a: "Thus says Yahweh: "For three

transgressions of Israel, and for four, I will not revoke the punishment." Cf. the similar clause directed at Moab (2:1a) and against Judah (2:4a).

10. Kratz, *Composition of the Narrative Books*, p. 314.

11. Ibid., p. 133, Kratz assigns the following elements to the Ur-Deuteronomy: Deut. 6:4–5; 12:13–28; 14:22–29; 15:19–23; 16:16–17; 16:18–20; 17:8–13; 19:1–13; 19:15–21; 21:1–9; 26:1–16.

12. See, e.g., Deut. 12:13–14, 18–19, 27; 14:27; 17:8–9; 18:1–5.

13. See Num. 21:1–3; Deut. 2:30–35; 3:3–7; 7:1–2; Josh. 6:17–21.

14. Kratz, *Composition of the Narrative Books of the Old Testament*, p. 318.

15. Ibid., Kratz writes "the tradition" but that is too abstract.

16. Ibid. Then follows the text: "Yhwh, the king of the gods and Lord of the earth, became king over Israel and the world, the one God became the only God, who in place of the Davidic king chooses the people of Israel and has obligated them to unconditional obedience, not only in the elect place, but throughout the world, wherever Jews are. In the framework of the 'Hexateuch,' which extends from Exodus to Judges, this development was recorded by the insertion of the Decalogue in Exod. 20 and afterwards in Deut. 5."

17. Exod. 20:2–17.

18. Kratz, *Composition of the Narrative Books of the Old Testament*, p. 318.

19. 2 Chron. 36:23: "Thus says Cyrus king of Persia: 'Yahweh the God of heaven has given me all the kingdoms of the earth, and he has charged me to build him a house at Jerusalem, which is in Judah. Whoever is among you of all his people, may Yahweh his God be with him. Let him go up.'" Cf Ezra 1:2–3.

20. Gen. 1:1.

21. Gen. 1:2.

22. Gen. 1:3.

23. See Emil Schürer, *The History of the Jewish People in the Age of Jesus Christ (175 B.C–A.D. 135)*, 3 vols., rev. and ed. Geza Vermes, Fergus Millar, and Matthew Black (Edinburgh: T & T Clark, 1973–87), 1:143.

24. For the political and social history of Palestine between Alexander the Great and Antiochus IV Epiphanes see Martin Hengel, *Jews, Greeks and Barbarians: Aspects of the Hellenization of Judaism in the pre-Christian Period* (Philadelphia: Fortress Press, 1980), pp. 1–48.

25. Hengel, *Judaism and Hellenism*, 1:72–78, 277–303.

26. Josephus *Jewish Antiquities* 12.239.

27. At the time of Antiochus's installment as king, Jason's brother Onias III was high priest (see 2 Macc. 4:7–10).

28. See 1 Macc. 1:13; 2 Macc. 4:9, 12, 14.

29. Elias Bickerman, *The God of the Maccabees: Studies on the Meaning and Origin of the Maccabean Revolt* (Leiden: Brill, 1979), p. 39.

30. See Henri-Irénéé Marrou, *A History of Education in Antiquity* (New York: New American Library, A Mentor Book, 1964), pp. 151–57.

31. For what follows see Hengel, *Judaism and Hellenism*, 1:278.

32. 2 Macc. 4:22.

33. Hengel, *Judaism and Hellenism*, 1:300.

34. Ibid., p. 85.

35. The phrase "by whom all live (in Greek, *di' hou pantes zôopoiountai*)" contains the Stoic etymology of the names "*Dis*" and "*Zeus*."

36. Translation based on James H. Charlesworth, ed., *The Old Testament Pseudepigrapha*, vol. 2, *Expansions of the "Old Testament" and Legends, Wisdom and Philosophical Literature, Prayers, Psalms, and Odes, Fragments of Lost Judeo-Hellenistic Works* (New York: Doubleday, 1985), p. 13 (R. J. H. Shutt). Shutt translates "Jove" instead of "Dis." Another translation by Hengel, *Judaism and Hellenism*, 1:264: "They worship the same God—the Lord and Creator of the Universe, as all other men, as we ourselves, O king, though we call him by different names, such as Zeus or Dis. This name was very appropriately bestowed upon him by our first ancestors, in order to signify that He through whom all things were endowed with life and come into being, is necessarily the ruler and lord of the Universe."

37. Cf. Hengel, *Judaism and Hellenism*, 1:265. Of a different opinion is John M. G. Barclay, *Jews in the Mediterranean Diaspora from Alexander to Trajan (323 BCE–117 CE)* (Edinburgh: T & T Clark, 1996), p. 143: "*Greek* recognition that the God whom the Jews worship is the one whom the Greeks call Zeus may seem logically reversible into *Jewish* recognition that the God whom Gentiles worship (as Zeus) is the same God honoured by Jews. But what is logically consequent may be psychologically intolerable. The strategy of Aristeas, here as elsewhere, is to illustrate Gentile recognition of Jewish religion, but that does not mean that Jews also recognize the validity of Gentile worship." Against this see John J. Collins, *Between Athens and Jerusalem: Jewish Identity in the Hellenistic Diaspora*, 2nd ed. (Grand Rapids, MI: W. B. Eerdmans, 2000), p. 192: "Pseudo-Aristeas was not suggesting the complete equivalence of Greek and Jewish religion by any means, only that the Greeks, too, had a place for the worship of a supreme god."

38. Hengel, *Judaism and Hellenism*, 1:265–66.

39. For an exemplary analysis of the different layers of tradition and the different perspectives see Bickerman, *God of the Maccabees*.

40. 2 Macc. 6:2.

41. Dan. 9:27; 11:31; 12:11; Mark 13:14a, etc.

42. See Hengel, *Judaism and Hellenism*, 1:175–80.

43. 1 Macc. 13:31–42.

44. Eduard Meyer, *Ursprung und Anfänge des Christentums*, vol. 2: *Die Entwicklung des Judentums und Jesus von Nazareth* (Stuttgart: Klett-Cotta, 1922), p. 279.

45. Schürer, *History of the Jewish People*, 1:145.

46. Hengel, *Judaism and Hellenism*, 1:77.

47. For more consequences that resulted from the monotheistic faith of the first Gentile Christian converts see above, pp. 44.

48. 1 Thess. 1:9.

49. 1 Cor. 8:5–6a.

50. See my *The Unholy in Holy Scripture: The Dark Side of the Bible* (Louisville, KY: Westminster John Knox Press, 1997), pp. 76–127, for the rise of anti-Judaism in the New Testament.

51. Origen *Against Celsus* 5.33. Translation after Henry Chadwick, ed., *Origen: Contra Celsum* (Cambridge: University Press, 1965), p. 289. Cf. Robert L. Wilken, *The Christians as the Romans Saw Them* (New Haven, CT: Yale University Press, 1984), pp. 112–17 ("An Apostasy from Judaism").

52. Some would deny the validity of contrasting a tolerant paganism and an intolerant Christianity. For what I consider a typically unsuccessful example of this position, see Peter Garnsey, "Religious Toleration in Classical Antiquity," in *Persecution and Toleration: Papers Read at the Twenty-second Summer Meeting and the Twenty-third Winter Meeting of the Ecclesiastical History Society*, ed. W. J. Sheils (Oxford: Basil Blackwell, 1984), pp. 1–27. In the view of Peter Brown, *Authority and the Sacred: Aspects of the Christianisation of the Roman World* (Cambridge: University Press, 1995), to propose that contrast indicates "a misapprehension of Greek and Roman religion" (p. 31). The balance of this chapter constitutes a refutation of such misinformed theses.

53. This was the second attempt in this matter. In 383 CE Symmachus had traveled to Milan as the speaker of the Roman senate to direct that request to Emperor Gratian. Yet Christian senators along with the bishops Damasus and Ambrose had prevented Symmachus from being received at the emperor's court. See Richard Klein, *Der Streit um den Victoriaaltar. Die dritte Relatio des Symmachus und die Briefe 17, 18 und 57 des Mailänder Bischofs Ambrosius* (Darmstadt: Wissenschaftliche Buchgesellschaft, 1972), p. 19. See also Ernst Dassmann, "Wieviele Wege führen zur Wahrheit? Ambrosius und Symmachus im Streit um den Altar der Victoria," in *Ist der Glaube Feind der Freiheit? Die neue Debatte um den Monotheismus*, ed. Thomas Söding (Freiburg: Herder, 2003), pp. 123–41.

54. Translation after R. H. Barrow, *Prefect and Emperor: The Relationes of Symmachus A.D. 384* (Oxford: Clarendon Press, 1973), p. 41 (*Third relatio 9*).

55. Ibid.

56. Richard Klein, *Symmachus. Eine tragische Gestalt des ausgehenden Heidentums* (Darmstadt: Wissenschaftliche Buchgesellschaft, 1986), pp. 134–37. My translation of Ambrosius's eighteenth letter.

57. See Bernhard Kötting, *Religionsfreiheit und Toleranz im Altertum* (Opladen: Westdeutscher Verlag, 1977), p. 39. Cf. Deut. 7:5: "But thus shall you deal with them: you shall break down their altars, and dash in pieces their pillars, and hew down their Asherim, and burn their graven images with fire." (RSV)

58. Scaevola. See Augustine *City of God* 4.27, and earlier the Stoic Panaitios.

59. Translation after Henry Bettenson, *St. Augustine Concerning the City of God against the Pagans* (New York: Penguin Books, Pelican Books, 1972), p. 234.

60. Ibid., pp. 234–35.

61. Ibid., pp. 235–36.

62. Ibid., p. 236.

63. Ibid.

64. For the aforementioned Scaevola's criticism of the mythical brand of theology, see the excerpt from his work in Augustine *City of God* 4.27: "The poets give such a distorted picture of the gods that such deities cannot stand comparison with good people. One god is represented as a thief, another as an adulterer, and so on; all kinds of degradation and absurdity in word and deed are ascribed to them. Three goddesses have a beauty contest; Venus wins the prize, and the disappointed candidates overthrow Troy. Jupiter himself is changed into a bull, or a swan, to enjoy the favors of some woman or other. A goddess marries a man; Saturn devours his children. Any imaginable marvel and every conceivable vice, however remote from the divine nature, can be found in this poetic tradition." Translation after Bettenson, *St Augustine Concerning the City of God*, p. 169.

65. See Thomas Baier, *Werk und Wirkung Varros im Spiegel seiner Zeitgenossen. Von Cicero bis Ovid* (Stuttgart: F. Steiner, 1997), pp. 46–48.

66. See ibid., p. 43.

67. Tertullian *To the Nations* 2.1.11–13.

68. See Jochen Bleicken, *Verfassungs- und Sozialgeschichte des Römischen Kaiserreiches*, vol. 2, 2nd ed. (Paderborn: Schöningh, 1981), p. 164.

69. See, e.g., Livy 39.8–19 on the Bacchanal conspiracy of 187 BCE. Cf. further W. H. C. Frend, *Martyrdom and Persecution in the Early Church: A Study of a Conflict from the Maccabees to Donatus* (Garden City, NY: Doubleday & Company, Anchor Books, 1967), pp. 77–93 ("Rome and Foreign Cults"); on the Bacchanal conspiracy, pp. 82–84.

70. Acts 13:50; 14:2–5, 19; 17:5–9, 13; 19:23–40.

71. Since for most people only sacrificed meat was available for purchase, this constituted another problem for the ordinary Christian. See Stanley K. Stowers, "Greeks Who Sacrifice and Those Who Do Not: Toward an Anthropology of Greek Religion." In *The Social World of the First Christians: Essays in Honor of Wayne A. Meeks*, ed. L. Michael White and O. Larry Yarbrough (Philadelphia: Fortress Press, 1995): 293–333.

72. Celsus in Origen *Against Celsus* 1.9. Translation after Chadwick, ed., *Origen: Contra Celsum*, p. 12.

73. For details see Wilken, *Christians as the Romans Saw Them*, pp. 31–47.

74. 1 Cor. 6:1–6.

75. Rom. 15:1 (written in Corinth).

76. The prohibition against eating meat offered to idols is Jewish (cf. Lev. 17:8; Ps. 105:28 LXX) and became the first part of the so-called Apostolic decree (Acts 15:20, 29; 21:25). See also Didache 6:3 and the comprehensive analysis

by Jürgen Wehnert, *Die Reinheit des "christlichen Gottesvolkes" aus Juden und Heiden: Studien zum historischen und theologischen Hintergrund des sogenannten Aposteldekrets* (Göttingen: Vandenhoeck & Ruprecht, 1997).

77. See the discussions in 1 Cor. 8–10 and Rom. 14–15.

78. See Rev. 2:14, 20; Justin *Dialogue with Trypho* 35.1–6; Irenaeus *Against All Heresies* 1.26.3 (on the Nicolaitans mentioned in Rev. 2).

79. 1 Cor. 7:12–16; see esp. verse 14c.

80. Pliny *Letters* 10.96.6 (see above, pp. 47–51).

81. Translation following Gerd Lüdemann and Martina Janssen, *Suppressed Prayers: Gnostic Spirituality in Early Christianity* (Harrisburg, PA: Trinity Press International, 1998), pp. 121–22.

82. On the negative implications of the death on the cross see Martin Hengel, *Crucifixion in the Ancient World* (Philadelphia: Fortress Press, 1977).

83. See Tacitus *Histories* 5.5 on the Jews as hostile to all human beings. See also my *Paul: The Founder of Christianity* (Amherst, NY: Prometheus Books, 2002), p. 152.

84. Differently Reinhard Feldmeier, *Der erste Brief des Petrus* (Leipzig: Evangelische Verlagsanstalt, 2005), p. 4.

85. See Tacitus *Annals* 15.44.2–5; Suetonius *Life of the Caesars*. Nero 16.2.

86. Thus the opinion of Melito of Sardis, Origen, Eusebius, and Lactantius.

87. Rev. 2:9.

88. Rev. 2:10.

89. Rev. 2:13.

90. Ibid.

91. Rev. 1:9.

92. 1 Pet. 1:1.

93. 1 Pet. 1:6–7; 5:4, 8, 10.

94. 1 Pet. 2:12, 19; 3:16.

95. 1 Pet. 4:15–16.

96. 1 Pet. 5:9. See Feldmeier, *Der erste Petrusbrief*, p. 167.

97. See Wilken, *Christians as the Romans Saw Them*, p. 15.

98. See by way of analogy the complaint of the silversmiths of Ephesus in Acts 19.

99. In Latin, *cognitiones*. "The term *cognitio* confirms what the later evidence indicates, that the form of trial was the personal judgement of the holder of *imperium* sitting formally *pro tribunali* to hear charges made in due form, and assisted by his consilium. He may be the proconsul or the imperial legate in provinces, or the city prefect who exercised the main police supervision at Rome with capital powers" (A. N. Sherwin-White, *The Letters of Pliny: A Historical and Social Commentary* [Oxford: Clarendon Press, 1966], pp. 694–95).

100. Translation after Pliny, *Letters and Panegyricus* in two volumes, II. Letters. Books VIII–X and Panegyricus with an English translation by Betty Radice,

Loeb Classical Library (Cambridge, MA: Harvard University Press and London: William Heinemann, 1969), pp. 285–93. See also the commentary by Sherwin-White, *The Letters of Pliny*, pp. 691–712.

101. Note that Trajan does not mention the sacrifice for the emperor as a test although Pliny had used it in such a way (*Letters* 10.96.5). This omission may constitute an indirect criticism.

102. This detail may represent another implied criticism of Pliny, inasmuch as he had acted against the Christians on the basis of anonymous notices.

103. Tertullian *To Scapula* 5. The proconsul's name was C. Arrius Antoninus.

104. On the foregoing see G. W. Bowersock, *Martyrdom and Rome* (Cambridge: Cambridge University Press, 1995), pp. 1–21.

Chapter II

THE SECOND LETTER TO THE
THESSALONIANS

*"I did that," says my memory. "I could not have done that," says
my pride and remains inexorable. Eventually—the memory yields.*[1]

—Friedrich Nietzsche

1. INTRODUCTION

To a greater degree than has heretofore been acknowledged, this
document of only forty-seven verses deserves the close attention
of those concerned with the issue of right belief and false belief in Primitive Christianity.[2] In 1903 William Wrede clearly demonstrated its
striking similarities to 1 Thessalonians in structure and vocabulary,[3]
concluding that 2 Thessalonians has employed 1 Thessalonians as a
model. This dependence is evident both from numerous verbal agreements[4] and from the fact that the most striking formal characteristic of
1 Thessalonians, the second thanksgiving found in 2:13, also appears in
2 Thess. 2:13. "If an interpreter wants to defend Pauline authorship for
both Thessalonian letters, he or she must somehow explain why so
many important words and phrases from 1 Thessalonians are found in
2 Thessalonians."[5] Wrede further suggested that the genuineness of 2
Thessalonians could not be asserted if one supposes it to have been
written to the same congregation only a short while after 1 Thessalonians—a supposition that has been generally accepted by those who
defend the authenticity of 2 Thessalonians in order to explain the agree-

59

ment between the two letters. Yet it makes little sense to write a second letter to the same congregation after a month or two and repeat portions of the first almost slavishly.[6]

One must also record the discrepancy between what the two letters say about the beginning of the end-time. According to 1 Thessalonians, the Second Coming of Jesus[7] will occur in the immediate future.[8] According to 2 Thessalonians, the day of the Lord can hardly be considered imminent. The general rebellion of the sinful must come first, and the man of lawlessness must be revealed, "the son of perdition who opposes and exalts himself against all that men call 'god' and anything that is worshipped, so that he takes his seat in the temple of God, proclaiming that he himself is God."[9] This discrepancy is an additional argument against the genuineness of 2 Thessalonians, especially since the other genuine Pauline letters also give a different calendar of the events before the end of time.[10]

We should further note in passing two desperate attempts that are sometimes made to refute the thesis that 2 Thessalonians uses 1 Thessalonians. The first contends that 1 Thessalonians, with its lack of explicit scriptural quotations, is addressed to the Gentile Christian part of the community of Thessalonica, while 2 Thessalonians, which often cites the Old Testament, is addressed to the Jewish Christians there.[11] This thesis is contradicted by the fact that Paul's predominantly Gentile Christian communities were instructed in scripture from the beginning. The second argues that 2 Thessalonians is in fact earlier than 1 Thessalonians,[12] a proposal that fails to explain the difficulty of the different expectations of the Second Coming of Jesus. Moreover, it is challenged by the clear evidence that 1 Thess. 2:1–3:5 looks back at what is clearly the quite recent visit during which Paul founded the congregation. In this case there could hardly have been time for an intervening letter.

But if Paul did not write 2 Thessalonians, and 1 Thessalonians is the earliest available writing of Paul and Primitive Christianity in general,[13] then we must ask when, why, and by whom 2 Thessalonians was composed.

The hypothesis currently favored by what is perhaps a majority of scholars derives from Wrede, and goes as follows: 2 Thessalonians seeks to revise the assumption in 1 Thessalonians that most Christians will survive until Jesus' Second Coming, an expectation seriously undermined by recent deaths within the community. It provides, as it were, the normative interpretation of the first letter.

Against this, a hypothesis developed as early as the nineteenth century seems to emerge as superior. It proposes that the author of 2 Thessalonians intended not to interpret 1 Thessalonians but to *supplant* it, because he regarded the hope for Jesus' imminent return in 1 Thessalonians as heterodox and therefore sought to repudiate the whole text as inauthentic. Thus, even according to the easy criteria of antiquity, the author of 2 Thessalonians purposely falsified a document. Yet since he obviously felt no qualms of conscience in this matter (he himself warns in 2 Thess. 2:2 against a forged letter of Paul), 2 Thessalonians must be considered a counterforgery. We shall now have to see whether a critical analysis of the letter can strengthen such a thesis.

2. TRANSLATION AND ANALYSIS OF 2 THESSALONIANS

1:1–2: Address and Greeting

(1) Paul, Silvanus, and Timothy to the church of the Thessalonians in <u>GOD our Father and the Lord Jesus Christ</u>. (2) Grace to you and peace from <u>GOD our father and the Lord Jesus Christ</u>.

COMMENT

Verse 1: Instead of "God the father" as in 1 Thess. 1:1a, this verse reads "God our father," which corresponds to the usage of the historical Paul.[14] The rest of the verse precisely matches 1 Thess. 1:1a.

Verse 2: A comparison with 1 Thess. 1:1b, "Grace to you and peace," shows that the greeting in this verse has been awkwardly enlarged by the phrase "from God our father and the Lord Jesus Christ." It seems that the author, knowing the extended greeting to be a standard element of Paul's letters,[15] has therefore added it at this point in order to suggest the text's authenticity.

1:3–12: The Tribulation of the Thessalonians and the Justness of God's Judgment

(3) We are bound to give thanks to GOD always for you, brothers, as is fitting, because your faith is growing abundantly, and the love of every one of you for one another is increasing. (4) Therefore we ourselves boast of you in the churches of GOD for your steadfastness and faith in all your persecutions and in the *afflictions* which you are enduring. (5) This is evidence of the **just** judgment of GOD that you may be made worthy of the kingdom of GOD, for which you are suffering.

(6) It is **just**, indeed, that GOD repays with *affliction* those who *afflict* you, (7a) and to grant rest with us to you who are *afflicted*,

(7b) when the **LORD JESUS** is revealed from heaven with his mighty angels in flaming fire, (8) inflicting severe _punishment_ upon those who do not know GOD and upon those who do not obey the gospel of our **LORD JESUS**, (9) who shall suffer the _punishment_ of eternal destruction and exclusion from the presence of the Lord and from the GLORY of his might, (10) when he comes on that day to be GLORIFIED BY his saints, and to be marveled at by all who have believed, because our testimony to you was believed (11) to which end we always pray for you, that our GOD may make you worthy of his call, and may fulfil every good resolve and work of faith by his power (12) so that the name of our **LORD JESUS** may be GLORIFIED in you, and you in him, according to the grace of our GOD and the **LORD JESUS** Christ.

COMMENT

The thanksgiving that in fact runs all the way from verse 3 to verse 12 seems at first glance to be completed in verse 4. In Greek, it consists of one convoluted sentence, a grammatical monstrosity that can be understood only after many readings. In the above translation I have tried to give the English reader an impression of the syntactic muddle found in the original.

Verse 3: "We are bound to give thanks to God" occurs also at 2 Thess. 2:13, yet at no other place in Paul's writings or in the rest of the New Testament. At 1 Thess. 1:2 and 2:13—both passages are models of 2 Thess. 1:3, 13—we read "we thank God."

Verse 4: Rather than reproduce the triad "faith," "steadfastness," and "hope" found in 1 Thess. 1:3b, the author leaves out "hope."[16] While "hope" is basic for 1 Thessalonians[17] the emphasis in 2 Thessalonians lies on "steadfastness."

Verse 5: "Suffering" clarifies the meaning of "persecutions" and "tribulations" in the previous verse. The author describes the persecutions and tribulations of the community as "evidence of the judgment." Indeed, the tribulations of the community are unjust and the consequence will be the punishment of the evildoers. Apparently the author's statements are based on experience of his own, especially since we find no parallel in 1 Thessalonians. It is noteworthy, though, that most members of Christian communities in the first century and beyond were hoping for a radical transformation of the social order that would signal the end of this world.[18]

Verses 6–7a: The wordplay with "afflict/affliction" picks up "affliction" from verse 4. Thus verse 6 is a continuation of verses 4–5. The author concludes from these unspecified afflictions two things: first, the evildoers who have caused the afflictions will be justly punished; second, the community will be rewarded for the injustice it has suffered.

Verses 7b–10: This section is a commentary of verses 6–7a. In verse 8 the people who have caused affliction are redefined as those who do not know God and verse 10 understands those presently being afflicted to be the holy ones and the believers who will rejoice at the Lord's coming. Making use of Old Testament and Jewish traditions,[19] the author solemnly describes the Second Coming. The historical Paul, on the other hand, while being very detailed about the items of punishment, does not spell out its details. He nowhere places emphasis on the punishment of unbelievers, but rather hints at the judgment from which he asserts the risen Jesus will save the believers.[20] In all the letters ascribed to Paul, the description of the pagans as those "who do not know God" at verse 8 is used only here and once in 1 Thessalonians.[21] The expression "who do not obey the gospel of our Lord Jesus Christ" surely refers to the pagans and possibly to opponents from within the community. At any rate, both groups are enemies of the "believing" Christian community. The term "gospel of our Lord Jesus Christ" occurs only here in the whole New Testament, and certainly derives from the author. Indeed, he regards "gospel" as a formula of truth,[22] having itself become a transmittable doctrine.[23] This doctrinal teaching and the witness of the "Paul" of 2 Thessalonians call for a faith that only those who have adopted the "love for truth"[24] are able to practice.

Verses 11–12: These verses assure the recipients of intercession and continue the thanksgiving of verses 3–4. "Glorified" picks up the same verb in verse 10. A possible background text is Isa. 66:5 LXX: "so that the name of the Lord be glorified."

2:1–2: Warning against a Forged Letter about the Day of the Lord

(1) We beg you, brothers, concerning the coming of our Lord Jesus Christ and our gathering with him, (2) not to be quickly shaken in mind or alarm yourselves, either by (supposed) spirit or by word of mouth, or by any letter purporting to be from us alleging that the day of the Lord has come.

COMMENT

The thanksgiving of 1:3–12 is followed by two sections—2:1–2 and 2:3–12—that pertain to the statements in the thanksgiving about the future judgment. Since these two passages are essentially without parallel in 1 Thessalonians, they can reasonably be taken to reflect the real purpose of the author.

Verse 1: This verse designates the theme of the following section: the Second Coming of the Lord Jesus and the union of the faithful with him. By proceeding in this way the author picks up the topic of 1 Thess. 4:13–5:11. The term "gathering"[25] occurs only here in Pauline literature.[26]

Verse 2: This verse suggests that the slogan "The day of the Lord has come" may have arisen by prophetic utterance in the spirit, either by quoting a saying of the apostle Paul or by referring to one of his letters. "Purporting to be from us" is the translation of the Greek *hôs di' hêmôn*. The Greek particle *hôs* implies a fabricated or objectively false property, and because *hôs di' hêmôn* immediately follows *epistolês* (letter), it is intended to indicate that the letter does not come from Paul. Even if one were to stretch a grammatical point to propose that it also referred to the two preceding elements (spirit, word), this would not alter the reference to "letter." Thus verse 2 warns the community not to allow itself to be confused about the Second Coming, "either by spirit (i.e., an exclamation in the Spirit) or by word of mouth or by letter purporting to be from us, alleging that the day of the Lord has come." As to the origin of this formula, one has to remember that the most striking characteristic of 1 Thessalonians is an ardent expectation of the coming of Jesus from heaven in the very near future.[27] Already during the founding of the community of Thessalonica Paul had indicated that the Christians there were expecting the advent of Jesus, whose imminent arrival would save them from the future judgment of wrath. Moreover, Paul expected to be alive—along with most of the other community members—at that time. Clearly, it is such a hope that the author of 2 Thessalonians rejects. To be sure, the phrase "The day of the Lord has come" cannot be found verbatim in 1 Thessalonians; still, one can imagine how in later times the reading of such specific passages as 1 Thess. 4:15, 17 could easily lead to the expectation that the day of the Lord was at hand. Indeed, a literal reading of these passages *had* to lead to such an interpretation, for in any other case one would have to reject the whole passage and others like it as an error.[28]

Two indications from the time of the Roman presbyter Hippolytus (late second century CE) give us an idea of what an appropriation of 1 Thessalonians may have looked like,[29] and how the expectation of an imminent end may have been expressed in practice.[30] In his *Commentary on Daniel*, Hippolytus writes:

> (IV 18) I can also relate something that happened recently in Syria. For a certain leader of the church in Syria . . . was himself deceived and deceived others . . . he misled many of the brothers so that they went out into the wilderness with women and children **to meet with Christ**.[31] These also wandered around in vain in the mountains, so that they would likely have been seized by a centurion as robbers and executed. Fortunately his wife was a believer. She persuaded him to desist from his recklessness, lest a general persecution take place because of them.

Immediately after that, Hippolytus gives another example:

> (IV 19) Similarly, (there was) another man in Pontus, who was also a leader of the church, a pious and humble man, but one who did not hold fast to scripture; rather, he believed more in the visions which he himself saw. . . . And then he once spoke in his error and said, "I want you to know, brothers, that the final judgment will take place after a

year." They heard him saying that **the day of the Lord has come**,[32] and prayed to the Lord with weeping and lamentation day and night, having the coming day of judgment before their eyes. And he led the brothers astray into such great anxiety and fearfulness that they left their lands and fields desolate, and most of them sold their possessions. And he said to them, "If what I have said does not happen, then no longer believe scripture, but let each of you do what he or she wills." So they waited for what was to come. And when a year was past and nothing of what he had said happened, he himself was ashamed that he had been wrong, but the scriptures seemed truthful. The brothers, however, were found to have been seduced to sin so that the virgins got married, and the men went to work on the land. But those who had sold their property in vain had to beg for their bread.

The above two cases illustrate two specific examples of how belief in the imminent end was annulled by the facts, and key vocabulary elements—printed in boldface—correspond word for word with 1 Thess. 4:17 and 2 Thess. 2:2. The expectation of meeting the Lord is rooted in the conviction that the day of the Lord has come; the catch phrase disparaged in 2 Thess. 2:2 matches the expectation of 1 Thess. 4:13–17.

The author of 2 Thessalonians not only attacks such an expectation but he preemptively nullifies an appeal to Paul by labeling 1 Thessalonians a forgery and putting his "authentic" letter to the Thessalonians into circulation (or introducing it to the community). 2 Thess. 2:2 and 2:15 make the point: Those who are leading people in Thessalonica astray "by spirit or by word of mouth" derive their authority from a *forged* text, 1 Thessalonians. Not only is the correct tradition about the end-time to be found in 2 Thessalonians, but the letter as a whole constitutes the ground for true Christian faith and must be so accepted without further discussion. Therefore, the author of 2 Thessalonians ordains, "If anybody disobeys what we say in this letter, note that man, and have nothing to do with him, that he may be ashamed" (3:14). Clearly, a correct understanding of Paul requires acceptance of 2 Thessalonians. See also below, pp. 74–75, on 2 Thessalonians' seal of authenticity at 3:17.

The questions that next demand our attention are these: How could the author of 2 Thessalonians have come to consider 1 Thessalonians a forgery—a letter that people had read in service and transmitted for many years? Did he *personally* believe in his theory? What criterion did he use to deny authenticity? Apparently the author assumed that 1

Thessalonians in its present shape did not stem from the apostle, and had so concluded because the "opponents" derived their theology from it. Therefore the end sanctified the means—composing a forgery—the dishonesty of which he may have soon enough repressed. If indeed his mind thus deceived him, it would be neither the first nor the last time that, as Nietzsche put it, memory yielded to pride.[33]

2:3–12: Teachings about the End-time

(3a) Let no one **DECEIVE** you in any way whatever. (3b) For (that day cannot come) unless the rebellion comes first, and the man of *lawlessness* is revealed, the son of perdition, (4) who opposes and exalts himself against all that men call "god" and anything that is worshipped, so that he takes his seat in the temple of GOD, proclaiming that he himself is GOD.

(5) Do you not remember that when I was still with you I told you this? (6) And you know <u>what restrains</u> him now, ensuring that he may be revealed in his time. (7) For the secret (power) of *lawlessness* is already at work—only until the <u>Restrainer</u> is out of the way.

(8) And then the *lawless* one will be revealed, and the Lord Jesus will kill him with the breath of his mouth and annihilate him by the manifestation of his (own) coming. (9) The coming (of the lawless one) will occur by the activity of Satan with all power and with signs and wonders (determined by the) <u>*LIE*</u>, (10) and with all **DECEPTION** of *unrighteousness* for those doomed to destruction, because they would not grasp the love of TRUTH and so be saved.

(11) Therefore GOD sends upon them the power of delusion, to make them <u>believe</u> the <u>*LIE*</u>, (12) so that all may be condemned who did not <u>believe</u> the TRUTH but had pleasure in *unrighteousness*.

COMMENT

Now the recipients of the letter are given the correct teaching about the end: it will come in the indefinite future, and only after the adversary has revealed himself. The true believers can rest assured that Jesus will kill the "lawless one" (verse 8) and that God will punish the sinners for their refusal to accept the truth (verses 11–12).

Verse 3a: Compare with the warning in Mark 13:5b about deception at the time that precedes the end of the world. First-century Jews and Christians alike considered every teaching that does not match religious truth to be fraud and deception.[34]

Verses 3b–4: The general apostasy and the arrival of the "man of lawlessness"[35] are necessary antecedents for the coming of the end. Both concepts are rooted in Jewish apocalyptic thought[36] and basic to Primitive Christian belief.[37] It remains unclear, though, whether a clear-cut myth of an eschatological opponent or of the Antichrist[38] can be combined with this personage and/or whether a specific historical figure is in view.[39]

Since neither event has taken place, the author concludes, the maxim he repudiated in verse 2 (the day of the Lord has [already] come) must be a deception.

Verse 5: The recipients of the letter should remember that "Paul" had already during the founding of the community sketched the two preconditions of the end. Yet we do not find these two items in 1 Thessalonians. What Paul did say there about the imminent coming of Jesus from heaven renders improbable the notion that he taught anything about the preconditions of the end. (Of course, it is at least a theoretical possibility that additional events may take place between the prediction of the imminent end and its actual occurrence.) Moreover, 1 Thessalonians contains several references to Paul's teachings and his exhortations to remember them.[40] The author of 2 Thessalonians pseudepigraphically employs this technique in claiming that during the founding of the community "Paul" had already noted these two preconditions of the end.

Verse 6: In addition to the two precursors of the end drama, the author adds another item—"the restraint"[41] that delays the end's coming. "Now" is used to distinguish the present from the past during which "Paul" told the community the content of verses 3–4. In the meantime the Thessalonians have learned of yet another factor that postpones the end. Yet we are not told how they have obtained that knowledge.

Verse 7: To refute the mistaken notion that the present situation has nothing to do with the expected end, the author introduces a secretly working force that is soon to be openly effective: the power of lawlessness. It is striking that in verse 7 he uses "the Restrainer," a masculine appellative, rather than the impersonal "restraint" found in verse 6. The reason for the change may be that the author is preparing the reader for the lawless person of verse 8. "Secret (power) of lawlessness" corresponds to "man of lawlessness" in verse 3. In the next verse "the lawless one" will pick up that thread.

Verse 8: "The lawless one" is identical with "the man of lawlessness" of verse 3. His arrival is one of the preconditions of the end. Writing, as it were, under the alias "Paul," the author predicts both this evil one's coming in the future and his destruction at the manifestation[42] of the advent[43] of the Lord Jesus.

Verses 9–10: Expanding on verse 8, the author adds that the coming of the lawless one occurs by the activity of Satan with all the power, signs, and wonders that falsehood is capable of producing. These signs and wonders seduce those who will be lost because they have not yet accepted the love of truth. Thus the last days will see the fulfillment of what has already begun to happen: as verse 3a warns, those who lack faith are being seduced in the present.

Verses 11–12: These verses explain and vary the content of verse 10 by arguing that God has assured the condemnation of unbelieving sinners by afflicting them with delusion so they will be more susceptible to the full power[44] of the lie.

2:13–15: Thanks and Consequences

(13) But we are bound to give thanks to GOD always for you, <u>*brothers*</u> beloved by the **Lord**, because GOD chose you from the beginning[45] to be saved through sanctification by the Spirit and belief in the truth. (14) To this he called you through our gospel, so that you may obtain the glory of our **Lord** Jesus Christ.

(15) So then, *brothers*, stand firm and hold to the traditions that you were taught, either by our word of mouth or by our letter.

COMMENT

Verses 13–14: Taking for his model 1 Thess. 2:13, the author attaches a second thanksgiving. Alluding to 1 Thess. 4:7 and 5:9, and creating a contrapuntal expansion of verse 10, verses 13b–14 formulate the state of salvation in the community: God has elected its members from the beginning and they have believed in the truth—quite the opposite of the lost ones whose fate is described earlier in verses 10–12.

Verse 15: This antithetical and summarizing echo of verse 2 admonishes the recipients of the letter to stand firm and to hold to the traditions that "Paul" taught them, "either by word of mouth or by letter." As in verse 5, "word" here refers to the preaching of Paul among the Thessalonians. The letter referred to is the present one—not 1 Thessalonians, but 2 Thessalonians, whose doctrine the recipients must observe and whose forged status is thus further camouflaged.[46] But in view of the doctrinal conflicts between the two, it is much more likely that the author is promoting the present letter—supposedly by Paul—as a vehicle of the tradition.

According to William Wrede, 2 Thess 2:15 "almost certainly refers to the first letter,"[47] and therefore the author of 2 Thessalonians cannot be describing 1 Thessalonians as inauthentic.[48] However, the context clearly requires that 2 Thess. 2:15 refers to 2 Thessalonians, "whose doctrine the Christians are to observe" and which is antithetically dissociated from the forged letter mentioned in 2 Thess. 2:2—probably signifying 1 Thessalonians. In short, the recipients of 2 Thessalonians are to maintain the valid end-time traditions, which have been communicated to them supposedly by word of mouth or by the present 2 Thessalonians.

2:16–17: Blessing of the Apostle

(16) Now may our Lord Jesus Christ himself, and God our Father, who loved us and gave us eternal *comfort* and **good** hope through grace, (17) *comfort* your hearts and establish them in every **good** work and word.

COMMENT

Verse 16: The expression "good hope" occurs in the New Testament only here. Compare "living hope" in 1 Pet. 1:3 and "blessed hope" at Titus 2:13.

Verse 17: The wish is rather general and would be suitable in almost any situation. "Word" finds an echo in verse 15.

3:1–5: Exhortation of Prayer

(1) Finally, brothers, pray for us, that the word of the **Lord** may spread rapidly and be glorified, as it did among you, (2a) and that we may be saved from wicked and *evil* people; (2b) for not all have faith. (3) But the **Lord** is faithful; he will strengthen you and guard you from *evil*. (4) And we have confidence in the **Lord** about you, that you are doing and will do the things which we command. (5) May the **Lord** direct your hearts to the love of God and to the steadfastness of Christ.

COMMENT

The style is rough, the train of thought unclear, and the expressions quite formulaic. Note that "Lord" is used four times.

Verse 1: Concerning the rapid spread of the word of the Lord, compare Ps. 147:4 (LXX). On "to be glorified," see earlier 1:9, 10, 12.

Verse 2: The note in verse 2b that "not all have faith"[49] serves as a reason for the statement of verses 1–2a. The author "provides a rationale for the urgent prayer for a successful missionary endeavor."[50]

Verse 3: This saying about the faithfulness of the Lord[51] picks up the wish of 2:17. Both the saying and the wish are as vague in substance as they are encouraging in tone.

Verse 4: The contextually discordant use of the verb "to command" is striking. It may point ahead to the next section, which contains a list of commands.

Verse 5: A general wish in the form of a prayer rounds off the unit. It is typical of a forged writing that the meanings of such genitives as "of God" and "of Christ" are not clear. If taken as subjective genitives, they would designate the love that comes from God and the steadfastness that comes from Christ. But they could be objective genitives, in which case the expressions denote love toward God and steadfastness toward Christ. Possibly the pseudepigraphic author has purposefully left the precise meaning open.

3:6–12: Rebuke of Idlers

(6) Now we COMMAND you, **brothers**, in the name of our ***Lord Jesus Christ***, that you keep away from any **brother** who is living in

an *undisciplined* manner and not in accord with the tradition that you received from us.

(7) For you yourselves know how you ought to <u>imitate</u> us; we were not *undisciplined* when we were with you, (8) we did not **EAT** any one's bread without paying, but with toil and labor we <u>worked</u> night and day, that we might not burden any of you. (9a) It was not because we have not that right, (9b) but to give you in our conduct an example to <u>imitate</u>.

(10) For even when we were with you, we gave you this COM-MAND: If any one will not <u>work</u>, let him not **EAT**. (11) For we hear that some of you are living *undisciplined* lives, mere busybodies, not doing any <u>work</u>. (12) Now such persons we COMMAND and exhort in the **<u>Lord Jesus Christ</u>** to do their <u>work</u> in quietness and to **EAT** their own bread.

COMMENT

The overall thrust of this section is its concurrent call for disciplined living and warning against idleness. See the italics in boldface in verses 6, 7, and 11.

Verse 6: The verse begins weightily, leading the reader to expect a deep-seated problem and/or a draconian solution. Yet "Paul" demands only that the community members withdraw from a brother who leads an undisciplined or disorderly life. (Note that the author can consider such a person still a "brother.") Both injunctions—keeping the offender as a brother and interrupting the personal relationship—are rooted in the situation of 2 Thessalonians, which becomes clear only in verse 11. The received tradition refers to the preaching of Paul in general, especially as preserved in 2 Thessalonians.

Verses 7–9: The admonition to imitate Paul[52] frames this section (verses 7, 9b). The author derives the content of verse 8 from 1 Thess. 2:9, which he thus declares an authentic—and perhaps normative—element of apostolic tradition. Verse 9b echoes 1 Cor. 9:4–5.

Verse 10: Concerning idlers, the author claims that he ("Paul") has already denounced them during the founding of the community: "If any one will not work, let him not eat." The phrase may derive from the author, especially since the historical Paul wrote nothing like this in 1 Thessalonians or in any other preserved letter.[53]

Verse 11: This verse reveals that the only concrete accusation in verses 6–12 is the charge of idleness. It is doubtful that this reproach has anything to do with the topic of the advent of Jesus discussed at 2:1–2, for the author does not connect these two items. Behind the warning of verse 11 is the situation of Christian communities around the end of the first century. More than one congregation had experienced problems with itinerant missionaries who sought to live in relative ease at the expense of the community.[54]

Verse 12: By way of summary, the author issues a command. Note in the translation my indications of the overlaps with what was said earlier.

3:13–15: Concluding Exhortations

(13) **Brothers**, do not be weary in doing what is right. (14) If anybody disobeys our instruction in this letter, note that man, and do not associate with him, that he may be ashamed. (15) Do not look on him as an enemy, but warn him as a **brother**.

COMMENT

Verse 13: After dealing with cases of idleness in the previous section verses 6–12, the author begins afresh. "Doing what is right" does not call for social work ("doing good") but means moral behavior in general.[55]

Verses 14–15: "Letter" in verse 14 refers to 2 Thessalonians: the right way to understand Paul is through acceptance of 2 Thessalonians. The author claims to have laid down both the foundation of faith and the ethical rules. For both he demands obedience.

The command to shun a disobedient person (verse 14) echoes the demand of verse 6 to keep away from the undisciplined. It is noteworthy, though, that both groups of persons continue to belong to the community. Oddly enough, verse 14 warns against a close personal association with wrongdoers, yet the brotherly admonition encouraged by verse 15 clearly requires such contact. This logical flaw is further evidence of the forged character of the writing. Its author does not have to take a concrete situation of an individual community into account, but from the outset writes with the general situation of the church in his mind. Besides, the great difference between the opponents he attacked in chapter 2 and those he reprimands in chapter 3 reveals rhetorical disorganization in addition to faulty logic. In the earlier case reconciliation is no longer possible, but in the latter correction may bring about reform. Even more fundamental, when the adversaries invoke Paul in claiming that the end has already arrived,[56] "Paul" accuses them of forgery,[57] and accuses them of trying to seduce the congregation.[58] Rather than attempt to bridge these differences, the author sketches a history of salvation that excludes the deceivers from the here-and-now salvation in the end-time. He seems to have forgotten his earlier invocation of a *brotherly* warning—to say nothing of the "peace" in the following verse.

3:16–18: Ending of the Letter: Repeated Wishes of Grace

(16a) Now may the <u>Lord</u> of **peace** himself give you **peace** at all times in all ways. (16b) The <u>Lord</u> be with you all. (17) I, Paul, write this greeting with my own hand. This is the mark in every letter of mine; it is the way I write. (18) The grace of our <u>Lord</u> Jesus Christ be with you all.

COMMENT

Verse 16: The blessing in verse 16a is somewhat changed from that of 1 Thess. 5:23. The blessing of verse 16b is condensed and serves as a sort of summation. It has few parallels in the Pauline literature, but compare Rom. 15:33: "The God of peace be with you all."

Verse 17: The forger's audacity is shown by the conclusion of the letter with its "seal of authenticity": "I, Paul, write this greeting with my own hand. This is the mark in every letter of mine; it is the way I write." Here the author surpasses even the historical Paul of 1 Thessalonians (which notwithstanding 1 Thess. 5:27 carries no mark of genuineness) and in this verse indelibly seals his letter's nonauthenticity for those who are familiar with the first letter as a genuine document. Still, one should not assume that Paul added 1 Thess. 5:16–18 or only 5:18 in his own handwriting. Even if that were the case, the author of 2 Thessalonians did not have access to the original manuscript of 1 Thessalonians (nor did the recipients of 2 Thessalonians).[59] Yet at the same time he promoted 2 Thessalonians by its imitations of 1 Thessalonians. This ruse was likely suggested by the indication of genuineness in 1 Cor. 16:21 and Gal. 6:11—two verses in which Paul makes an addition in his own hand—or the pseudo-Pauline letter to the Colossians, where a similar ploy is employed.[60]

Verse 18: Except for the addition of "all," this blessing is identical with 1 Thess. 5:28.

3. INTOLERANCE AND THE GOSPEL IN 2 THESSALONIANS

Historical Situation

The preceding analysis of the relationship of 2 Thessalonians to 1 Thessalonians probably sheds new light on a conflict between two branches of the Pauline school, a controversy that is perhaps best set at the end of the first century, though a later date is also possible.[61]

(a) One group developed the Pauline tradition of 1 Thessalonians by accepting and reformulating indisputable statements of the apostle about the nearness of the end—similar to the two examples from Hippolytus quoted earlier.[62] In such a case the community would have experienced a sudden groundswell of apocalyptic expectation: the day of the Lord would be seen to be immediately at hand. But since the author of 2 Thessalonians does not mention such a mistake, that scenario must be rejected. The other and more likely option is that those followers of Paul who were attacked in 2 Thessalonians had in fact proclaimed that redemption and the end were present: the day of the Lord had already dawned. They would no doubt be properly described as Gnostics or enthusiasts, and may have had ties with the groups represented by Colossians,[63] Ephesians,[64] and the Pauline teachers attacked in 2 Tim. 2:16b–18, all of whom claimed that the spiritual resurrection had already happened.[65] In that case, not only the statement "the day of the Lord has come" (2 Thess. 2:2) must be understood in such a way, but the possibility recommends itself that the formulation derives from the author of 2 Thessalonians. (Similarly, Hippolytus himself probably formulated the same statement in the second of his examples.)

(b) The other group, followers of the author of 2 Thessalonians and representatives of a proto-orthodox early Catholic Christianity, distinguished Paul from the heretics by interpreting him in accordance with the spirit of this later time, and thus retained for him a place within the developing doctrine of the church. Indeed, our author may have been a churchman who resorted to such draconian measures out of a concern to preserve and develop the legacy of Paul, but who also may have acted to spare ordinary Christian people from the threat of confusion.

Andreas Lindemann disputes that "a controversy between 'orthodoxy' and 'heresy' is emerging"[66] behind 2 Thessalonians; contrary to Philipp Vielhauer, he denies that 2 Thessalonians was written with the aim of "snatching Paul from the enthusiasts, interpreting him in accord with the time, and thus keeping him useful for the church."[67] Indeed—thus Lindemann—2 Thessalonians "has no polemical features at all. The letter rather gives the impression that its author simply wants to warn the Christians he is addressing against taking 1 Thess. 4:15 literally."[68] Yet, if with Lindemann[69] we accept the exegetical result achieved above—namely that 2 Thessalonians seeks to replace 1 Thessalonians and designates it a forgery—then from a historical perspective 2 Thessalonians is highly polemical.[70] Its author "saves" the heritage of Paul by adopting a prototype, editing it extensively, and trying to obliterate it with the claim that it is an imposture.

In any case, the adversaries attacked as deceivers seem in reality to be true heirs of Paul and have 1 Thessalonians on their side. But we need not decide whether our vote should be cast for 2 Thessalonians or the Paulinists whom the author attacks, for a lie remains a lie, even if it is part of a Holy Scripture. Still, the forger could hardly have imagined (any more than could Paul himself) that ultrapolemical 2 Thessalonians would at one time find itself in the New Testament canon beside 1 Thessalonians, a work that he considered such a danger that it must be repudiated. Thus even in the course of the apostle's domestication, his "resurrection" and rescue have been undertaken. Indeed, by laying claim to at least fragments of the apostle, the forger helps to keep him alive.

Occasionally scholars have expressed doubt that a forged letter could possibly have replaced an authentic letter of Paul. Thus Yale professor Abraham Malherbe remarks: "The notion, that someone should write under the name of Paul to secure apostolic authority in order to undermine a genuine Pauline letter, is stunning in its boldness. And it exhibits an understanding of what the use of apostolic 'authority' meant in pseudonymous letters that does not do justice to the phenomena."[71] But this argument is less than persuasive, for it overlooks the harsh expedients of the Christian use of literature in times of conflict in order to silence adversaries.

Two examples will suffice to make the point. At the end of the second century, Bishop Irenaeus expressed fears that heretics might change his writings;[72] and Bishop Dionysios of Corinth, who had composed catholic letters to all churches,[73] responded bitterly to their falsification:

> When Christians asked me to write letters, I wrote them, and the apostles of the devil have filled them with tares by leaving out some things and putting in others. But woe awaits them. Therefore it is no wonder that some have gone about to falsify even the scriptures of the Lord when they had plotted against writings so inferior.[74]

On this Walter Bauer offers the following comment: "If it was possible for the heretics to falsify writings of an orthodox 'bishop' without having their project spoiled by opposition from the Christian public, then it must have been even easier for them to withdraw from circulation considerable amounts of 'ecclesiastical' literature, which was disturbing and uncomfortable to them."[75] The same applies, then, to an "orthodox" author like the "Paul" of 2 Thessalonians.

The Reason for the Intolerance of the Gospel in 2 Thessalonians

Being asked why he had to destroy 1 Thessalonians, the author of 2 Thessalonians might answer that he had to do the job thoroughly because the forger of 1 Thessalonians was a deceiver. He might have added that he was called on to be a savior of correct teaching in a situation of great danger. Indeed, he was obliged to protect the church against seducers and seduced alike, for they lacked obedience to the truth and to the gospel. If he had had the power to do so, he would have commanded the burning of 1 Thessalonians, using the same reasoning as that of Emperor Theodosius when in 448 CE he ordered the burning of the books of the philosopher Porphyry and of all the other enemies of Christianity. He declared: "It is my will that all writings which make God angry and spoil the souls shall not be heard by human beings."[76] Thus is it ever with those who are secure in their exclusive rectitude.

NOTES

1. Friedrich Nietzsche, *Beyond Good and Evil*, trans. Helen Zimmern (Amherst, NY: Prometheus Books, 1989), p. 86 (no. 68).

2. For the history of research see Robert Jewett, *The Thessalonian Correspondence: Pauline Rhetoric and Millenarian Piety* (Philadelphia: Fortress Press, 1986), pp. 3–16; Frank Witt Hughes, *Early Christian Rhetoric and 2 Thessalonians* (Sheffield, UK: Sheffield Academic Press, 1989), pp. 13–16.

3. William Wrede, *Die Echtheit des zweiten Thessalonicherbriefs untersucht* (Leipzig: J. C. Hinrich'sche Buchhandlung, 1903).

4. Cf. 1 Thess. 1:1 with 2 Thess. 1:1–2; 1 Thess. 3:11 with 2 Thess. 2:16; 1 Thess. 5:23 with 2 Thess. 3:16; 1 Thess. 5:28 with 2 Thess. 3:18.

5. Hughes, *Early Christian Rhetoric*, p. 14.

6. Abraham J. Malherbe, *The Letters to the Thessalonians: A New Translation with Introduction and Commentary* (New York: Doubleday, 2000), plays down the agreements between the two letters, claiming that "the differences between the letters are far more striking than their similarities" (p. 359). Moreover, he regards 2 Thessalonians as genuine. He supposes that Paul dispatched it only few months after 1 Thessalonians (pp. 364, 375).

7. Note that the expression "Second Coming of Jesus," which for the sake of convenience I am using throughout the book, does not occur in Paul, who prefers to speak of the arrival (in Greek, *parousia*) of Jesus.

8. 1 Thess. 4:13–17.

9. 2 Thess. 2:3c–4.

10. Cf. 1 Cor. 15:22–28; 15:50–52; 2 Cor. 5:1–10. Indeed, since 1 Cor. 15:51–52 seems to be a direct continuation of the thought of 1 Thess. 4:13–17 (see my *Paul: The Founder of Christianity* [Amherst, NY: Prometheus Books, 2002], pp. 50–51), the resulting timetable of 2 Thessalonians would be rather odd.

11. On this and related theories of separate recipients, see the survey by Jewett, *Thessalonian Correspondence*, pp. 21–24.

12. Ibid., pp. 24–26, and more recently John C. Hurd, *The Earlier Letters of Paul—and Other Studies* (Frankfurt: Peter Lang, 1998). Hurd claims that on the basis of inner criteria 2 Thessalonians is the earliest letter of Paul (p. 149). Referring to 1 Thess. 1:8, Hurd quite unconvincingly rejects the thesis that 1 Thessalonians was written in Corinth (p. 107).

13. This remains true whether you date 1 Thessalonians with the majority opinion to around 50 CE or with the minority opinion to around 40 CE (see

my *The Acts of the Apostles: What Really Happened in the Earliest Days of the Church* [Amherst, NY: Prometheus Books, 2005], pp. 257–60). In any case, this fact deserves more attention from both scholars and the interested public than it has received.

14. See Rom. 1:7b; 1 Cor. 1:3; 2 Cor. 1:2; Gal. 1:3; Phil. 1:2; Philem. 3.

15. Ibid.

16. "Hope" is used in 2 Thessalonians only at 2:16 (which is based on a traditional formula).

17. See 1 Thess. 1:3; 2:19; 4:13; 5:8.

18. See Mark 10:31; Luke 6:20b–23.

19. Zech. 14:5; Exod. 3:2; Isa. 66:15–17.

20. 1 Thess. 1:9–10.

21. 1 Thess. 4:5b.

22. See 2 Thess. 2:10, 12, 13.

23. See 2 Thess. 2:15; 3:6.

24. See 2 Thess. 2:10.

25. In Greek, *episynagôgê*.

26. When elsewhere used in the New Testament, it designates a gathering of the church members (see, e.g., Heb. 10:25).

27. 1 Thess. 4:15, 17.

28. See Andreas Lindemann, "Zum Abfassungszweck des Zweiten Thessalonicherbriefes," *Zeitschrift für die neutestamentliche Wissenschaft* 68 (1977): 39.

29. Note that Hippolytus's examples have no causal connection with the opponents of 2 Thessalonians but stem from a Montanist context. (Montanism goes back to the prophet Montanus from the Christian church of Phrygia in Asia Minor who in the middle of the second century claimed to be the embodiment of the Paraclete [John 14:16, 26; 15:26; 16:7].) This is an analogy, not a genealogy.

30. I have offered a fresh translation on the basis of the new edition by Marcel Richard, ed., Hippolyt, *Kommentar zu Daniel*, Die griechischen christlichen Schriftsteller der ersten Jahrhunderte, n.s. 7 (Berlin: Akademie-Verlag, 2000), pp. 234, 236, 238. See an earlier translation in my *Heretics: The Other Side of Early Christianity* (Louisville, KY: Westminster John Knox Press, 1996), pp. 114–15.

31. In Greek, *eis synantesin tô Christô*.

32. In Greek, *enestêken hê hêmera tou kyriou*.

33. See the epigraph to this chapter, p. 59.

34. See Wrede, *Echtheit des zweiten Thessalonicherbriefs*, p. 64.

35. "Lawlessness" (in Greek, *anomia*) does not mean licentiousness or rejection of the Mosaic Law, but behavior *against* God's law in general. See 1 John 3:4: "Everybody who commits sin commits lawlessness, and sin is lawlessness." See further Ps. 88:23 (LXX).

36. Dan. 11:32, etc.

37. Matt. 24:1–2; 1 Tim. 4:1–2, etc.

38. See below, pp. 89–91, on 2 John 7, and G. W. Lorein, *The Antichrist Theme in the Intertestamental Period* (London: T & T Clark, 2003); Heike Omerzu, "Wer ist dieser? Wilhelm Boussets Beitrag zur Erforschung des Antichrist-Mythos," in *Studien zur Johannesoffenbarung und ihrer Auslegung: Festschrift für Otto Böcher zum 70. Geburtstag,* ed. Friedrich Wilhelm Horn und Michael Wolter (Neukirchen-Vluyn: Neukirchener Verlag, 2004), pp. 93–119 (a comprehensive survey).

39. See Malherbe, *Letters to the Thessalonians,* pp. 431–32, for a critique of historical identifications of the restrainer, such as the Roman emperor Nero.

40. For example, 1 Thess. 2:9; 3:3b, 4; 4:2.

41. In Greek, *to katechon*. See the most recent massive work by Paul Metzger, *Katechon: II Thess 2,1–12 im Horizont apokalyptischen Denkens* (Berlin: Walter de Gruyter, 2005). Metzger detects a reference to the Roman Empire in this term. Yet in most cases apocalyptic thought does not allow such a historical interpretation. Besides, such an explanation offers little help for the exploration of the meaning of the text and its author's purpose.

42. In Greek, *epiphaneia*. Apart from this passage, the term occurs in the New Testament only in the pastoral Epistles. See below, pp. 136–37, on 2 Tim. 1:10.

43. In Greek, *parousia*.

44. In Greek, *energeia*.

45. In Greek, *ap' archês*. Other ancient codices have *aparchên* ("first fruit"), a reading that is likely secondary to the original text. See the remarks by Maarten J. J. Menken, *2 Thessalonians* (London: Routledge, 1994), p. 8.

46. Wolfgang Trilling, *Der zweite Brief an die Thessalonicher* (Neukirchen-Vluyn: Neukirchener Verlag, 1980), pp. 128–29, 155.

47. Wrede, *Echtheit des zweiten Thessalonicherbriefs,* p. 60.

48. Ibid.

49. Cf. Rom. 10:16a: "Not all obeyed the gospel."

50. Earl J. Richard, *First and Second Thessalonians* (Collegeville, MN: Liturgical Press, A Michael Glazier Book, 1995), p. 370.

51. Cf. 1 Cor. 1:9.

52. Cf. 1 Thess. 1:6; 1 Cor. 4:16; 11:1; Phil 4:9.

53. Yet one should not a priori deny the Pauline source of such a saying, for it is typical of the didactic Wisdom literature with which Paul was acquainted.

54. See, e.g., Didache 11:5–9; 12:1–8. On hospitality among Christians see below, p. 99.

55. Cf. Gal. 6:9.

56. 2 Thess. 2:2.

57. Ibid.

58. 2 Thess. 2:3a.

59. Against Menken, *2 Thessalonians*, pp. 35–36.

60. Col. 4:18.

61. Possibly the parallel in 2 Pet. 3:15–16, which indicates two reactions to Paul, may help us to locate 2 Thessalonians more precisely.

62. See above, pp. 65–66.

63. See Col. 2:12.

64. See Eph. 2:6.

65. Cf. my *Heretics: The Other Side of Early Christianity* (Louisville, KY: Westminster John Knox, 1996), pp. 122–30.

66. Andreas Lindemann, *Paulus im ältesten Christentum: Das Bild des Apostels und die Rezeption paulinischer Theologie in der frühchristlichen Literatur bis Marcion* (Tübingen: J. C. B. Mohr/Paul Siebeck, 1979), p. 133.

67. Thus Philipp Vielhauer, *Geschichte der urchristlichen Literatur: Einleitung in das Neue Testament, die Apokryphen und die Apostolischen Väter* (Berlin: Walter de Gruyter, 1975), p. 101.

68. Lindemann, *Paulus im ältesten Christentum*, p. 134

69. Lindemann, "Zum Abfassungszweck des Zweiten Thessalonicherbriefes" (see above, p. 61).

70. Cf. also Andreas Lindemann, *Apostel und Lehrer der Kirche: Studien zu Paulus und zum frühen Paulusverständnis* (Tübingen: J. C. B. Mohr/Paul Siebeck, 1999), p. 185n6.

71. Malherbe, *Letters to the Thessalonians*, p. 371.

72. Eusebius *Ecclesiastical History* 5.20.2.

73. Ibid., 4.23.1–11.

74. Ibid., 4.23.12.

75. Walter Bauer, *Orthodoxy and Heresy in Earliest Christianity* (Philadelphia: Fortress Press, 1971), p. 166. Bauer afterward suggests that the author of the New Testament book of Revelation "had similar anxieties in his conflict with the heretics. He levelled a curse on anyone who would alter his prophetic book by additions or deletions (Rev. 22.18f.). Although such language reflects to some degree stylistic conventions, it is nevertheless motivated by John's actual situation" (p. 167).

76. Wolfgang Speyer, *Büchervernichtung und Zensur des Geistes bei Heiden, Juden und Christen* (Stuttgart: Hiersemann, 1981), p. 34.

Chapter III

THE SECOND AND THIRD LETTERS OF JOHN

In the proposition "God is love," the subject is the darkness in which faith shrouds itself; the predicate is the light, which first illuminates the intrinsically dark subject. In the predicate I affirm love, in the subject faith. Love does not alone fill my soul: I leave a place open for my uncharitableness by thinking of God as a subject in distinction from the predicate.[1]

—Ludwig Feuerbach

1. INTRODUCTION

The following analyses[2] join recent attempts to use the two very brief Johannine letters titled 2 and 3 John, as well as the conflict they reveal, as "windows" on the inner life and history of the Johannine circle. These investigations are concerned above all with gaining insight into that dispute by means of a careful analysis of these most personal documents among the Johannine writings.[3]

2 John and 3 John as Early Accessible Documents of the Johannine Circle

What follows is based on two well-founded assumptions: that the Johannine writings originated in Asia Minor, specifically Ephesus, and that 2 and 3 John are among the earliest extant writings of the Johannine circle, reflecting a time close to the origin of this sectlike fellowship of male and female friends of Jesus. The key concepts of this circle are "truth," "love," and "knowledge"; we also find references to the "beginning," the inculcation of the "commandment," and the so-called immanence formulas, which describe "abiding" or "being" in the new reality. Equally characteristic is the Johannine dualism seen in the thematic contrasts of truth and lie, life and death, love and hatred.

Of course, proximity to the origin of the Johannine community can mean no more than a proximity to the beginning that we can perceive. In other words, whatever may be the real chronological relationship of the four Johannine writings, it makes the most sense to start from the most personal documents attributable to the community, the two brief letters, and to attempt to find our way from there. In short, I try to offer an analysis that does not presuppose any specific chronological sequence. Besides, the Fourth Gospel as we have it, to say nothing of the current state of research into its editorial process, also tells against too narrow an assumption about the relationship of the four Johannine texts to one another.[4] Indeed, the conflict in the three Johannine letters can be traced in the probable course of the Gospel's composition while "a good deal of it may already have been fixed."[5] Thus we might very well have to posit a Johannine Ur-Gospel at the beginning and the finished Gospel (with or without chapter 21) at the end of the chronological sequence of Johannine writings. In that case, both the Gospel of John in its final form (i.e., chapters 1–21) and 1 John (a "homily in the form of a letter,"[6] as Georg Strecker described it) would have later developed out of the confederation of the Elder's communities; indeed, both bear the stamp of the process of the consolidation of the Johannine circle. In other words, both show antidocetic features, but at the same time a synthesizing of earlier Gnostic motifs with the "catholic" elements.

If we assume that the earliest parts of the Gospel of John derive from the beginning of the Johannine community, docetic elements must be inevitable.[7] The original parts of the Fourth Gospel include all those passages that are stamped by a present eschatology.[8] They correspond to the "I am" sayings of Jesus, in which he portrays himself as bread,[9] vine,[10] light of the world,[11] and resurrection and life.[12] Here the salvation present in Jesus does not need any future supplementation, but is present in the follower's acceptance of his or her Lord. It depends on no more than a simple formula of reciprocity in which believer stands in the same relation to the revealer and Father as these do to each another: "I am in my Father and you in me and I in you."[13] Another question is whether the Gospel of John as a whole has an anti-docetic interest.[14] This may be unequivocally answered in the affirmative, since the final editor emphasizes the factuality of baptism[15] and Eucharist[16] and the fleshly nature of the risen Jesus.[17]

The publication of the three letters of John—with the general homily at the beginning (1 John), the letter to the church (2 John) second, and the private letter (3 John) at the end—could well reflect the pattern of the collection of Paul's letters; in addition the number three matches the triad of the pastoral Epistles, 1, 2 Timothy, and Titus.

The Elder[18] mentioned in 2 and 3 John is the recognized head of the Johannine circle, and for that reason his name does not need to be mentioned. For those receiving the letter "the Elder" was enough indication, as they knew the writer of the letter by this unmistakable title. It may well be due ultimately to the reputation of this figure among early Christians that 2 and 3 John found their way into the canon. From there it is no great step to regarding these two letters as original documents from the founder of the Johannine school.

To this can be added conjectures, which, while they do not underlie the subsequent analysis, should at least be kept in view as possibilities. First, the Elder who is the ostensible author of 2 and 3 John could be identical with the disciple who, according to John 21:20–24, presumably died in extreme old age, and to whom this appended chapter attributes the composition of the Fourth Gospel. Second, we cannot rule out the possibility that the Elder of 2 and 3 John is to be identified with the elder named John from Asia Minor whom Bishop Papias of Hierapolis mentions.[19] If sustainable, these two suppositions would add a welcome element of ecclesiastical history to the controversies behind the Johannine letters.

Be that as it may, our author, the Elder, is evidently a figure who had authority in the Johannine association of communities. He addresses a private letter to Gaius (= 3 John) and in it refers to a letter to the community (verse 9). In my view it is simplest to identify this letter with 2 John. If that is correct, then 3 John was prompted by the effect that 2 John had on the members of the community, and that would explain why 3 John was addressed to an individual. This person, Gaius, was apparently a member of the community to which 2 John was addressed, as well as being a friend of the presbyter, and as such was able to serve as a go-between who could support brothers sent by the Elder (3 John 6). In this way, the Elder hopes to regain influence over these elements of the community that have fallen away from him because of the discord sown by Diotrephes, who both calumniates the presbyter and forcefully cultivates his own authority.

2. TRANSLATION AND ANALYSIS OF 2 JOHN[20]

Verses 1–3: The Salutation

(1) The Elder to the elect lady and her children, whom I *love* in the **truth**, and not only I but also all who know the **truth**, (2) because of the **truth** which abides in us and will be with us for ever. (3) Grace, mercy, and peace will be with us, from God the Father and from Jesus Christ the Father's Son, in **truth** and *love*.

COMMENT

2 John clearly addresses itself to a definable community of people.[21] The prescript names the sender ("the Elder") and the addressees ("the elect lady and her children) in verse 1 and presents a greeting in verse 3. This structure follows the pattern found in Pauline community letters, which no doubt served as its model.

　　Still, the prescript's traditional structure does not mask its decidedly Johannine flair. "Truth," a central Johannine concept, appears four times, the distinctively Johannine preposition "from"[22] is used twice, and we find both the characteristic verb "to abide" (see verse 9) and the typical phrase "Jesus Christ, the Son of the Father" (instead of "the Lord Jesus Christ"). The prescript concludes with John's favorite terms: "truth" and "love."

　　Verse 1: The sender is evidently a well-known figure; indeed, "the Elder" seems to be a title expressing the dignity in which the community holds him. Further, the remark that he loves the children of the community in truth, as do those who know the truth, clearly implies a relationship far more intimate than these few words explicitly state. "The church is described as *kyria* (lady), because by its election it participates in the kingship exercised by the *kyrios* (Lord) Jesus Christ."[23] The claim of election permeates the primitive Christian religion in general.[24]

Verse 2: The phrase "because of the truth which abides in us and will be with us for ever" confirms the impression that the sender shares with the recipients of the letter a common basis of faith to which he need only allude. "Truth" is in any case a central concept for both the sender and the receivers, as is "abide."[25]

Verse 3: The greeting of peace is traditional, but is supplemented with two Johannine words, "truth and love," which also run through the following verses. According to verses 4–5, the Elder has found the members of the congregation "walking in the truth" and now admonishes them to love one another.

Verses 4–6: Walking in the Truth

(4) I rejoiced greatly to find some of your children WALKING in the truth, just as we have received a **command** by the Father. (5) And now I beg you, lady, not as though I were writing you a new **commandment**, but the one we have had from the beginning, let us *love* one another. (6) And this is *love*, that we WALK according to his **commandments**; this is the **commandment**, as you have heard from the beginning, and you must WALK in it.

COMMENT

This exhortation to mutual love is a summary of Johannine admonition in its equation of walking in the truth, walking according to the Father's commandments, and loving one another.

Verse 4: The Elder "found" some members of the community walking in the truth in accordance with the command of the Father. (It will become clear from verses 9–11 that the right teaching about Christ is part of walking in the truth.) This refers either to a visit by the Elder or to a meeting with a group sent by the congregation to notify him about its situation. In any case, the Elder did not simply receive messages from members of the church, but met with them.

Verse 5: "Lady" as a designation for the community takes up the expression from verse 1. The accentuation is on the claim that the community had the commandment "from the beginning." This is thus not in contradiction to verse 4, where the author has made an unconditionally positive statement about the community's present way of life. For the commandment to love one another as coming from the beginning see 1 John 2:7: "Beloved, I am writing you no new commandment, but an old commandment which you had from the beginning; the old commandment is the word which you have heard." Note that the Elder's concept of tradition orients itself on the foundational belief. Those who deviate from it—as have the false teachers who "run on ahead" (see below, verse 9) or those who had left the congregation (1 John 2:19)—have violated the command to love one another.

Verse 6: This expands on verse 5: note that "this is love" is rhetorically echoed by "this is the commandment," and that "commandment" (singular) repeats "commandment" in verse 5. The community's devotion to preserving the tradition is praiseworthy, especially inasmuch as true doctrine (verse 9) distinguishes between the orthodoxy of the community (i.e., the teaching of the Elder) and the heterodoxy of the false teachers.

1 John provides an important parallel for the present section:

1 John 2:7–11

(7) Beloved, I am writing you no new **commandment**, but an old **commandment** which you had from the beginning; the old **commandment** is the word which you have heard. (8) Yet I am writing you a new **commandment**, which is true in him and in you, because the darkness is passing away and the true *light* is already shining. (9) He who says he is in the *light* and HATES HIS BROTHER is in the darkness still. (10) He who loves his brother abides in the *light*, and in it there is no cause for stumbling. (11) But he who HATES HIS BROTHER is in the darkness and walks in the darkness, and does not know where he is going, because the darkness has blinded his eyes.

"The 'commandments' [in 1 John 2:3–4] concentrate on the one 'old' commandment, i.e. the one which was given at that time by Jesus and observed by the community (2.7f.), which Jesus himself first made possible."[26] Yet despite the repeated invocation of love, the polemical character of 1 John 2:7–11 is noteworthy. For example, the author does not offer examples to define hatred of one's brother. Did he postulate hate on the part of the opponents simply because they had a different view of Christ or because they had "left" the community? In 2 John, conversely, the deception of the false teachers is specified, but hate is not mentioned.

Verses 7–8: Rejection of Other Christians because of False Teaching

(7) For many **deceivers** have gone out into the world, men who will not acknowledge the coming of Jesus Christ in the flesh; such a one is the **deceiver** and the antichrist. (8) Look to yourselves, that you may not lose what we have worked for, but may win a full reward.

COMMENT

Verse 7: The Elder warns against being led astray by false teachings and offers detailed instructions as to how they are to be countered. The "false teachers" are termed "Antichrist" in keeping with the systems of eschatological coordinates. They are part of the collectively understood Antichrist whose appearance shortly before the end of the world the Elder expects. Jewish traditions had transmitted this idea to the Primitive Christians.[27] According to the Elder, then, false teachers have already appeared in the present extremity of time, just before the end; they deny that Jesus Christ appeared in the flesh.[28]

The statements about the Antichrist in 1 John allow us to further reconstruct the position of the opponents.

1 John 2:18

Children, it is the last hour! As you have heard that Antichrist is coming, so now many Antichrists have come. From this we know that it is the last hour.

Thus the coming of false teachers occurs in the end-time. 1 John 2:19 gives the additional information: "They went out from us, but they were not of us; for if they had been of us, they would have continued with us." Later 1 John 2:22 adds: "Who is the liar but the one who denies that Jesus is the Christ?"

One should understand this statement as referring to Christ's coming in the flesh. The contrary stand, the position taken by the opponents, can probably be reconstructed thus: Jesus cannot be the Christ because he has come in the flesh. The Christ in whom we believe and whom we confess has *not* come in the flesh. A polemical comment that strongly supports this reconstruction appears in 1 John 4:2b–3a: "Every spirit that confesses that Jesus Christ has come in the flesh is from God, and every spirit that does not confess Jesus is not from God."

In 2 John 2 the participle "coming" (in Greek, *erchomenos*) can be understood as future, present, or past[29] tense. For the latter, see 1 John 4:2 as well as John 1:9: "The true light that enlightens everyone was coming into the world." Consider also John 11:27: "Yes, Lord; I believe that you are the Christ, the Son of God, the one coming into the world," a case in which the present participle "coming" can be taken to imply past events, since the Christ who is coming into the world is the one who already has come into the world. While that is largely a quibble based on the slippery nature of grammatical tenses, the present participial form—which NRSV renders as a present perfect verb in 2 John 7 but in the above text functions as a gerund—may have been intended to emphasize Jesus' personal presence in the incarnation.

A statement by Bishop Polycarp of Smyrna may shed further light on the controversy about Jesus' coming in the flesh. Echoing (but not quoting) 1 John 4:2 and 2 John 7, sometime around 140 CE he makes the following comments in his letter to the Philippians 7:1a: "Everyone who does not confess that Jesus has come in the flesh is an Antichrist." Polycarp's confession is "a well-tried battle cry which comes from a Johannine doctrinal tradition which is not yet very old."[30] Besides, Polycarp's next sentence also sounds Johannine: "And whosoever does not confess the testimony of the cross is of the devil."[31] Indeed, even the taunt Polycarp evidently flings at Marcion in calling him "firstborn of Satan" has Johannine coloring.[32] In other words, Polycarp stands with the heirs of the Elder and the Elder himself in a battle against Christian heretics who deny the fleshliness of Jesus.

Verse 8: The community is admonished not to repudiate what "we" (the Elder, using the ceremonial plural) have created lest it fail to receive its reward at the last judgment. Of course, the "false teachers" alias "the antichrist" who do not confess Jesus as coming in the flesh have no part in any reward but will be destroyed beforehand.

Accordingly, the clash between heresy and orthodoxy goes back to a split in the Johannine association of communities. The "false teachers" broke away from the circle of Johannine communities before 1 John was written. The Elder represents one element in the Johannine community and the "false teachers" whom he attacks are the other. He thinks it necessary to confess that Jesus Christ comes in the flesh, while the others evidently teach a Docetism according to which Christ's coming is/was not a completely fleshly occurrence. As R. Alan Culpepper explains, they "held to the divinity of the Christ, but either denied or diminished the significance of his humanity."[33] Writing at about the same time as our author, Ignatius of Antioch expresses this even more drastically: real Christians ought to confess Jesus as the one who "bore flesh."[34] He continues: "The one who refuses to say this denies him completely, as one who bears a corpse."[35]

Verses 9–11: The Strict Command to Separate from False Christian Teachers

(9) Any one who runs on ahead instead of abiding in the (right) **teaching** about Christ does not have God; whoever abides in the **teaching** has both the Father and the Son. (10) If anyone comes to you and does not bring this **teaching**, do not receive him into the house or give him any <u>greeting</u>, (11) for whoever <u>greets</u> him shares his wicked deeds.

COMMENT

Verse 9: As the fundamental consequence of verses 7–8, the Elder states that only those who hold fast to the teaching of Christ (as the one who comes in the flesh) have a share in Father and Son. The negative side of this is that anyone, who runs on ahead[36] of the accepted belief, that is, adopts a progressive doctrine, has no part in God. At the same time, this prepares for verse 10, in which a possible enemy is in view. As earlier in verse 5, the Elder "introduces the concept of tradition as means of opposing the false teachers. The essence of the false teaching lies precisely in its departure from the teaching that had been the foundation of the community and that has been preserved by it."[37]

Verse 10: Here the Elder orders harsh action against those former brethren who have developed a new teaching about Christ. One should avoid not only welcoming them into the house, but even greeting them, lest one thereby abet the wickedness of the false teachers. This sharp injunction clearly represents a change from the previously noted ideal (implied in verses 1–3, 5–6) of welcoming all Christian brothers and sisters. Indeed, it drives home the point implied in verse 6 that love is contingent upon doctrinal orthodoxy!

But what were the circumstances surrounding the discovery of this unorthodoxy? There are but two possibilities. The first is that visitors were first welcomed and then examined for doctrinal propriety in the course of worship and/or a community assembly where they could be required to affirm Jesus' coming in the flesh. The second is that it was possible to recognize and reject them as heretics upon first contact. In the latter case, of course, the specific nature of their heterodoxy must already have been known. Be that as it may, the examination of teachers became a rule in the Johannine circle; on this see 1 John 4:1: "Beloved, do not believe every spirit, but test the spirits to see whether they are from God; for many false prophets have gone out into the world."[38]

Walter Bauer calls the Elder's command an "anxious instruction," and sees in it a retreat into orthodoxy with the aim of preserving "what could be protected from entanglement with 'the world.'"[39] But surely this way of expressing the situation is too negative. After all, the writer's prime concern was for clarity of self-assertion in order to mark out a positive position within the association of Johannine communities by defining the correct teaching. In short, he intends to draw a sharp and permanent line between heresy and church. The term "truth" used so often in 2 John (and 3 John) has taken on a close connection with "teaching."

Verse 11: Here the Elder caps his radical exhortation by insisting that anyone who so much as greets a false teacher shares in his wicked deeds. We have what amounts to a clash of two hostile spheres of influence—truth and lie, light and darkness, good and evil.

A recent commentator, Georg Strecker, remarks that one "can obviously also argue, in reverse, that the agapê of the Christian community must be strong enough to support different teachings: for not only can doctrine be a guide to agapê, but agapê can also contribute to the definition of doctrine."[40] Then he continues: "In view of the fact that the continuing existence of his work is evidently at stake, such a relativizing of his teaching could scarcely be expected of the presbyter at this crucial moment. In his opinion, 'the teaching of Christ' that he represents has an unconditional claim to be heard."[41]

Rebuttal: Strecker wants to understand the Elder's action from a cognitive level ("could scarcely be expected of the presbyter") and deprives the text of its ontological depth, including its palpable sense of hatred. According to the Elder, a hidden reality corresponds to what he enunciates. He must have felt that he therefore had no choice but to draw a line.

The apostle Paul similarly consigns an incestuous Christian to Satan[42] in order to protect the holiness of the congregation, and insists on a total disconnection between the realm of Christ and the sphere of demons. And we see an archaic pattern of thought that allows no interim solutions, but knows only the antithesis between death and life. No doubt this seems strange to the conscious mind of the "enlightened" person of today, but not to the subconscious—nor, for that matter, to the modern religious fanatic. Certainly, to use Martin Hengel's words, "the roots of this conduct, strange though it may seem to us, are basically Jewish and dualistic."[43] Hengel suggests making "a fundamental distinction between the historical question and the problem of ethical justification or even imitation of the presbyter's attitude today."[44] But we might wish to reexamine John 8:44, where the Jews are children of the devil,[45] or Phil. 3:2, where Paul's opponents are "dogs," in the light of key Johannine sayings like John 3:16 or 1 John 4:8—or according to the standards of Jesus' message.[46] Hengel has, of course, foreseen the objection, for he continues: "But before we condemn the greatest teachers of the primitive church, Paul and John, we should try to understand them as men of their time and in special critical situations against which they had to react. Here in particular the Pauline corpus and the Johannine corpus are closely connected. Both know radical grace, but also the inexorable 'no' against any falsification of the message of salvation."[47]

Still, one might respond by asking first whether "heretics" could not know "radical grace," and second to whom we shall turn to provide the criteria for determining whether the message of salvation has been falsified.

Verses 12–13: Final Greetings

(12) Though I have much to write to you, I would rather not use paper and ink, but I hope to come to see you and talk with you face to face, so that our joy may be complete.

(13) The children of your elect sister greet you.

COMMENT

These verses form the conclusion to the letter.

Verse 12: Again with Johannine flair ("so that our joy may be complete"), the elder expresses a wish to pay a visit.

Verse 13: This brief greeting at the end of the letter links up with the "children of the elect sister" in verse 1. This time, however, the expression denotes the community of the Elder from whom the greetings comes, while in verse 1 it relates to the community being addressed. In this way the unity of the two communities is implicitly asserted.

3. TRANSLATION AND ANALYSIS OF 3 JOHN

3 John is a private letter to Gaius, concerning whom the traveling brothers have given a good report to the associated Johannine communities. Demetrius, who evidently has carried the letter, gets an equally good report.[48] The letter itself abounds in typically Johannine language: truth,[49] testimony/testify,[50] joy,[51] and beloved/love.[52]

Verses 1–4: Prescript and Greeting

(1) The Elder to the beloved Gaius, whom I love in the **TRUTH**.

(2) Beloved, I pray that all may go well with you and that you may be in health; I know that it is well with your soul. (3) For I greatly rejoiced when some of the brothers arrived and testified to your **TRUTH**, as indeed you do **walk in the TRUTH**. (4) No greater joy can I have than this, to hear that my children **walk in the TRUTH**.

COMMENT

Verse 1: This is the prescript. Gaius is beloved by the Elder and is addressed as such three times in the letter (verses 2, 5, 11). "Whom I love in the truth" (verse 1b) corresponds to 2 John 1b ("whom I love in the truth"). Note the key Johannine terms "love" and "truth."

Verse 2: Instead of the blessing found in 2 John 3, this verse contains a formal prayer for the well-being of the recipient.

Verse 3: Here the Elder expresses his joy that the Christian brothers have reported to him that Gaius is walking in the truth (cf. the close parallel in 2 John 4).

Verse 4: Expanding on the individual report the author expresses his even greater joy at hearing that his "children" are also remaining faithful to his teaching

Verses 5–8: Support of Missionaries

(5) **Beloved**, you do faithfully whatever you do for the brothers, even though they are strangers to you; (6) they have testified to your **love** before the church. You will do well to send them on their journey in a manner worthy of God, (7) for they went out in the name (of Christ) accepting no <u>support</u> from the Gentiles. (8) We ought to <u>support</u> such people, so that we may be fellow workers in the truth.

COMMENT

Verse 5: After verses 1 and 2, the Elder for the third time addresses the recipient, Gaius, as "beloved" and in verse 5 indicates the meaning of "walking in the truth" (verses 3 and 4): it denotes demonstrations of love and support toward previously unknown fellow believers.

Verse 6: These brothers have born witness to Gaius's love before the (assembled local) community, and therefore should be well received and helped to continue their journey.[53]

Verse 7: The Elder adds an explanation about these missionaries: having gone out in the name of Christ, they naturally accept nothing from Gentiles. This reflection of Jewish behavior corresponds to earliest Christian practice. See the missionary rule that was placed on the lips of Jesus: "Do not go among the Gentiles."[54] At the same time we may conclude that they are engaged in a mission to Gentiles from whom they will neither seek nor accept support.

Verse 8: This verse explains the need to support these missionaries: those who receive them as guests become fellow workers in the truth. A play on words that cannot be reproduced literally ties this verse to the preceding one.[55]

Verses 9–10: Reprimand of Diotrephes

(9) I did write a letter to the **church**; but Diotrephes, who likes to put himself first, does _not welcome_ us. (10) So if I come, I will call attention to what he is doing, prating against me with vicious words. And not content with that, he himself does _not welcome_ the brothers, and also stops those who want to do so and expels them from the **church**.

COMMENT

Verse 9: This gives the reason for the present letter and refers to a letter that the author previously wrote to the community—one we should identify as 2 John.[56] An influential member of the community, Diotrephes, does not accept the Elder's authority, nor has he welcomed the brothers who carried that letter.[57] The Elder then gives the reason for this nonacceptance: Diotrephes seeks to make himself their leader.

Verse 10: Here the Elder expresses his desire to chastise Diotrephes, explaining his reason for this by developing the key term "not welcome" in verse 9 to indicate Diotrephes' misdemeanors (for the details see below).

Verses 11–12: Recommendation of Demetrius

(11) Beloved, do not imitate _evil_ but imitate _good_. He who does _good_ is of GOD; he who does _evil_ has not seen GOD.(12) Demetrius has _testimony_ from every one, and from the **truth** itself; I _testify_ to him too, and you know our _testimony_ is **true**.

COMMENT

Verse 11: After admonishing the addressees not to imitate the evil but the good, the Elder explains the origins of good and evil in people: if good, the person is from God; if evil, he has never known God. Similar statements appear in 1 John 3:6b ("No one who sins has either seen him [Jesus? God?] or known him") and 1 John 3:10b ("All who do not do what is right are not from God, nor are those who do not love their brothers").

Verse 12: This is a triple commendation of Demetrius the letter bearer. He has not only received favorable testimony from everyone (as did Gaius, verse 3), but truth itself testifies in his behalf, as does the sender of the letter.

Verses 13–15: Final Greetings

(13) I had much to write to you, but I would rather not write with pen and ink. (14) I hope to see you soon, and we will talk together face to face. (15a) Peace be with you. (15b) The friends greet you. Greet each of the friends there by name.

COMMENT

Verses 13–14: See 2 John 12 for a similar wording.

Verse 15a: The same greeting of peace occurs in John 20:19, 21, 26.

Verse 15b: At the end, personal greetings are sent. "The friends"—a term indicating those who greet and those who are greeted—is evidently a technical term for the members of the Johannine community. Compare with John 15:13–15 and also Luke 12:4a.

4. INTOLERANCE AND THE GOSPEL IN 2 AND 3 JOHN

Historical Setting

The letter that called for uncompromising rejection of false teachers was evidently not well received by Diotrephes. He probably sympathized with the brothers it inveighed against and therefore responded with a counterattack. Just as the Elder calls for a repudiation of the false teachers, now Diotrephes deprecates the emissaries of the Presbyter[58] and underlines his intransigence by outlawing "those of good will" who wanted to offer hospitality to the Presbyter's emissaries.[59] At the same time he spreads malicious rumors about the Elder, who in return charges him with being egotistical and power hungry.[60]

Diotrephes probably had a leading role in a group that incurred the Elder's wrath by advocating a Docetic view of Christ.[61] As 2 John demonstrates, its members had not separated themselves from the other Johannine Christians, but the Elder initiated and demanded a separation because, in his view, the dualistic theology of the schismatics abrogated the history of salvation. Accordingly, he charges that these Docetic teachers represent the realm of darkness and *are* the Antichrist. Historically speaking, however, both groups clearly belonged to one and the same circle of churches. Furthermore, Diotrephes' influential position in one congregation was sufficiently recent that he was unknown to the Elder when 2 John was composed. Ironically enough, this very letter may have contributed to a consolidation of Diotrephes' authority, for afterward the community remained in his hands.[62]

Two objections have been made to this reconstruction:

> **First objection:** Since 3 John contains no mention of false teachers and the "letter itself nowhere reproaches Diotrephes with doctrinal error,"[63] he cannot be the representative of a Docetic Christology condemned by the Elder in 2 John 7.

Rebuttal: This argument is not convincing, since "heresy" was but one element in a struggle that included a desire for personal power. Walter Bauer describes the situation thus: "And the assurance repeated no less than five times in this brief writing that the brethren who support the elder possess the 'truth'—that entity which in 2 John and also in 1 John distinguishes the orthodox believer from the heretic—renders it very unlikely, to my way of thinking, that we are here dealing merely with personal frictions between the elder and Diotrephes."[64] A little later Bauer remarks: "Since 2 John shows the elder to be a determined opponent of a docetic interpretation of Christ, we need not spend time in searching for the real reasons that time and again prompt him to renew his efforts to maintain contact with the beloved Gaius through letters like 3 John, and with the church of Diotrephes through emissaries."[65] Moreover, we are at a stage when the struggle is still in its developing stages, as is clearly expressed by the fact that Diotrephes does not welcome the Elder and his "brothers," but the Presbyter is nevertheless seeking a dialogue with his adversary.

Second objection: The issue in 3 John is not theology but hospitality.[66]

Rebuttal: This misses the point, since controversies in early Christianity often have a theological background, and the more so since in 2 John correctness of doctrine is a stated criterion of the division between Christians. Besides, since 3 John explicitly refers to 2 John,[67] it "thus becomes especially valuable and instructive for us in that it represents the attempt of an ecclesiastical leader to gain influence in other communities in order to give assistance to likeminded persons within those communities, and if possible, to gain the upper hand."[68]

Thus, early second-century church history in Asia Minor erupts in a conflict that produces two distinct faith traditions: one of them converges with other forms of Christianity and becomes the Catholic Church, while the other gets swallowed up in the Gnostic maelstrom. When—following John and 1 John—the two short letters of John became part of the New Testament and thus attained the status of Holy Scripture, so thick a veil lay over their earliest purpose that they almost ceased to exist.

The Intolerance of the Gospel in 2 and 3 John

The human and theological conflict moves toward a climax that envisions the Elder meeting Diotrephes personally in order to restore order. But wouldn't that call for love and compromise? Has the Elder made a tactical blunder here? Would Diotrephes be easily mollified and theologically flexible? Or does the Elder offer to confer with Diotrephes only in order to appear reasonable and conciliatory? In view of his harsh injunctions and his stated intent not to compromise but to confront (3 John 10), such a ploy would not be surprising.

It was, after all, the Elder who introduced the intolerance of exclusive truth into the communities that he had founded, and in addition he added practical consequences. Henceforth, Christians from that circle who differed from the founding father on even one specific point concerning Christ would no longer be welcome. In the person of Diotrephes the other side responded and declared the messengers of the Elder to be no longer welcome. What was taking place was a split in a church founded on the gospel of love. To be sure, the intolerance was strictly an intramural phenomenon concerning correctness of doctrine,

and entailed consequences only for church members who held a different view of Christ—but the seed that was planted was unequivocally
a product of the leadership and the guiding spirit of the community,
and the poisonous weed it produced flourished all too well in the centuries to come.

As for relations with those outside the church, 3 John 7 clearly
demonstrates the communities' negative attitude toward the nonbelieving Gentiles. Given the covert dualism that underlies all Johannine
writings, one may go so far as to say that the nonbelieving Gentiles had
been assigned to the realm of darkness, from which they could escape
only through baptism and faith in Jesus Christ. Such a view betrays a
very twisted notion of tolerance indeed!

Concerning the unbelieving Jews whom neither 2 John nor 3 John
mentions, one may glean from passages in the Gospel of John indications of the Elder's viewpoint and summarize the Johannine perspective
thus: Though salvation has come from the Jews,[69] many of them have
not believed in the name of the Son of God[70] and have thus missed
eternal life. Becoming more specific and comparing John's account of
the passion with the accounts in the other synoptic Gospels, it is clear
that John not only outdoes the other evangelists in his exculpation of
Pilate, but almost as if to compensate for this astigmatic portrait he
takes the lead in incriminating the Jews for their role in the death of
Jesus.[71]

No wonder, then, that antagonism between Jesus and the Jews runs
like a scarlet thread through the Fourth Gospel. Polemically, it comes to
a head when Jesus describes the Jews as children of the devil.[72] From the
beginning, John repeats and emphasizes Jewish resolutions to kill
Jesus[73] and continues this defamatory pattern throughout his
account.[74] The embittered dispute between Jesus and the Jews reaches a
provisional climax in John 8:37–45.

John 8:37–45

(37) (Jesus:) "I know that you are descendants of Abraham; yet *you
seek to kill me*, because my word finds no place in you. (38) I speak
of what I have seen in the Father's presence; you ought to do what
you have heard from the Father." (39) They answered him,
"Abraham is our father." Jesus said to them, "If you were Abraham's
children, you would do what Abraham did, (40) but now *you seek*

to kill me, a man who has told you the TRUTH which he heard from God. This is not what Abraham did. (41) You do the works of your father." They said to him, "We were not born of fornication; we have one Father, God." (42) Jesus said to them, "If God were your Father, you would love me, for I proceeded and came forth from God; I came not of my own accord, but he sent me. (43) Why do you not understand what I say? It is because you cannot bear to hear my word.

(44) You are from your father, the devil, and you want to do your father's desires. He was a murderer from the beginning, and has nothing to do with the TRUTH, because there is no TRUTH in him. When he lies, he speaks according to his own nature, for he is a liar and the father of lies.

(45) But because I tell the TRUTH, you do not believe me."

COMMENT

The Jesus of this text[75] calls the unbelieving Jews children and sons of the devil; the bitterness of the conflict between Johannine Christians and their Jewish neighbors here portrayed can scarcely be exceeded. Without doubt its acrimony can be explained by conflicts between members of Johannine congregations and unconverted Jews. In that respect, of course, the views we find here were governed by their time; nonetheless, the author is convinced of what he puts into Jesus' mouth, and that means that he intends to demonize the Jews. This action need not indicate a significant local distance between them and the Johannine community. Indeed, we may be witnesses to a controversy within Judaism that only later culminated in a final separation. Clashes between groups that retain some common bond are always nastier than those between parties who have little interest in each other. None of this, of course, reverses the totality of the denunciations proclaimed.

It is clear, then, that the Jews play a significant role in the framework of Johannine dualism, with its contrasts between God and the world, light and darkness, truth and lie. As representatives of the world, Jews become allegorical stand-ins for those who do not believe. They represent the darkness,[76] the lie,[77] and death.[78] They are "of this world" and come "from below."[79] Since they have not confessed to the one who comes "from above" but is not "of this world" they must die in their sins.[80] They neither know God,[81] nor can they know him, for God can be known only through the Son.[82] Because they judge "according to the flesh,"[83] they remain in bondage, for only through the Son can people be really free.[84] "Salvation does indeed come from the Jews (4:22), but this statement is valid only in a preliminary sense in that it applies to the historical appearance of Jesus as Jew, for true worship is a matter of Spirit and in truth (4:23)."[85]

The other side of this uncompromising hostility to the Jews lies in John's understanding of Christ; this we can see, for example, in John 14:6: "I am the way, the truth, and the life; no one comes to the Father but by me." But it should not be difficult to recognize that this claim to exclusivity is radically Jewish, since its roots are to be found in Jewish exclusivism, and the age-old bitterness of intra-Jewish controversy.[86]

In the foregoing I have extensively used the Fourth Gospel in order to establish the thought world of 2 and 3 John. Indeed, these brief letters contain only a segment of the faith they represent. And for much the same reason it is worth a brief detour into 1 John in order that we may further fill in some of the remaining gaps in 2 and 3 John. One issue that demands special attention is the method of dealing with members of the community who, while innocent of sympathizing with the false teachers, have committed some other sin.

1 John 5:16–17

(16a) If anyone sees his brother committing what is not a <u>mortal</u> sin, he will ask, and God will grant life to such a one whose sin is not <u>mortal</u>. (16b) There is sin which is <u>mortal</u>; I do not say that one is to pray for that. (17) All wrongdoing is sin, but there is sin which is not <u>mortal</u>.

This text[87] is based on a community rule distinguishing between mortal[88] and venial sins—that is, the possibility or impossibility of repentance[89]—that the elder may have known of. Indeed, 1 John "documents a vigorous debate within early Christianity on the issues of whether a baptized Christian can sin, and how the church is to relate to sinners in their midst."[90] The very early Christian belief that a baptized person can no longer sin was originally shared by the circle of Johannine communities;[91] yet when the unblinkable reality of sin had at last to be acknowledged by the church, ways of differentiating among and dealing with sins had to be devised.[92] It remains important to see that the proto-orthodox party of the Johannine community did distinguish between sins that could yield to intercessory prayer (and repentance)[93] and those that permanently excluded the wrongdoer from the community. Indeed, the struggle to retain the supposedly holy world of revelation necessarily involved radical and implacable separation from "sin" ontologically understood, while at the same time making a compromise with the sinful reality of this world.[94]

Theological theories were devised to support the struggle. Proto-orthodox Johannine theologians concluded that the dissenters had never really belonged to the church: "They went out from us, but they were not from us; for if they had been from us they would have continued with us" (1 John 2:19). To be sure, this happened before the Elder took measures against the dissidents, yet he displays the same dualistic thinking as the Johannine theologians who wrote 1 John 2:19. No wonder, then, that in his mind the dissidents had to commit evil deeds: after all, they were the personification of evil, namely the Antichrist.[95] This, of course, made any further dialogue impossible since any contact was strictly forbidden in order to avoid infection. Therefore, a theological consequence was necessary. After all, a radical understanding of grace leads necessarily to an intolerant preaching of the gospel, one that includes practical, and if necessary harsh, consequences. Yet thereby the love command that is more central to the Johannine writings than to any other New Testament text loses much of its credibility, because it is restricted to loving the brothers[96] (all dissidents having been deprived of brotherhood). At that point, of course, the repeated invocation of truth begins to sound like nothing so much as a desperate attempt at self-justification by damning other Christians.

A Final Note

Yet questions remain: What was the real reason for the Elder to damn other Christians? And what was the real reason for those other Christians to dismiss the fleshly Jesus? While the Elder does not provide a clue to this question, Bishop Ignatius—who in his thinking has many affinities with the Elder—does. Apparently he requires the corporeal suffering and fleshly resurrection of Jesus Christ in order to give his own suffering a meaning, for he writes as follows: "But if, as some who are atheists—that is, unbelievers—say, that he only appeared to suffer—it is they who are the appearance—, why am I in bondage, and why also do I pray to fight the wild beasts? I am then dying in vain and am, even more, lying about the Lord" (*Letter to the Trallians* 10).

However, since the Johannine literature nowhere connects personal suffering with Jesus' death and resurrection, we have to look for another explanation for the insistence on the fleshly nature of both Jesus' coming into this world and his resurrection from the dead. Most likely the "opponents" questioned the gospel and creedal formulae of Jesus' bodily presence and resurrection on the basis of their Greek education, which excluded a bodily resurrection.[97] The predictable response of the Catholic tradition represented by church leaders like the Elder was to cling ever more tenaciously to the received tradition, insisting that Jesus had walked the earth and risen from the dead not only in a body, but also in the flesh. Once the controversy had begun, other factors came into play—and of course, power and authority were two of them. Having thus given due acknowledgment to the issues of authority and education in the split of the Johannine community, I suggest that the same may be true for controversies that affected other communities studied in this book.

NOTES

1. Ludwig Feuerbach, *The Essence of Christianity* (Amherst, NY: Prometheus Books, 1989), p. 264.

2. See the earlier preliminary studies on the Johannine circle and the listing of further literature in my *Heretics: The Other Side of Early Christianity* (Louisville, KY: Westminster John Knox Press, 1996), pp. 170–83, 300–309.

3. For details see Udo Schnelle, *The History and Theology of the New Testament Writings* (Minneapolis, MN: Fortress Press, 1998), pp. 434–516.

4. The relationship of chapter 21 to the rest of the Fourth Gospel would remain a subject for yet further discussion.

5. Martin Hengel, *The Johannine Question* (Philadelphia: Trinity Press International, 1989), p. 177.

6. Georg Strecker, *The Johannine Letters: A Commentary on 1, 2, and 3 John* (Minneapolis, MN: Fortress Press, 1996), p. 3.

7. One too easily forgets that Paul's view of Christ occasionally verged on Docetism. Nor should we expect otherwise for the early Christianity in which Paul lived and worked. What was later consolidated was then still fluid, alive, and open-ended. For example, according to Paul, the Son of God is "born of a

woman" (Gal. 4:4) and yet he assumed only the "form of a servant" (Phil. 2:7) and merely "a human likeness" (Phil. 2:7) or "the likeness of flesh" (Rom. 8:3).

8. John 3:17–18, 36; 5:24–27; 11:25–26; 14:18–24.

9. John 6:35.

10. John 15:1–8.

11. John 8:12.

12. John 11:25–26.

13. John 14:20; cf. 10:14–15; 17:21, 23.

14. See Udo Schnelle, *Antidocetic Christology in John: An Investigation of the Place of the Fourth Gospel in the Johannine School* (Minneapolis, MN: Fortress Press, 1992).

15. John 3:5.

16. John 6:51c–58; 19:34b, 35.

17. John 20:27.

18. In Greek, *presbyteros*.

19. Eusebius *Ecclesiastical History* 3.39.4.

20. In passing, let me reiterate that 2 John is a real letter despite the curious recent appearance of a number of publications disputing its authenticity. No less a scholar than Helmut Koester writes about 2 John, "It is not a true letter but a rather superficial compilation of Johannine sentences in the form of a catholic epistle; the 'elect lady' of 2 John 1 is the church in general. From the Third Epistle of John the author of 2 John draws the title of 'the Elder,' and from the First Epistle he copies the confession that Jesus has come in the flesh (2 John 7), which he propagates as right teaching (*didache*, 2 John 9–10). 2 John is important because it demonstrates how Johannine Christianity, following in the footsteps of 1 John, becomes an advocate of anti-Gnostic theology" (Helmut Koester, *Introduction to the New Testament*, 2 vols., 2nd ed. [New York: Walter de Gruyter, 1995–2000], 2:202). The best counterargument to this is to read the document itself repeatedly, for one thereby gains the indelible impression that a real person is writing to a specific and familiar group of people. Indeed, among "all the letters of the New Testament 2 and 3 John (along with Philemon) have a breath of originality and freshness among them. Their length (2 John: 1,126 letters; 3 John: 1,105) reveals that each filled a single sheet of papyrus of the same size. The design of both epistles, their style, including certain phrases common in Hellenistic letter writing . . . , the concise treatment of concrete questions, the mention of specific individuals . . . all this guarantees that they were designed as letters from the outset" (Rudolf Schnackenburg, *The Johannine Epistles: Translation and Commentary* [New York: Crossroad, 1992], p. 267).

21. Against Elisabeth Schüssler Fiorenza, *In Memory of Her: A Feminist Theological Reconstruction of Christian Origins* (New York: Crossroad, 1983), who suggests that "elect lady" of 2 John 1, like the "elect sister" of 2 John 13, is the female leader of a house church (p. 300) and not the symbolic name for a

church in Asia Minor of which the writer was a member. But as the two-part prescript (2 John 1–3, which recalls the letters of Paul) shows, 2 John is not a personal letter like 3 John but a letter to a community. Verse 13 contains the greetings of the members ("children") of the sister church to which the Elder belongs.

22. In Greek, *para* instead of *apo.*

23. Schnelle, *History and Theology of the New Testament Writings,* p. 443.

24. 1 Pet. 1:1; Rev. 17:4.

25. See John 5:38; 8:31, 35, etc. See the rich excursus in Strecker, *Johannine Letters,* pp. 44–45.

26. Hengel, *Johannine Question,* p. 171n64.

27. See the tyrannical king of the end-time in Daniel 11–12 and his interpretation as Antiochus IV Epiphanes. See further Mark 13:22.

28. In Greek, *erchomenon en sarki.*

29. Cf. 3 John 3: "The brothers who have come to the Elder."

30. Hengel, *Johannine Question,* p. 16.

31. Cf. 1 John 3:8: "Everyone who commits sin is of the devil."

32. Cf. John 8:44: "the Jews have the devil as their father."

33. In James L. Mays, ed., *The HarperCollins Bible Commentary,* rev. ed. (San Francisco: HarperSanFrancisco, 2000), p. 1178.

34. In Greek, *sarkophoros.*

35. Ignatius *To the Smyrneans* 5.2. "Who bears a corpse" is the translation of the Greek *nekrophoros.*

36. In Greek, *proagein.*

37. Schnelle, *History and Theology of the New Testament Writings,* p. 445.

38. For the testing of the spirits in Primitive Christianity see further 1 Cor. 14:29; 1 Thess. 5:21; Rev. 2:2b; Ignatius *To the Ephesians* 9:1. Note that Didache 11:7 forbids an examination of the prophets who speak in the spirit. Their examination is based on their way of life (Didache 11:8).

39. Walter Bauer, *Orthodoxy and Heresy in Earliest Christianity* (Philadelphia: Fortress Press, 1971), p. 92.

40. Strecker, *Johannine Letters,* p. 244.

41. Ibid.

42. 1 Cor. 5:5.

43. Martin Hengel, *Johannine Question,* pp. 44–45.

44. Ibid., p. 45.

45. On this passage see further above, pp. 100–102.

46. E.g., the authentic words of Jesus contained in Matt. 5:43–48 and Luke 6:27–36.

47. Hengel, *Johannine Question,* pp. 44–45.

48. 3 John 12.

49. 3 John 1, 3 (twice), 4, 8, 12.

50. 3 John 3, 6, 12 (three times).

51. 3 John 4.

52. 3 John 1 (twice), 2, 5, 6.

53. Cf. Rom. 15:24; 1 Cor. 16:6. The Greek verb *propempein* means "to equip for a journey."

54. Matt. 10:5b.

55. In Greek, *hypolambanein* (verse 8) picks up *ou lambanontes* (verse 7): the Christian community "should receive" those who are "not receiving" anything from the Gentiles.

56. Those unwilling to accept 2 John as the letter mentioned in 3 John 9 must assume that the communication there referred to has been lost or was destroyed by Diotrephes.

57. Against Schnelle, who comes to the puzzling conclusion that Diotrephes *clearly acknowledged* the Elder's authority: *History and Theology of the New Testament Writings*, p. 450.

58. 3 John 9.

59. 3 John 10.

60. 3 John 9.

61. Bauer, *Orthodoxy and Heresy in Earliest Christianity*, pp. 92–93. See further Strecker, *Johannine Letters*, pp. 261–63.

62. It would be far-fetched to describe Diotrephes "with confidence as a bishop, and as one who is fighting, just as Ignatius has required, for the solidarity of his congregation around himself" (thus Hans von Campenhausen, *Ecclesiastical Authority and Spiritual Power in the Church of the First Three Centuries* [Stanford, CA: Stanford University Press, 1969], p. 122).

63. Ibid., p. 122n324.

64. Bauer, *Orthodoxy and Heresy in Earliest Christianity*, p. 93.

65. Ibid.

66. Abraham J. Malherbe, "The Inhospitality of Diotrephes," in *God's Christ and His People: Studies in Honour of Nils Alstrup Dahl*, ed. Jacob Jervell and Wayne A. Meeks (Oslo: Universitetsforlaget, 1977), pp. 222–32.

67. 3 John 9a.

68. Bauer, *Orthodoxy and Heresy in Earliest Christianity*, p. 93.

69. John 4:22b.

70. See John 20:31; 1 John 5:13.

71. See my *The Unholy in Holy Scripture: The Dark Side of the Bible* (Louisville, KY: Westminster John Knox Press, 1997), pp. 95–96.

72. John 8:44.

73. John 5:16, 18; 7:1, 19.

74. John 10:31–39; 11:45–53; 19:7.

75. For illustrative parallels see the following: "You seek to kill me" (verse 37) takes up word for word John 5:18; 7:1, 19–20, 25; for "my word finds no place in you," cf. John 5:38a.

76. John 8:12.

77. John 8:44.

78. John 8:51.

79. John 8:23.

80. John 8:24.

81. John 5:19–47; 7:28; 15:21; 16:3.

82. John 8:14, 19, 42.

83. John 8:15.

84. John 8:32–36.

85. Georg Strecker, *Theology of the New Testament* (New York: Walter de Gruyter, 2000), p. 495.

86. See my *Unholy in Holy Scripture*, pp. 113–14.

87. 1 John 5:14–21 seems to be an addition to 1 John, which most likely ended with 1 John 5:13 (see the correspondence with John 20:31). Yet 5:14–21 can still be used for the description of Johannine Christianity, for it seems to be a straightforward development.

88. In Greek, *pros thanaton.*

89. See the rich excursus "Second repentance" in Strecker, *Johannine Letters,* pp. 203–208.

90. Schnelle, *History and Theology of the New Testament Writings,* p. 466.

91. 1 John 3:9.

92. 1 John 1:8–10.

93. However, according to Schnackenburg, *Johannine Epistles,* "[t]he idea of mortal sin implies nothing about the possibility or impossibility of repentance" (p. 250).

94. Other communities such as the one represented by Hebrews were not as flexible. "A focal point of Hebrews' parenetic instruction is found in the statement that excludes a second repentance. Neither apostates nor wanton sinners can 'be restored again to repentance' (6:4–6; 10:26–31; 12:16–17). The once-for-all character of Christ's sacrifice leaves no room for a repeated forgiveness of flagrant sins" (Strecker, *Theology of the New Testament,* p. 620).

95. 2 John 9 warns against the evil deeds of the false teachers who were earlier identified with the Antichrist.

96. See especially 1 John 2:7–11.

97. See my *Paul: The Founder of Christianity* (Amherst, NY: Prometheus Books, 2002), pp. 123–25.

Chapter IV

THE FIRST AND SECOND LETTERS TO TIMOTHY, AND THE LETTER TO TITUS

The leadership claimed by the apostles and their successors aimed at total control—*not only over the faithful's belief, but also over all their possessions. That control could take on Orwellian dimension, extending to their very lives. Religious segregation, intolerance, and internal control had found their way into Christianity.*[1]

—Bernhard Lang

1. INTRODUCTION[2]

Since the eighteenth century 1 and 2 Timothy and Titus have been known as the pastoral Epistles, or simply the Pastorals. This designation arose because all three writings contain instructions, prophecies, and admonitions for leading the community, that is, for carrying out the office of pastor. The collective labeling is justified, because these three works have a unitary stamp that distinguishes them from the other epistles commonly referred to as "Pauline": they presuppose the same organization, similar conditions in the community, and the same adversaries. They also show close correspondence in language, style, and theological focus. But Paul did not write them.

In terms of the history of the canon, they are attested only relatively late, but always as a unity. Since they do not appear in Marcion's collection of Paul's letters (c. 130 CE), we can infer with at least reasonable assurance that he did not then know them; and since later followers of Marcion accepted the Pastorals, it seems certain that he had issued no explicit condemnation of them. Bishop Irenaeus (125–202 CE) is the first to know and use them. Indeed the very title of his work against heretics, "Unmasking and Refutation of the Gnosis Falsely So-called" (180 CE) contains an explicit allusion to 1 Tim. 6:20. In the Muratorian Canon, the earliest extant list of canonical writings (c. 200 CE),[3] the Pastorals follow Philemon—a strong indication that they were a later addition to an already existing collection of Paul's letters. That they are three in number no doubt reflects the important motif of three found throughout the Hebrew and Christian scriptures[4] and indicates the author's conscious design to enhance thereby their acceptance and authority. Evidently they were originally planned as a corpus and disseminated with a claim to be valid throughout the Pauline mission. But the Pastorals further claim their interpretation of Paul to be final and authoritative: they represent themselves as the apostle's abiding testament.

The author of the Pastorals urges the congregations to remain faithful to the legacy of their Pauline tradition. See, for example, 2 Tim. 2:2 ("Paul" to Timothy): "And what you have heard from me before many witnesses entrust to faithful people who will be able to teach others also." Clearly, this seeks to establish a chain of tradition from Paul through his disciple Timothy to the author of the Pastorals, one of the competent persons mentioned there. 2 Tim. 2:2 and 1 Tim. 6:20a— "O Timothy, guard the deposit entrusted to you"—show that the author seeks to ensure the unimpaired continuity of the Pauline tradition as he conceives it. Indeed, the author probably saw this direct succession to be in danger—hardly an unreasonable concern in view of the highly divergent interpretations of Paul in other contemporary writings from the Pauline school.[5]

The Pastorals employ the genre of the testament to make Paul speak to the author's time. Since Luke had already done that in his account of Paul's speech in Miletus,[6] the development from a sermon ascribed to Paul to an epistle written in his name was quite natural. Clearly, here, as in the Miletus speech, Paul is portrayed as one of the elders who are issuing directives for the contemporaries of the pastor. These instructions consist partly of church ordinances[7] aimed at organizing the community through the disciples commissioned by the apostle, and partly of detailed remarks about the battle against heretics.[8]

I shall first discuss 1 Tim. 6:20–21 and its historical background, because verse 20 may contain a reference to Marcion's main work

(*Antitheses*, c. 140). After that I shall try to determine whether Polycarp (c. 70–156 CE), who was bishop of Smyrna and mentor of Irenaeus, composed the pastoral Epistles. If one or both of these questions can be answered in the affirmative, we will have gained an important chronological datum to work from.[9]

1 Timothy 6:20–21 and Its Historical Background

The text reads: (20) "O Timothy, guard the deposit entrusted to you. Turn away from the godless chatter and contradictions[10] of what is falsely called knowledge,[11] (21) which some have professed and have fallen away from faith." Grace be with you.

It is striking that many words appearing in this text are found elsewhere in the Pastorals, but nowhere else in the New Testament.[12] For "entrusted deposit"[13] see 2 Tim. 1:12, 14; for "to turn away from" (or, "to avoid")[14] see 1 Tim. 1:6 and 5:15; 2 Tim. 4:4 (and Heb. 12:13). For "godless chatter"[15] see 2 Tim. 2:16; for "miss the mark"[16] see 1 Tim. 1:6 and 2 Tim. 2:18.

What particularly stands out is the formula "antitheses of what is falsely called knowledge," a phrase that appears here in the accusative as the object of "avoid" but in no other biblical text. Moreover, *epignôsis* (knowledge) is elsewhere found instead of *gnôsis*, and always connected with "the truth."[17] For the expression "falsely" or "falsely called"[18] compare with the "false speakers" at 1 Tim. 4:2, as well as the following phrases of the historical Paul: "false brothers,"[19] "false apostles,"[20] "false witnesses."[21] "What is falsely called knowledge," therefore, denotes knowledge not worthy of the name. The specification "for by professing it some have missed the mark as regards the faith" suggests that "knowledge" here picks up the opponents' terminology.[22] While the author sometimes adds names,[23] here he is purposely expressing himself in general terms. Therefore it may be inadvisable to see too specific a reference in 1 Tim. 6:20–21. Moreover, we should note that this passage stands at the end of the letter, and therefore is likely intended to utter a general warning against heresies.

Even if the emphatically general and polemical character of 1 Tim. 6:20–21 is clear, the question nevertheless resurfaces whether verse 20 may not, like 2 Tim. 2:18 (see above), have been coined on the basis of a slogan formulated by the opponents. "Knowledge" may have Gnostic heirs of Paul in mind, and "Contradictions" could be an explicit refer-

ence to Marcion's principal work, *Antitheses*. In that case, 1 Tim.
6:20–21 would be an evocative formulation by the author of the Pastorals, who at once derogates both Marcion and Gnostic disciples of
Paul by taking up their terminology.[24] But of course finding an allusion
to Marcion's title here would require a late dating of Pastorals. The next
section strongly encourages such a step.

Is Bishop Polycarp the Creator of the Pastorals?

The following remarks cite and summarize the work of Hans von
Campenhausen,[25] who seeks to demonstrate both philologically and
theologically the likelihood of Polycarp's authorship.

"Four so-called hapax legomena* which the Pastorals have as compared with the New Testament also occur in Polycarp's short letter to
the Philippians."[26] Moreover, the author of the Pastorals describes the
present world-age regularly as *ho nyn aiôn*. This term "occurs only twice
in Polycarp's letter[27] and three times in the pastoral Epistles,[28] and is
absent from all the other writings of the earliest Christian, apostolic,
and post-apostolic period."[29] Admittedly, two other passages are constantly cited in favor of Polycarp's dependence on the Pastorals, but
they are not convincing: Polycarp *Philippians* 4:1: "The love of money is
beginning of all difficulties. . . . We know we brought nothing into the
world and can take nothing out of it." This has parallels in 1 Tim. 6:7,
"We brought nothing into the world, and we cannot take anything out
of the world," and 1 Tim. 6:10a, "The love of money is the root of all
evils." But since Polycarp and the author of 1 Timothy are quoting com-
monplaces that have the character of wisdom sayings, a dependence of
one on the other cannot be thus demonstrated. Still, the evidence does
point to a church tradition common to Polycarp and the Pastorals.[30]

Moreover, the most remarkable feature shared by the Pastorals and
Polycarp's letter is to be found "not in individual points of contact but
in their whole character, i.e. in their content and to a certain degree also
in the form of their structure which is conditioned by this."[31] To be
more specific, one finds in Polycarp *Philippians* 4:1–6:2 codes of conduct and instructions similar to those in Titus 1:5–6. The fight against
heretics in Polycarp *Philippians* 6:3–7:2 corresponds to that in 1 Tim.

---

*A *hapax legomenon* ("once spoken") is a word that occurs only one time
in a specific body of literature, here the New Testament.

1:3–20 and 4:1–2 as well as in Titus 3:8–11. Furthermore, "The word stands firm and is worthy of full acceptance," a clause that often appears in the Pastorals,[32] may recall the phrase in Polycarp *Philippians* 7:2: "The word handed down to us from the beginning."

Therefore, even if it cannot be certified that Polycarp is the author of the Pastorals, it is a foregone conclusion that both reflect the same milieu. The writer of the Pastorals "must at least have been intimately connected with Polycarp."[33] And that further suggests that the Pastorals were written around 140 CE.

The Pastorals as Pseudepigraphical Letters

Here we must once again examine the view of the Pastorals as pseude-pigraphical documents. Before all else, let me emphasize that the "Pastor" cannot be considered a personal disciple of the apostle Paul. If, therefore, he purposely creates the impression that the apostle wrote this letter, his product must be termed a forgery every bit as bluntly as 2 Thessalonians. Attempts to pass it off as a well-intentioned reprise of the apostle's tutelage or validate it on the grounds of doctrinal paral-lelism are intellectually dishonest. And it is beyond cavil that had con-temporary readers seen through his mask, they would have condemned the imposture.

As an example one might refer to the case of the elder in Asia Minor about whom Tertullian reports:

> But if certain women use the falsely so titled Acts of Paul [by referring to Thecla's example] as a license for women's teaching and baptizing, let them know that, in Asia, the elder who composed that writing as if he were augmenting it by the title "About Paul" from his own store, after being convicted, and confessing that he had done it from love of Paul, stepped down[34] from his office. For how credible would it seem that he who has not permitted a woman even to learn, with overbold-ness should give a female the power of teaching and of baptizing? "Let them be silent," he says, "and at home consult their own husbands."[35]

COMMENT

What was the reproachable action of this presbyter? He wrote a piece that, according to Tertullian, falsely carried the title "Acts of Paul."

This—Tertullian opines—the apostle Paul would have rejected, since the community that used the "Acts of Paul" permitted baptism and teaching by women. Against this Tertullian refers to Paul's statement in 1 Cor. 14:35, and the contrast indicates to him that the work is inauthentic. Obviously the author of the Acts of Paul would have been expected to come from the immediate environment of Paul ("love" of Paul was not enough). And consider a further significance: if at a later time "epistles of Paul" were to be written by Christians who had not been personally acquainted with him, this would constitute an affront even by the principles of Primitive Christianity. Compared with such an explicit plagiarism, the Acts of Paul were an innocent case. Its author did not attribute them to Paul as an author, nor did he for himself claim participation in the events described. Our elder in Asia had merely had less luck than his numerous predecessors who, like the author of the Pastorals, produced forged letters that became part of Christianity's sacred scripture.[36]

2. TRANSLATION AND ANALYSIS OF 1 TIMOTHY

1:1–2: Prescript

(1) Paul, an apostle of Christ Jesus by command of GOD our Savior and of *Christ Jesus* our hope, (2a) to Timothy, true child in faith. (2b) Grace, mercy, and peace from GOD the Father and *Christ Jesus* our Lord.

COMMENT

This section exhibits the so-called *oriental form* of the prescript, which consists of two parts. The first part gives the name(s) of the sender(s) (verse 1) and then identifies the person(s) to whom the letter is sent (verse 2a). The second part is a blessing (verses 2b–3), which here corresponds to Jewish benedictions[37] and may echo the priestly blessing of the Old Testament book of Numbers.[38] The oriental form is used in all the extant Pauline letters—whether genuine or not—and also in Revelation.[39] In contrast, the *Greek form* of the letter prescript contains only one part. It can be found in Acts[40] and James.[41] The distinction between the two types of prescripts helps to determine the relationship of early Christian documents to one another.[42]

Verse 1: This verse begins weightily by deriving Paul's apostleship directly from God and Christ Jesus.

Verse 2: The statement in verse 2a is based on 1 Corinthians 4:17 and sets the stage for the letter. It is to his child in faith, his disciple, that "Paul" addresses the writing.

1:3–11: Attack upon Heretics and the Right Use of the Law

(3) As I did when I was going to Macedonia, I urge you to remain in Ephesus in order that you may charge certain persons not to **teach** any different doctrine, (4) nor to occupy themselves with myths and endless genealogies that promote speculations rather than the divine training that is in FAITH. (5) For the purpose of the instruction is love that issues from a pure heart and a good conscience and sincere FAITH, (6) from which certain persons have swerved and wandered away into vain discussion. (7) They desire to be **teachers** of the law without understanding either what they are saying or the things about which they make assertions.

(8) But we know that the *law* is good, if any one uses it *law*fully. (9a) We know this, that the *law* is not laid down for the righteous (9b) but for the

(1-2) lawless and disobedient,
(3-4) ungodly and sinners,
(5-6) unholy and profane,
(7-8) murderers of fathers and mothers,
(9) manslayers, (10)
(10) immoral persons,
(11) sodomites,
(12) kidnappers,
(13) liars,
(14) perjurers,

and whatever else is contrary to the sound doctrine (11) that conforms to the gospel of the glory of the blessed GOD which was entrusted to me.

COMMENT

Verse 3: The author imposes on the reader two presuppositions: first, that the letter was written in Macedonia,[43] and second, that "Paul" is in Ephesus[44] and had made travel plans as outlined at 1 Cor. 16:5–7. The phrase "to teach any different doctrine"[45] can be found in the New Testament only here and later in 1 Tim. 6:3. Its necessary premise is the existence of a body of normative doctrines against which any other doctrine can be measured.

Verse 4: "Myth" is to be understood negatively here and at other places in the Pastorals[46] and in 2 Peter. According to 2 Pet. 1:16, a myth is a fiction or a fairy tale as opposed to the historical reality to which the author has been an eyewitness. The pastoral Epistles consider myths to be cosmic-metaphysical speculations of Gnostic origin that are opposed to the right doctrine and to truth. There are many myths, but only *one* truth. Since Titus 1:14 speaks of "Jewish myths," one may think of Gnostic interpretations of the Old Testament to which the Nag Hammadi texts offer many parallels.[47] However, one must not use the modern understanding of myth[48] at this point. The author of the Pastorals does not mean that the opponents are propagating mythic accounts of the origin of the world, but rather that their tales are untrue and silly. After all, his own doctrine of salvation is itself based on a myth.

Verse 5: The author designates love to be the aim of Christian preaching while suggesting by the context that the heretics are unable to reach that goal because the content of their doctrines differs from the church's preaching. The threefold specification of love—that it issues from a pure heart, a good conscience, and sincere faith—reflects the author's tendency to use edifying language.

Verses 6–7: In a sarcastic tone the author accuses the false teachers of total ignorance. Their complete lack of understanding, he implies, stems from the fact that they have abandoned the true belief. Thus their "heresy" receives no specific refutation but is derogated by authoritarian name-calling. The term "teachers of the law" is not necessarily a self-designation of those attacked, but serves to introduce the following section, verses 8–11.

Verse 8: For the content compare with Rom. 7:12. The author opposes the false teaching with what he considers correct doctrine. It is noteworthy that he neither characterizes nor discusses the opponents' specific interpretation of the law, but simply asserts his own understanding of the law to be that of the church catholic.

Verse 9a: For the content compare with Rom. 3:21, 28. A righteous person has no need of the law because he or she has not only received sound doctrine but also lives according to it.

Verses 9b–10: This catalogue[49] consists of fourteen vices (see the numbering in the translation); two times seven is a stylistic device.[50] The expression "sound doctrine" appears in the New Testament only in the Pastorals.[51] Similar expressions which only this author uses are "sound words"[52] and "to be sound in faith."[53] Though there is no direct contrasting between "sound" doctrine and "sick" doctrine, this concept may well underlie the author's argument. Indeed, he regards his teaching and preaching as "sound" because it thwarts the wicked influence of the false teachers and keeps them from further destroying the church catholic. And recollect that 6:4a describes the consequences of the heresy as sickness.

Verse 11: This verse serves both as a conclusion and as a transition. Note that in this context "gospel" suggests "'the Christian message as a whole,' especially in its moral aspect, with which the 'sound teaching' accords."[54] One might observe parenthetically that the lofty self-assurance the writer displays in designating himself—in the guise of Paul—as God's specially ordained agent may indicate that while he often distorts Paul's teaching, he has accurately if unwittingly captured the apostle's swagger.

1:12–17: Christ Jesus Has Made Paul His Servant

(12) I thank him who has given me strength, Christ Jesus our Lord, because he judged me faithful and put me into service, (13) though I once was a blasphemer and a persecutor and a scorner. **But I received mercy** because I had acted ignorantly in unbelief, (14) and the grace of our Lord was greater, with the faith and love that are in Christ Jesus. (15) The word stands firm and is worthy of full acceptance: "Christ Jesus came into the world to save sinners"—of whom I am the foremost. (16) **But** for this reason **I received mercy**, that in me, as the foremost, Jesus Christ might display the fullness of his patience as an example to those who will in the future believe in him for eternal life. (17) To the King of ages, immortal, invisible, (the) only God, be honor and glory forever and ever. Amen.

COMMENT

Verse 12: This picks up verse 11 and introduces the thanksgiving in which "Paul" looks back on his conversion and twice emphasizes the mercy that he received.

Verse 13: Like the historical Paul[55] and like the members of the community whom he persecuted,[56] the Paul of the Pastorals employs a "that was then, this is now" scheme to describe the change in his life. An important difference, however, is that the author of the Pastorals attributes his persecution of the church to unbelief rooted in ignorance, while the historical Paul identifies zeal for the law as his motivation.[57]

Verse 14: "Paul" claims the content of the grace that he has supposedly received to be "The faith and love that are in Christ Jesus."

Verse 15: The grace afforded to "Paul" is further described in a confessional statement, "The word stands firm and is worthy of full acceptance," and can be found at other places in the Pastorals.[58] Since the original historical setting (Sitz im Leben) of this affirmative or confirmatory formula can no longer be determined, one can well imagine it as an element of community jargon.

Verse 16: As someone whose sins were forgiven, "Paul" claims to be an example for all who in the future would believe in Christ Jesus. In Paul's genuine letters we do not find any similar pretense to be a model for all future believers. Rather, the historical Paul assigns himself a quite different though obviously decisive role in salvation history—that of the apostle to the Gentiles.[59]

Verse 17: A benediction glorifying the oneness and exclusivity of God rounds off the section.

1:18–20: Exhortation and Admonition of Timothy

(18) This charge I commit to you, Timothy, my child, in accordance with the prophetic utterances which pointed to you: that by taking them to heart you may fight the good fight, (19) holding (fast to) FAITH and a good conscience. By rejecting the claims of conscience, certain persons have made a shipwreck of their FAITH, (20) among them Hymenaeus and Alexander, whom I have delivered to Satan that they may be taught not to blaspheme.

COMMENT

Verse 18: "This charge" refers both to the previous sections (it picks up the verb in verse 3 and the noun in verse 6) *and* to the following ones. The personal address "my child Timothy" echoes 1 Tim. 1:2 ("Timothy, true child in faith"). The term "prophetic utterances"[60] looks back to Timothy's ordination, an event described in a later section.[61] Indeed, many key elements of this book have the character of a renewal of ordination.[62] The expression "fight the good fight" is an obviously military image, and recalls 4 Macc. 9:24 in which martyrdom by torture is "fighting the sacred and noble fight for piety (or, [true] religion)."

Verses 19–20: The way of life of the ordained person has been shaped by faith and good conscience. "Paul" blames Hymenaeus and Alexander—who likely had been earlier ordained as functionaries of the church catholic—for deserting their faith. By alluding to the consignment to Satan stipulated in 1 Cor. 5:5, "Paul" hopes by chastisement to lead them back to the church. For the historical Paul it was a very different story: "handing over to Satan" involved the death of the sinner in order to save his soul.

2:1–7: Prayers for All People, especially for the Government

(1) First of all, therefore, I urge that supplications, prayers, intercessions, and thanksgivings be made for all people, (2) for kings and all who are in high positions, that we may lead a quiet and peaceable life, in all piety and dignity. (3) This is good, and it is acceptable in the sight of GOD our *Savior*, (4) who desires all people to be *saved* and to come to the knowledge of the TRUTH.

(5) For there is **one** GOD, and there is **one** mediator between GOD and humans, the human being Christ Jesus,

(6a) who gave himself as a ransom for all,

(6b) the testimony at the proper time. (7) For this I was appointed a preacher and apostle—I am telling the TRUTH, I am not lying—a teacher of the Gentiles in faith and TRUTH.

COMMENT

Verse 1: "Therefore" takes up "I entrust this charge to you" in 1:18, disregarding 1:19b–20. The obligation to pray for all human beings noted in verse 1 is specified in verse 2. The use of various terms signifying prayer—supplications, prayers, intercessions, thanksgivings—is simply rhetorical pleonasm.

Verse 2: The Christian community should pray for kings and all who are in high positions. For the obligation to observe piety see below, pp. 125–26, on 1 Tim. 4:8. Clearly, the purpose of these injunctions is to allay any Gentile suspicion of wrongdoing that could prompt denunciations to the Roman authorities and thus threaten the Christian community.[63]

Verses 3–4: Praying for everyone is analogous to the will of God, whose aim is the salvation of all. "Knowledge of truth"[64]—a technical term in the communities of the Pastorals[65]—is a short formula of Christian faith.

Verses 5–6a: This liturgical piece, which is similar to 1 Cor. 8:5–6, substantiates the thesis of verse 4. It proclaims the oneness of God and, more specifically, his exclusiveness. Also emphasized is the exalted nature of Christ, whose self-sacrifice has made him the sole mediator between God and humans. (On the Gnostic criticism of the oneness of God—that is, exclusive monotheism—see below, pp. 213–28, appendix 1.)

Verses 6b–7: The phrase "the testimony at the proper time" has the appearance of an appendix whose syntax is a bit awkward. In the Pastorals the adverb "at the proper time" designates the predetermined time of revelation.[66] Verse 7 interprets verse 6b: as in 1:15, the "objective" revelation, proclaiming the oneness of God and of the salvation by Christ in accordance with the divine plan, is the preacher's ordained function.

2:8–15: Rules for Men and Women

(8) I wish therefore that the men in every place should pray, lifting holy hands without anger or strife.

(9) Likewise WOMEN should adorn themselves in appropriate dress _with_ chastity and _prudence_: not with braided hair or gold or pearls or costly attire, (10) but rather with good works, as is fitting for WOMEN who profess reverence for God.

(11) A WOMAN should learn in **silence** with all submissiveness. (12) I permit no WOMAN to teach or to have authority over a man; she is to keep **silent**. (13) For Adam was formed first, then Eve; (14) and Adam was not deceived, but the WOMAN was deceived and became a transgressor. (15) However, she will be saved through bearing children—if she perseveres in faith and love and holiness, _with prudence_.

COMMENT

Verse 8: This brief injunction directed at men demands prayer that is free from wrath and strife. The author seems to be transferring a code from the Jewish-Hellenistic synagogue to the Christian community.

The ensuing section (verses 9–15)—a surprisingly long and detailed prescription for women—aims to thwart their activity in church service and to enforce their submission to men.

Verses 9–10: The author uses a topos from the moral philosophy of his time. He calls on women to eschew frivolous self-adornment and to observe modesty and propriety in dress and behavior.

Verses 11–12: These verses match the post-Pauline interpolation in 1 Cor. 14:33b–35[67]—a passage that may in fact derive from the author of the Pastorals.

Verses 13–14: Two proof-texts from scripture[68] further defend the commands. In this passage we find a notable contrast to 2 Cor. 11:3, in which the historical Paul compares misleading the whole congregation (men and women) with Eve's seduction by the serpent. He has no wish to equate Eve with women in general. Here, however, the author emphasizes the difference between Adam and Eve: Adam's primacy derives from his having been created first; nor was he the one deceived, but rather Eve, who became the first transgressor of God's commands.

Verse 15: The one function that affords women salvation is childbearing—a statement that is likewise substantiated in scripture—for it "transforms the punishment of Gen. 3:16 into a means of salvation."[69] The author evidently encourages childbearing in an effort to rebut the asceticism of the heretics (see 4:3) and thereby to protect women of the community from having their faith undermined by the call to celibacy.[70] Gnostic teachers are likely behind the argument in verses 9–15. Against them the author defines the role of the Christian woman both negatively (not to teach) and positively (to bear children). The opposite of both commands is richly documented in Gnostic sources. Indeed, women in Gnostic circles were accorded more freedom and respect than those in the second-century church, for they not only served as teachers but also were deemed worthy to receive revelations. The portrait of Mary Magdalene in the Gospel of Mary—in which she appears as Jesus' foremost disciple—is a striking example.[71]

3:1–13: Demands on the Offices of the Bishop and the Deacon

(1) The word stands firm: If any one aspires to the office of BISHOP, he desires a noble task. (2) Now a BISHOP must be without reproach, the HUSBAND OF ONE WIFE, temperate, sensible, dignified, hospitable, skillful in teaching, (3) no drunkard, not violent but gentle, not quarrelsome, and no lover of money. (4) He must manage his own household well, keeping his children submissive and respectful with complete _dignity_—(5) for if a man does not know how to manage his own household, how can he care for God's church? (6) Nor should he be newly converted, lest he become puffed up and **fall into** the condemnation **of the devil**. (7) He should also have a good reputation among those outside, so that he may not **fall into** reproach and the snare **of the devil**.

(8) **DEACONS** likewise must be _dignified_, not double-tongued, not addicted to much wine, not greedy for gain; (9) they must hold the mystery of the **faith** with a pure conscience. (10) And let them also be tested first; then if they prove themselves blameless let them serve as **DEACONS**.

(11) The women likewise must be _dignified_, no slanderers, but temperate, faithful in all things.

(12) Let **DEACONS** be the HUSBAND OF ONE WIFE, and let them manage their children and their households well; (13) for those who serve well as **DEACONS** gain a good standing for themselves and also great confidence in the **faith** which is in Christ Jesus.

COMMENT

Verse 1: For the affidavit "The word stands firm," see above, p. 118, on 1:15. The author assumes that one does not become bishop by seniority or reputation, but that anyone may strive for that distinction. This seems to presuppose the developed constitution of a church, because such a phenomenon does not seem likely to represent the earliest phase of community formation.[72]

Verses 2–3: Besides monogamy, the requirements for a bishop include a catalogue of positive and negative moral norms that reflect the general ideals of ancient society.[73]

Verses 4–5: The household is a model for both the local community and the church catholic.

Verses 6–7: The discourse on the specific behavior of the bishop must be seen against the background of early Christian experience in pagan society. The good witness and opinion of Gentile neighbors was especially important for the positive image and consequent growth of Christian congregations.[74]

Verse 8: "Paul" formulates requirements for the office of a deacon that are similar to those for a bishop.

Verse 9: It is a noteworthy departure from the historical Paul[75] that the author uses the term "mystery" in a formulaic way for what Christians must believe.

Verse 10: "Paul" can hardly be seen to have a regular examination procedure in mind—we learn nothing of its details—but simply urges the community's attention during the selection process.

Verse 11: Since verses 8–10 and verse 12 deal with the duties of a deacon, the wives in verse 11 are likely those of the deacons. Note that as with husbands (verse 8) and bishops (verse 4) the demand for dignity stands in first place.

Verse 12: The duties of the deacons parallel those of the bishops. They should marry only once and exercise proper governance over their households.

Verse 13: Two promises are held out: high rank and esteem within the congregation, and inner confidence founded on the assurance of salvation.[76]

3:14–16: The Basis and Goal of the Apostolic Command

(14) This I am writing to you in the hope to come to you soon, (15) but so that if I am delayed, you may know how one ought to behave in the house of GOD, which is the church of the living GOD, the pillar and bulwark of the truth. (16a) Great indeed, we confess, is the mystery of our religion:

(16b) He was manifested in the *flesh*—vindicated in the <u>Spirit</u>,
Seen by <u>angels</u>—preached among the *nations*, Believed on in the
world—taken up in <u>glory</u>.

COMMENT

Verses 14–15: As "Paul" now notes by way of addition, he has given the
directions found in 2:13–3:13 in case his plans for a visit should fail.[77]
This is simply a ruse to help camouflage his forgery. Note that in his
eyes the house of God is the church of the living God, the very pillar
and bulwark of the truth. This claim is no doubt intended to establish
and perpetuate the authority of the officers of the church catholic.

Verse 16a: This affirmation serves as a transition to the kerygmatic
element that follows. As for the "mystery of our religion," compare with
the "mystery of faith" in verse 9.

Verse 16b: This contains the fragment of a hymn in praise of the
exaltation of Christ that was likely recited during church services. It consists of three double lines with three opposite pairs in a chiastic pattern:
that is, the successive pairs describe the earthly and the heavenly world,
but in reverse order.[78] In the translation I have marked the nouns that
correspond to each other by italics and underlining.

4:1–5: The Coming of Heretics in the End-time and Their Preaching

(1) Now the <u>Spirit</u> says explicitly that in future times some will
depart from the faith. They will give heed to deceitful <u>spirits</u> and
doctrines of demons, (2) based on the hypocrisy of liars whose consciences are seared, (3) who forbid marriage and enjoin abstinence
from foods that GOD created to be received with *thanksgiving* by
those who believe and know the truth. (4) For everything created by
GOD is good, and nothing is to be rejected if it is received with
thanksgiving; (5) for then it is consecrated by the word of GOD and
prayer.

COMMENT

Verse 1: The idea that demonic antagonists will rise up at the beginning
of the end-time is an oft-repeated theme of early Christian texts.[79] The

historical Paul also considered the rise of heresies necessary,[80] but he did not relate their appearance to the apocalyptic drama. To be sure, like the author of the Pastorals he regarded the devil and his demonic helpers as real entities, but in the apostle's view, they worked their evil not by fomenting heresies, but through the machinations of his opponents[81] or through his illness.[82]

Verse 2–3a: The polemic against the adversaries is extreme. Because they cling to "false" teachings—such is the conclusion of the author—there must be some secret sin behind what they do.

Verses 3b–5: Here we find the only argument leveled against the adversaries, a demonstration based on the correctness of accepting the good gifts of God the creator. Oddly enough, "Paul" attacks the dietary code of the opponents, but does not apply the same logic to rebut their ban on marriage, even though it would seem to apply equally well and verse 3a names both as objectionable elements in their teaching. Both are ascetic features of a doctrine that is predicated on a dualism of divinities: the highest God and the inferior creator God of the Old Testament.

4:6–11: The Task of Timothy as the Good Teacher and the Servant of Jesus Christ

(6) If you put these instructions before the brothers, you will be a good minister of Christ Jesus, nourished on the words of the faith and of the good *teaching* you have followed. (7) Shun the godless and silly myths. TRAIN yourself in **piety**; (8) for while bodily TRAINING is of some value, **piety** is of value in every way, as it holds promise for the present life and also for the life to come. (9) The word stands firm and is worthy of full acceptance. (10) For to this end we toil and strive, because we have our hope set on the living God, who is the Savior of all human beings, especially of those who believe. (11) Command and *teach* these things.

COMMENT

Verse 6: As elsewhere[83] the author here introduces a separate section with special commands for Timothy. The task of the community's leader consists in giving instructions about correct belief and correct doctrine.

Verse 7: Elsewhere in the Pastorals the author employs the verb "to shun" or "to reject"[84] in connection with the fight against heresy.[85] This always takes the form of simple condemnation that never deigns to present arguments. "Myth" stands in opposition to "piety."

Verse 8: The depreciation of bodily exercise picks up the demands of the false teachers from verse 3. The author confronts them with piety (in Greek, *eusebeia*), which holds promise for the present as well as the future life. Not only is piety an important theological term in the Pastorals,[86] but elsewhere in the New Testament the term appears only four times in 2 Peter[87] and once in Acts.[88] It is shaped by the Hellenistic environment and, generally speaking, designates respect for binding values. By appealing to the ethical aspect of the concept, the author combines it with his specific view of Christ and the history of salvation.

Verses 9–10: After inserting the confirmatory formula in verse 9, the author creates verse 10 (introduced by "For to this end") in order to complement and extend the assurance of verse 8. The confession of God the savior is the main thrust of verse 10. The designation "God the savior" has already been used at 1:1 and also occurs in connection with the living God at 3:15. On the difference between "all human beings" and "those who believe" see the historical Paul at 1 Thess. 5:15.

Verse 11: The author concludes the section with two orders. The verbs "to command" and "to teach" suggest the two primary functions of a community leader struggling against "heretics."

4:12–16: The Community Leader Exhorted to Be an Example

(12) Let no one despise your youth, but set the believers an example in speech and conduct, in love, in faith, in purity. (13) Till I come, pay attention to (public) reading, to preaching, to *teaching*. (14) Do not neglect the gift you have, which was given you by prophetic utterance when the council of elders laid their hands upon you. (15) Practice these duties; devote yourself to them, so that all may see your progress. (16a) Take heed to yourself and to your *teaching*; (16b) hold to that, for by so doing you will save both yourself and your hearers.

COMMENT

Verse 12: In Primitive Christianity a bishop's youth was occasionally a matter of concern.[89] On the model character of a church official see 3:1–13.

Verse 13: The phrase "till I come" harks back to 3:14. The second part of the verse gives the details of Timothy's task in acting for "Paul." In contrast to private study, "(public) reading" is reading aloud to others.[90] One assumes that the content of public reading would be Jewish scripture, apostolic or episcopal letters, and accounts of the words and deeds of Jesus.[91] Although it is highly unlikely that anything resembling the New Testament existed at the time of the Pastorals, we find in 1 Tim. 5:18–19 quotations from the Old Testament: Deut. 25:4; 24:15; 19:15.

Verse 14: This verse alludes to the dignity conferred on Timothy by his ordination; the "prophetic utterance" and "laying on of hands" were most likely elements of this rite.

Verses 15–16: In verse 15 the author stresses the importance of the commands given in the previous verse. The command in verse 16a once again underlines the importance of teaching. God bestows salvation through the leader of the community; acting through Christ he has made possible the salvation of mankind (verse 16b).

5:1–2: Rules for Relating to Different Age Groups

(1) Do not rebuke an older man but exhort him as you would a father; treat younger men like brothers, (2) older women like mothers, younger women like sisters, in all purity.

COMMENT

Verses 1–2: One could be tempted to connect these two verses to what follows, especially since the subsequent statements about widows follow smoothly. On the other hand, the code concerning widows (verses 3–16) governs the behavior of the church as a whole, whereas here we find general regulations to guide the behavior of a community leader toward older and younger men and women. The content of the instructions is conventional.[92] See Titus 2:2–8 for more developed instructions on various age groups.

5:3–16: Rules for Widows

(3) Honor WIDOWS if they are real WIDOWS. (4) If a WIDOW has children or grandchildren, let them first learn to show piety to their **own family** and make a return to those who brought them up; for this is acceptable in GOD's sight. (5) She who is a real WIDOW, and is left all alone, has set her hope on GOD and continues in supplications and prayers night and day; (6) whereas she who is self-indulgent is dead even while she lives. (7) Issue these commands so that all may be without reproach: (8) If any one does not provide for his relatives, and especially for **his own family**, he has denied the faith and is worse than an unbeliever.

(9) Let a WIDOW be enrolled if she is not less than sixty years of age, having been the wife of one husband; (10) and she must be well attested for her good deeds, as one who has brought up children, shown hospitality, washed the feet of the saints, relieved the afflicted, and devoted herself to doing good in every way.

(11) But refuse to enroll younger WIDOWS; for when sensuality alienates them from Christ, they desire to marry (12) and thereby incur condemnation for having violated their first pledge. (13) Besides that, they learn to be idlers, gadding about from house to house, and not only idlers but gossips and busybodies, saying what they should not. (14) So I would have younger WIDOWS marry, bear children, rule their households, and give the enemy no occasion to revile us. (15) For some have already turned away to follow after Satan.

(16) If any believing woman has relatives who are WIDOWS, let her assist them; let the church not be burdened, so that it may assist those who are real WIDOWS.

COMMENT

Verse 3: The author takes great pains to define the status of a widow and to formulate clear criteria for deciding who is a "real" widow. It would appear that many women sought to be acknowledged as widows in order to ensure their support.

Verse 4: A first case applies to widows who have a family.

Verses 5–6: Here a contrast between true and false widows follows. On verse 5 compare with the widow in the parable Luke 18:2–5 who,

Jesus suggests in verse 7, will be heard by the God she calls on day and night. See further the prophetess Hannah, likewise a widow, who does not leave the temple and serves God by fasting and prayer (Luke 2:36–37).

Verse 7: Like the bishop in 3:2, the widow should be without blame.

Verse 8: By way of addition the author addresses the possibility that his command of verse 4 is not being followed. Surprisingly, he equates neglect of family with denying the faith and thereby declares Christian evildoers even worse than people with no faith. I assume that by "denying the faith" (in Greek, *arneisthai tên pistin*) he means apostasy.[93]

Verses 9–13: In verses 9–10 "Paul" enumerates the criteria for real widowhood and in verses 11–13 explains why younger widows should be rejected.

Verse 14: Compare with 1 Tim. 2:15. Perhaps the adversaries offered younger widows freedom from traditional roles as mothers and house-wives; perhaps the author either had been or feared being taunted that some of his members had adopted the heretics' way of life.

Verse 15: In this verse we hear about widows who have taken a deci-sive step toward "heresy" by falling away from the orthodox faith of the author. As in 1 Tim. 1:16 and 2 Tim. 2:4, the verb "to turn away" (in Greek, *ektrepesthai*) signifies a turn toward "heresy."

Verse 16: The author reiterates the command of verse 4 that a Chris-tian woman should support widowed family members in her own house.

5:17–25: Rules for Elders and Exhortations for Timothy

(17) Let the ELDERS who govern well as presiding officers be deemed worthy of a double compensation, especially those who labor in preaching and teaching; (18) for the scripture says, "You shall not muzzle an ox when it is treading out the grain," and, "The laborer deserves his wages." (19) Never admit any charge against an ELDER except on the evidence of two or three witnesses. (20) As for those (elders) who persist in sin, rebuke them in the presence of all, so that the rest may stand in fear.

(21) In the presence of God and of Christ Jesus and of the elect angels I charge you to keep these rules without favor, doing nothing from partiality. (22) Do not be hasty in the laying on of hands, nor participate in another man's sins; keep yourself pure. (23) No

longer drink only water, but take a little wine for the sake of your stomach and your frequent ailments.

(24) The sins of some men *are conspicuous*, pointing to judgment, but the sins of others come to light later. (25) So also good deeds *are conspicuous*; and even when they are not, they cannot remain hidden.

COMMENT

Verses 17–18: While in verse 17 the author suggests a compensation double that of other elders who do not serve as presiding officers, in verse 18 he adduces two scriptural proofs[94] to back up the command from the previous verse.

Verses 19–20: Here the author sets forth a community rule—also backed by scriptural citation—on how to deal with elders who have sinned.[95]

Verse 21: The author employs a solemn, triadic formula of confirmation.

Verse 22: "Timothy" should not lay the hands on anybody prematurely. It remains uncertain whether this is part of a ritual of repentance or of ordination.

Verse 23: Picking up the term "pure" of verse 22c, the author warns against an ascetic attitude and encourages a moderate use of wine. (The reference to Timothy's health problems derives from the fictional frame of 1 Timothy.) The criticism of asceticism is likely directed at the same dissidents assailed in 4:3–5.

Verses 24–25: A pair of sayings rounds off the section. It supplements and adds to the requirement of verse 22c that "Timothy" must keep himself pure.

6:1–2: Commands for Believing Slaves

(1) Let all who are under the yoke of slavery regard their masters as worthy of all honor, so that the name of God and the <u>teaching</u> may not be defamed. (2a) Those who have **believing** masters must not be disrespectful on the ground that they are brothers; rather they must serve all the better since those who benefit by their service are **believers** and beloved. (2b) <u>Teach</u> and urge these duties.

COMMENT

Here the author requires that a slave respect his or her master—even if the latter is a believer and therefore a "brother." On the rule for slaves compare with Titus 2:9–10.

Verse 1: This rule holds for all Christian slaves.

Verse 2a: The author clearly deems important the case of Christian slaves serving Christian masters and urges Christian slaves to be especially zealous to fulfill their duties. It is very possible that the "opponents" concluded from specific passages of Paul's authentic letters (see, e.g., Gal. 3:28 and Philemon 16) that he favored an egalitarian relationship between slaves and masters. Were this opinion to become known, or worse yet made the basis of community practice, the result would no doubt be to alienate outsiders or even incur their enmity. (See the comment on 2:2 concerning the author's unwillingness to arouse social disapproval that might jeopardize the community's security.) Yet the reaction of outsiders is neither the only nor perhaps even the primary concern that led the author of the Pastorals to adopt such a stance in the case of slavery. His rigidly conservative policy in part reflects a theology shaped by Old Testament and Primitive Christian thought.[96]

Verse 2b: The author urges "Timothy" to convey his commands to the slaves.

6:3–10: Love of Money as the Main Motive of the Heretics

(3) If any one <u>teaches</u> otherwise and does not agree with the sound precepts of our Lord Jesus Christ and the <u>teaching</u> which accords with **piety**, (4a) he is puffed up with conceit, he knows nothing, but is addicted to disputation and quibbling, (4b) which produce envy, dissension, slander, base suspicions, (5) and wrangling among people who are depraved in mind and bereft of the truth, imagining that **piety** is a SOURCE OF PROFIT.

(6) Of course, **piety** is a great SOURCE OF PROFIT, but only for those who find profit in contentment. (7) For we brought nothing into the world, and we cannot take anything out of the world; (8) but if we have food and clothing, with these we shall be content. (9) But those who desire to be rich fall into temptation, into a

snare, into many senseless and hurtful desires that plunge men into ruin and destruction. (10a) For the love of money is the root of all evils.

(10b) It is through this craving that some have wandered away from the faith and pierced their hearts with many pangs.

COMMENT

Verses 3–5: This condemnation of "heretics" renews the attacks seen at the beginning of the letter (1:3–7). False teaching is to be repudiated because it results in immoral conduct. The description in verse 3 of catholic teaching as "the sound precepts of our Lord Jesus Christ" stands in contrast with verse 4a, in which "Paul" associates false teaching with sickness—by which he means, as verse 4b shows, various harmful behaviors.

Verses 6–9: Building on the charge of greed he has laid against the dissidents, the author develops an ideal of piety combined with contented self-sufficiency that has a sapiental basis.[97]

Verse 10a: The citation of a proverb widely used in antiquity[98] aptly concludes the preceding section.

Verse 10b: This part of the verse, which is artificially appended to the preceding section, accuses the opponents of love of money. Having assigned that motive to their actions, the author can allege that they "have wandered away from the faith."[99]

6:11–16: The Ordinational Confession as the Basis for the Episcopal Charge

(11) But as for you, man of GOD, shun [all] this; aim at righteousness, godliness, faith, love, steadfastness, gentleness. (12a) Fight the good fight of the faith; take hold of the eternal life to which YOU were called (12b) when YOU **made the good confession** in the presence of many witnesses.

(13) I charge YOU in the presence of GOD who gives life to all things, and of Christ Jesus who in his testimony before Pontius Pilate **made the good confession**

(14) to keep the commandment unstained and free from reproach until the appearance of our Lord Jesus Christ.

(15) And this will be made manifest at the proper time by the blessed and only Sovereign, the King of kings and Lord of lords,

(16) who alone has immortality and dwells in unapproachable light, whom no one has ever seen or can see.

To him be honor and eternal dominion. Amen.

COMMENT

This passage contains a discrete and separate moral exhortation; except for verse 11 ("shun [all] this!"), which refers generally to 6:3–10, this section has no ties with the context.

Verse 11: Although the term "man of God" typically designates every baptized person,[100] here only Timothy can be meant, for it is to him that the author addresses the catalogue of virtues that stand in contrast to the vices listed in verses 4–5.

Verse 12: This verse introduces the confession of ordination that follows in verses 13–16. Indeed, verse 12b explicitly refers to that rite.

Verses 13–16: This section derives from liturgical tradition and was probably used in an ordination ritual. Verse 13 may echo John 18:36–37. Verse 14 attests the validity of hope in Jesus' future coming.[101] Yet the phrase "at the proper time" (verse 15a) shows that this hope is no longer an imminent expectation but refers to an indeterminate future; hence the need for fixed and lasting institutions. The traditional praise of verses 15b–16 matches that in 1 Tim. 1:17. Indeed, the predicates of God reflect a strict monotheistic confession.

6:17–19: Exhortation of the Rich

(17) As for the **rich** in this world, charge them not to be haughty, nor to set their hopes on uncertain **riches** but on God, who **richly** furnishes us with everything to enjoy. (18) They are to do good, to be **rich** in good deeds, liberal and generous, (19) thus laying up for themselves a good foundation for the future, so that they may embrace true life.

COMMENT

Verses 17–19: "The rich" connects to the phrase "to become rich" in verse 9. Although the author ostensibly speaks about rich persons in general, he seems to be addressing wealthy members of his own congregation. Moreover, "Paul" has a positive attitude to wealth; its only danger is that it may cause the rich to put their hopes not in God but in the false security of money. Generosity, on the other hand, will ensure them eternal life.

6:20–21: Final Warnings against False Knowledge and Benediction

(20) O Timothy, guard the deposit entrusted to you. Turn away from the godless chatter and contradictions of what is falsely called knowledge, (21) which some have professed and have fallen away from faith. Grace be with you.

COMMENT

Verses 20–21: As was noted earlier (see above, p. 111) a number of words used in these two verses do not appear in the rest of the New Testament. Hence it appears that verses 20–21 aim at specific targets. Verse 20 seems to pick up a key word—"knowledge"—used by opponents who claim to derive from the apostle Paul, while the term "contradictions" probably alludes to the literary work of Marcion.[102] Verse 20, then, is a pithy formulation of the author of the Pastorals that he directs against both Pauline Gnostics and Marcion.

3. TRANSLATION AND ANALYSIS OF 2 TIMOTHY

1:1–2: Prescript

(1) Paul, an apostle of Christ Jesus by the will of GOD according to the promise of the life which is in Christ Jesus, (2) To Timothy, beloved child: Grace, mercy, and peace from GOD the Father and Christ Jesus our Lord.

COMMENT

Verses 1–2: The prescripts of Romans[103] and 1 Corinthians[104] are the direct literary model.

1:3–5: Thanksgiving

(3) I thank God whom I serve with a pure conscience, as did my fathers, when I <u>remember</u> you constantly in my prayers. (4) <u>Remembering</u> your tears, I long night and day to see you that I may be filled with joy, (5) and I <u>remember</u> your sincere faith, a faith that dwelled first in your grandmother Lois and your mother Eunice and now, I am sure, in you.

COMMENT

Verses 3–5: Differently from 1 Timothy and Titus—which both follow the prescript with orders to the recipient to be carried out in Ephesus and Crete respectively—yet in accordance with most of the other Pauline letters, the prescript is followed by a thanksgiving that consists of a thrice-repeated remembrance of the addressee in prayer, an expressed wish to see him again, and a recollection of the faith of the addressee and of his ancestors. "Faith" is a transmitted gift of piety. Later we learn that "Timothy" has known the Holy Scriptures from childhood.[105]

1:6–14: Encouragement to Fresh Effort and Preservation of Spiritual Heritage

(6) Hence I remind you to rekindle the gift of GOD that is within you through the laying on of my hands; (7) for GOD did not give us a spirit of timidity but a spirit of power and love and self-control. (8) ***Do not be ashamed***, then, of testifying to our Lord, nor of me his prisoner, but share in SUFFERING for the **GOSPEL** in the power of GOD,

(9) Who <u>saved</u> us and called us
    With a holy calling
    Not according to our own works
    But his own purpose and grace,

Given us in Christ Jesus
>   Before times eternal,
>   (10) But revealed now
>   Through the appearance of our _Savior_

Christ Jesus,
>   Who has destroyed death
>   But revealed life and incorruption
>   Through the **GOSPEL**

(11)—for which I was appointed a herald and apostle and teacher.

(12) Therefore I SUFFER all this. But _**I am not ashamed**_, for I know in whom I have put _FAITH_, and I am certain that he is able to _guard the deposit entrusted_ to me until that Day.

(13) Follow the pattern of the sound words which you have heard from me, in the _FAITH_ and love which are in Christ Jesus; (14) _guard the_ splendid _deposit entrusted_ (to you) by the Holy Spirit who dwells within us.

COMMENT

Verse 6: According to 1 Tim. 4:14, the author received God's gift (of the pastoral office) when the group of elders laid their hands on him. In this verse, however, "Paul" declares that it was _his_ laying on of hands that conferred the ordination. While 1 Tim. 4:14 is presumably based on the custom followed at the time of the Pastorals, the present verse seeks to emphasize the personal closeness between the author and the recipient of the letter.

Verse 7: The thought of the previous verse is reinforced by a paraphrase of Rom. 8:15.

Verse 8: Compare with Rom. 1:16. The author uses the verb "to be ashamed" in the same way as Paul did there, namely in connecting it with "gospel" and "power of God." Heretofore we have not heard of "Paul's" imprisonment, but his sufferings serve as a model for "Timothy."

Verses 9–10: Both verses stem from tradition; we may leave open the question of how much is due to direct quotation and how much to paraphrasing of tradition. In any case, the nouns "savior" and "appearance" derive from the author.[106]

The thesis that the author is indebted to tradition can be substantiated mainly for two reasons: (a) the participial forms that I have translated by relative clauses[107] and (b) the use of the "once-now scheme" in the text. This scheme—earlier seen in 1 Tim. 1:13—corresponds to the style of Primitive Christian preaching in contrasting the present reality of the revelation of "grace" with the past, during which the "grace" was hidden.[108]

Verse 11: "Paul" is part of the Gospel;[109] indeed, he is its herald, apostle, and teacher. Note that the sequence places "herald" at the head of the list. "Herald"[110] occurs elsewhere in the New Testament only at 2 Pet. 2:5.

Verse 12: This verse points back to verse 8. Here the "apostle" is himself doing what he there enjoined his pupil to do, namely to suffer without feeling ashamed. Furthermore, he expresses his assurance that God (or Christ) will safely guard the deposit entrusted to him.

Verse 13: The preaching of the "apostle" should be the model for the preaching of his pupil.

Verse 14: "Paul's" pupil must guard[111] the splendid deposit entrusted to him with the help of the Holy Spirit.[112] Note that the formulation—indicated in italics—is parallel to verse 12; like "Paul" like "Timothy." Both have received a deposit of faith and truth. Yet according to verse 12, God (or Christ) will guard the deposit of the "apostle," whereas in verse 14 "Timothy" is to guard the deposit vouchsafed to him by the Holy Spirit.

1:15–18: Instances of Apostasy and Fidelity

(15) You know that all who are in Asia have turned away from me, including Phygelus and Hermogenes.

(16a) *May the* **Lord** *grant* <u>mercy</u> to the household of Onesiphorus, (16b) for he often refreshed me; he was not ashamed of my chains, (17) but when he arrived in Rome he searched for me eagerly and found me.

(18a) *May the* **Lord** [= Jesus Christ] *grant* him to find <u>mercy</u> from the **Lord** [= God] on that Day. (18b) And you know full well how much his service has accomplished in Ephesus.

COMMENT

Verse 15: In order to introduce a deterrent example, the author refers to the general revolt against "Paul" in Asia—a mutiny in which Phygelus and Hermogenes participated and that apparently was general knowledge among the Pastoral communities.

Verses 16–18: "Paul" is in prison in Rome (note the earlier allusion in verse 8 and subsequent references in 2:9 and 4:6–8, 17). Onesiphorus, who along with his household has remained faithful and who thus stands in contrast to the deserters, is an example of how to follow the earlier commands not to be ashamed (verses 8, 12), as the author points out in verse 16b. Verse 18a is a parenthesis following from and further developing verse 16a. Note the two parallel sections verses 16a–17 and 18a–b. A wish for mercy for Onesiphorus is followed by a reference to his present and previous support of "Paul."

2:1–13: *Renewed Encouragement of Faithful Service, and Its Promised Rewards*

(1) You then, my son, be strong in the grace that is in <u>Christ Jesus,</u> (2) and what you have heard from me before many witnesses entrust to faithful people who will be able to teach others also. (3) Share in **suffering** as a good *soldier* of <u>Christ Jesus.</u>

(4) No *soldier* on duty gets entangled in civilian pursuits, since his aim is to satisfy the one who enlisted him.

(5) An athlete is not crowned unless he competes according to the rules.

(6) It is the hardworking farmer who ought to have the first share of the crops.

(7) Think over what I say, for the Lord will grant you understanding in everything.

(8) Remember Jesus Christ, risen from the dead, descended from David, as preached in my gospel, (9) for which I am suffering and wearing chains like an evildoer. But the word of God is not chained. (10) Therefore I endure everything for the sake of the elect, that they also may obtain salvation in Christ Jesus with its eternal glory. (11a) The word stands firm.

(11b) **If we have died with him, we shall also live with him.**

(12a) **If** we endure, we shall also reign with him.

(12b) **If** we _deny_ him, he also will _deny_ us.

(13a) **If** we are faithless, he remains faithful.

(13b) For he cannot _deny_ himself.

COMMENT

Verse 1: "Timothy" should himself become strong in order to transmit to other potential teachers what he has learned from "Paul" and other reliable witnesses.

Verses 3–7: The command in verse 3 to suffer as a good soldier of Christ is followed in verses 4–6 by three arguments for doing so. The first argument (verse 4) is connected with verse 3 by the keyword "soldier," but other than that the relevance of the three images—which derive from 1 Cor. 9:7, 24–25—is not clear. Perhaps this explains the author's apparently arbitrary change of subject and assurance of God's gift of right understanding in verse 7.

Verses 8–10: Verse 8 is a Christological introduction, which derives from a creedal formula. Note the author's citation of "my gospel" as the source of the phrase and the significant agreement between the present text and Rom. 1:3b–4a, where the historical Paul also employs a creedal formula.[113] The description of "Paul's" sufferings in verses 9–10 is the prelude to the hymnic text of verses 11b–13. In 1 Tim. 5:21, the noun "the elect" designates elected angels; here, however, as in Titus 1:1, Christians constitute the elect. In the Old Testament, God elected the Israelites;[114] the earliest Christians claimed the same for themselves. Among them "the elect" was an honorary title for the members of the first congregations.[115]

Verse 11a: On the formula of affirmation see above, p. 118.

Verses 11b–13a: This is a fragment of a tradition. (Because of its use in verse 10, the name of Christ, which must have preceded the piece, was unnecessary and therefore dropped.) A strong indication of its traditional origin is the fourfold repetition of "if" (set in boldface); yet since an overall structure cannot be identified, it is safer to suppose that the author has modeled the passage on some well-known tradition that subsequently vanished. Clearly, it was formulated to explain the content of verse 8 and affirm the promise of verse 10.[116] On verse 11b compare with Rom. 6:8; on verse 12a compare with Rom. 8:17.[117] On verse 12b compare with Matt. 10:33. Verses 12b and 13a stand in considerable tension, for while verse 12b envisages retribution, verse 13a points out that human faithlessness encounters divine faithfulness as a response.

Verse 13b: The author supports the thesis of verse 13a: Christ remains faithful because he cannot deny himself.[118] Note the contextual variation of "deny" and its poetic effect in verses 12b–13b.

2:14–21: Proper Conduct toward Heretics; the Firm Foundation of the Faith

(14) Remind them of this, and charge (them) before GOD not to dispute about <u>words</u>, for that does no good, but only destroys the listeners. (15) Do your best to present yourself to GOD as one approved, a worker who does not need to be ashamed, guiding the <u>word</u> of truth along a straight path.

(16a) Avoid profane and empty talk, (16b) for it will lead people into more and more impiety, (17a) and their infectious ideas will spread like a plague. (17b) Among them are Hymenaeus and Philetus, (18a) who have swerved from the truth by holding that (our) resurrection has already occurred (18b) and are thereby upsetting the faith of some.

(19) But GOD's firm foundation stands, bearing this seal: "The **Lord** knows those who are his," and, "Let every one who names the name of the **Lord** depart from iniquity." (20) In a great house there are vessels not only of gold and silver, but also of wood and earthenware, and some <u>for noble use</u>, some for *ignoble*. (21) If any one purifies himself from what is *ignoble*, then he will be a vessel <u>for noble use</u>, consecrated and useful to the master of the house, ready for any good work.

COMMENT

Verses 14–15: The author decrees that the right behavior for "Timothy" and his communities is to avoid any contact with the dissidents. The remark that the addressee has no need to be ashamed echoes the admonition in 1:8 that "Timothy" ought not to be ashamed and the corresponding remark in 1:12 that "Paul" is not ashamed.

Verses 16–17a: The author likens the teaching of the "heretics" to a serious illness, a contagious pathology that threatens the author and his flock.

Verses 17b–18b: Hymenaeus and Philetus may have been dangerous apostates in the Pastoral communities because of their poisonous teachings. "Paul" offers a synopsis of their doctrine: the resurrection has already taken place.[119] The remark in verse 18b that "they are upsetting the faith of some" seems both to indicate and to qualify the success of the heretics.

Verses 19–21: The first quotation is from Num. 16:5, the second cannot be identified, but it may be a paraphrase of Isa. 26:13. The author admits that in the house of the church there are quite a few "heretics" who do not belong there. Yet he does not offer the details that one might have expected, especially after referring by name to two renegades in verse 17. Of primary importance, according to "Paul," are two basic issues: the church's foundation in faith and the readiness of the "vessels for noble use" to serve the master of the house.

2:22–26: Directions for Right Behavior toward Heretics

(22) You must flee the youthful passions and aim at righteousness, faith, love, and peace, along with those who call upon the **Lord** from a pure heart. (23) Shun all stupid, senseless controversies, knowing that they breed _quarrels_. (24) And the **Lord's** servant should not be _quarrelsome_ but kindly to every one, an apt teacher, forbearing, (25a) gently correcting opponents. (25b) God may perhaps grant that they will repent and come to know the truth, (26) and they may escape from the snare of the devil, after being held captive by him to do his will.

COMMENT

Verse 22: The leader of the community receives general instructions and, in a sort of ecumenical aside, is united with all who call upon the name of the Lord—that is, *all Christians*.[120] This prepares for the instructions on dealing with heretics in the following verses.

Verse 23: "Timothy" must avoid controversies and quarrels that deal with speculations about myths and genealogies.[121] This is a variant of the commands found in verses 14, 16a.

Verses 24–25a: Here follow general commands concerning what a servant of the Lord must do.[122] It goes without saying that the servant of the Lord will find it easier to attract converts when friendly or at least respectful contact has been established. Yet there is a tension when the author as in verse 23 and elsewhere repudiates all controversies but at the same time wants to befriend and even correct opponents with whom he refuses to discuss disagreements, and about whom he will only a little later[123] say that they will never arrive at a knowledge of truth. This tension may be explained by the use of traditional language about what a servant of the Lord must do.

Verses 25b–26: On the granting of repentance in verse 25b, see Polycarp Phil. 11:4: "May the Lord give them (the fallen presbyter Valens and his wife) true repentance." The idea that God/the Lord confers repentance on people is common in Primitive Christianity[124] and derives from Judaism. See Sib. Oracles 4:168–70: "God will grant repentance and will not destroy. He will stop his wrath against you if you all practice honorable piety in your hearts."

The instruction of the opponents and those deceived by them has two aims. First, their repentance may lead them to recognize the truth of the Christian message.[125] Second, it may release them from the snare of the devil after a captivity during which he forced them to follow the path of evil.[126] However, since contact with the dissidents has been interrupted before, this seems to be only theoretical, pious talk, the more so in view of the negative characterization of them in the next section.

3:1–9: Heretics as Sinners of the Last Days

(1) But understand that the last days will be a time of troubles. (2) For people will be <u>lovers</u> of self, <u>lovers</u> of money, proud, arrogant, abusive, disobedient to their parents, ungrateful, unholy, (3) inhuman, implacable, slanderers, profligates, fierce, haters of good, (4) treacherous, reckless, swollen with conceit, <u>lovers</u> of pleasure rather than <u>lovers</u> of God, (5a) making a pretense at piety but denying its power.

(5b) Turn away from such people. (6) For among them are those who worm their way into houses and capture weak women burdened with sins and swayed by various impulses, (7) (women) who will listen to anybody and can never arrive at knowledge of the **truth**. (8) As Jannes and Jambres opposed Moses, so these (people) also oppose the **truth**, people of corrupt mind and counterfeit faith; (9) but they will not make further progress, for their folly will be plain to all, as was that of those two (people).

greetings to you, as do Pudens and Linus and Claudia and all the brothers. (22) **The Lord** be with your spirit. Grace be with you (all).

COMMENT

Verse 9: The request that "Timothy" come to "Paul" in the near future picks up the motif from the beginning of the letter that the apostle longs to see his pupil once more.[239]

Verses 10–11: "Paul's" loneliness and desertion by his followers similarly hark back to an earlier statement.[140]

Verse 12: On Tychicus compare with Eph. 6:21; Col. 4:7; Acts 20:4–5, and also Titus 3:12. By having "Paul" send Tychicus to Ephesus, the author expresses the enduring cordiality between his church and the one in Ephesus at this time.

Verse 13: In terms of content, this verse and 1 Tim. 5:13 are the most trivial in the New Testament letters; here the only aim is to create an impression of authenticity.

Verses 14–15: Alexander was identified as an opponent in 1 Tim. 1:20. Clearly, the action against him described there was a failure, because he continues to be an antagonist.

Verses 16–17: The very general description of events incident to "Paul's" trial intensifies the impression of his loneliness expressed in verses 10–11.

Verse 18: The statement that the Lord will save "Paul" for his heavenly kingdom evokes an echo of verse 8.

Verses 19–21: Listing the many coworkers of "Paul"—which is in contradiction with the situation painted in verses 10–11 and 16–17—has the sole aim of suggesting the authenticity of the writing.

Verse 22: The concluding benediction—an appropriate finale of the epistle—is twofold. "Paul" extends the blessing of his successor "Timothy" to all who are with him, that is, the proto-orthodox church of that time.

4. TRANSLATION AND ANALYSIS OF TITUS

1:1–4: Prescript

(1a) Paul, a servant of GOD and an apostle of Jesus Christ

(1b) according to the **faith** of GOD's elect and to the knowledge of the truth which is in accordance with piety, (2) on the basis of the hope of eternal life, which GOD, who is free from all deceit, promised ages ago (3) and at the proper time revealed in his word through the preaching with which I have been entrusted by command of GOD <u>our Savior</u>, (4) to Titus, my true child in a common **faith**: Grace and peace from GOD the Father and Christ Jesus <u>our Savior</u>.

COMMENT

On the form of the prescript see the comments on 1 Tim. 1:1–2 and 2 Tim. 1:1–2. The prescript found in Titus is by far the most elaborate of the three. Further, it is composed in liturgical language (verses 1b–3), possibly in order to remind the readers of the content of the faith held in common. Doubtless the ornate preface signals the author's desire to make especially emphatic the messages that follow.

Verse 1: The faith of the "elect"[141] and the "knowledge of truth"— the latter specified to be "in accordance with piety," thereby stressing the unity of faith and deed—define the content of "Paul's" call. Any faith that does not match his and that of the church catholic leads away from sound teaching to disruptive error, the various heresies that are falsely called knowledge.

Verse 2: The adjective "free from all deceit"—literally, "without lie"[142]—occurs only here in the New Testament. That Gnostics accused the Old Testament God of lying might have been the reason for its use.[143] While it is true that the Platonic tradition also regarded God to be without lie,[144] that fact can hardly explain a nonpolemical use at this place. Given the scarcity of "without lie" as a predicate of "God" in Primitive Christianity, its use in this preface is extraordinary, especially since it is not part of the author's customary repertoire of terms.

Verse 3: God's message of hope for eternal life is present in the apostle "Paul's" ministry.

Verse 4: The common faith is the bond that unites the apostle and "Titus," his pupil and an official of the church catholic.

1:5–9: *The Choice of Elders at Crete Assigned to Titus*

(5) This is why I left you in Crete, that you might see to what needed to be done, and appoint elders in every town as I ordered you—(6) each of them **blameless**, the husband of one wife, and whose children are believers and not open to charges of immorality or insubordination. (7) For a bishop, as God's steward, must be **blameless**; he must not be arrogant or quick-tempered or a drunkard or violent or greedy for money, (8) but

(1) hospitable,

(2) a lover of goodness,

(3) master of himself,

(4) upright,

(5) holy,

(6) self-controlled, (9)

(7) holding firm to the reliable word as taught,

so that he may be able to present sound <u>teaching</u> and also to reprove those who contradict it.

COMMENT

Verse 5: "Titus" receives the order to organize churches in Crete. This is in addition to achieving the doctrinal soundness that is commanded of "Timothy" in 1 Tim. 1:3, and represents the other side of the struggle against "heretics." Indeed, only intact church organizations enable orthodox teachers to cleanse their memberships of dissenters and thereby get rid of heretics.

Verses 6–8: This list of duties applies to all church officials in prominent positions.[145] The seamless transition from "elder" to "bishop" suggests that the author equates the two offices.

Verse 9: A church official—whether elder or bishop—must ensure respect for sound teaching in the congregation.

1:10–16: Against the Deceitful Heretics

(10) For there are many insubordinate people, empty talkers and deceivers, especially those of the circumcision; (11) they must be silenced, since they upset whole families by teaching what they have no right to teach simply to satisfy their greed.

(12) One of them, one of their own prophets, said, "Cretans are always liars, evil beasts, lazy gluttons." (13a) That testimony is **true**.

(13b) Therefore reprove them sharply, that they may be sound in the faith (14) instead of giving heed to Jewish myths or to commands of people who reject the **truth**. (15a) To the <u>pure</u> all things are <u>pure</u>, (15b) but to the *corrupt* and unbelieving nothing is <u>pure</u>; their very minds and consciences are *corrupted*. (16) They profess to know God, but they deny (him) by their deeds; they are abominable, disobedient, and unfit for any good work.

COMMENT

These statements about the opponents interrupt the community rules at 1:5–9 and 2:1–10. From 3:9 on the author will again turn to the issue of "heretics."

Verses 10–11: By referring to "those of the circumcision" (verse 10b) the author points to the Jewish background of the "heretics." Yet rather than designating their ethnic origin, he may mean only that these people have adopted a particular interpretation of the Old Testament. (From the beginning Gentile Christians showed a great interest in Jewish scriptures.) The author is attacking those he considers opponents both because of their refusal to submit to his authority and because what they are teaching often destroys family harmony. In addition, their greed is contrary to the magnanimity required of a bishop (verse 7). While the last charge is simply polemical exploitation of the obvious, the first two charges have a kernel of historical truth. The dissidents did indeed question the authority of bishops, whose power was based on the command of obedience, and their challenges were partly successful. This in turn led to the upset of many a family. The author of Titus, on the other hand, essentially equated obedience to God and obedience to the bishop. Since under these circumstances any discussion was fruitless, the only way to achieve spiritual unity was to silence[146] the opponents. Orthodoxy had to demand submission lest the Pastoral communities fall apart.

Verses 12–13a: To confirm his polemic against the dissidents the author quotes a highly negative assessment by the Cretan author Epimenides[147] of his own people. (Remember that according to the fiction of the letter "Titus" is presently on Crete.[148]) Indeed, says our author, the Cretan philosopher was prophetic in his judgment about the Cretan heretics.

Verses 13b–14: The verb "to reprove"[149] picks up the same word in verse 9. But what is "Titus" expected to do? Surely he is not to enter into a dialogue with the opponents, for in verse 11 "Paul" had told him to silence these people, a task that might conceivably have included the use of force—if such were available. Since the church is grounded on the truth, it need not risk debate.

Verse 15: For the wording of the epigram in verse 15a compare with the saying of the strong brothers to whom Paul belonged at Rom. 14:20: "All things are clean" (cf. Mark 7:15).[150] "The ironic tone of the Pastor more than suggests that the Gnostics were using the words in the sense, 'To us who are clean, anything is permitted; for nothing can now defile us.'"[151]

Verse 16: On this reproach compare with 2 Tim. 3:5. Heretical teaching and moral misconduct belong together.

2:1–10: Commands for Various Groups in the Communities

(1) But as for you, proclaim what is consistent with sound teaching.

(2) Older men should be sober, serious, sensible, sound in faith, in love, and in steadfastness. (3) The older women likewise: reverent in behavior, not slanderers or slaves to drink, teachers of all good things, (4) in order **that** they may advise the young women to love their husbands and to love their children, (5) to be *prudent*, chaste, domestic, kind, and submissive to their husbands, **in order that** the word of GOD may not be blasphemed. (6) Likewise urge the younger men to be *prudent* (7a) in all respects.

(7b) Offer yourself as a model of good works, in your teaching display integrity, seriousness, (8) and a wholesome message that is beyond reproach, **in order that** any opponent may be put to shame, having nothing bad to say of us.

(9) Slaves should be submissive to their masters and in every respect well pleasing, never talking back. (10) They should not pilfer, but show complete loyalty, **in order that** in every way they may prove adornments to the doctrine of GOD our Savior.

COMMENT

Verse 1: This command once again enjoins the leader of a congregation to proclaim sound doctrine in order to combat the "heretics." "The emphatic 'you' and the 'things that accord with the sound teaching' are in contrast to the teachers and teachings condemned in 1.10–16."[152]

Verses 2–7a: This section contains a catalogue of virtues for older men, older women (and indirectly younger women), and younger men. The list derives from the stock of general values in the Hellenistic world and transfers it to the Christian community. At other places in the Pastorals its author had directed similar demands to bishops, deacons, and their wives.[153]

Verses 7b–8: As the leader of the community "Titus" receives special instructions.[154] He has a special responsibility to be a model with respect to conduct and teaching. (Note the expression "wholesome message," in Greek, *logon hygiê.*) The opponent who must have no opportunity to criticize the congregation is the "heretic."

Verses 9–10: On the rule for slaves see the exegesis of 1 Tim. 6:1–2.

2:11–15: The Appearance of Grace as the Basis for Proper Conduct

(11) For the grace of GOD *appeared* bringing **salvation** to all, (12) teaching us to renounce *impiety* and worldly passions, and to lead a prudent, upright, and *pious* life in this age, (13) awaiting our blessed hope, the *appearing* of the glory of our great GOD and **Savior** Jesus Christ, (14a) who gave himself for **us** (14b) in order that he might redeem **us** from all lawlessness and

(14c) purify for himself a chosen people

(14d) eager for good works. (15) Declare these things forcefully; exhort and reprove with full authority; and let no one look down on you.

COMMENT

Verse 11: The statement that God's grace brings salvation to all amplifies the expression in verse 10, "the doctrine about God our Savior." The author's reference in this verse to the appearance of God's grace instead of the appearance of Christ (2 Tim. 2:10) matches his way of introducing the "revelation of the word" (Titus 1:3). See also on 1 Tim. 2:4. In each case the "grace" of God is for all.

Verse 12: Here the author likens the grace of God to "instruction," later in 3:4–7 to "righteousness."

Verse 13: The author formulates the Christian hope for the future. It may be disputed whether he distinguishes between "great God" and "savior Jesus Christ" or whether he designates Jesus Christ as the great God for whose appearance[155] the church is waiting. The present text no doubt supports the latter option. Not only do other New Testament texts likewise identify Jesus Christ with God,[156] but also at the beginning of the second century this identification was widespread in Primitive Christianity.[157]

Verse 14: Verses 14a–c constitute a creedal formula introduced by a relative pronoun.[158] "[V]erses 14b and 14c, reflect the Semitic style of synthetic parallelism. None of the key words in this clause— 'redeem,' 'purify,' 'lawlessness,' 'people,' and 'chosen'—appear elsewhere in the Pastorals, let alone this epistle."[159] In verse 14d the author adds "eager for good works"[160] and thus offers his synopsis of the Christian life.

Verse 15: In addressing these three admonitions—to declare, exhort, and reprove with full authority—to the leader of the congregation under the name of "Titus" the author picks up the imperative from 2:1: "Proclaim what is consistent with sound teaching." The verb "to reprove" was used twice before: 1:9, 13.

3:1–7: Christian Conduct and Its Motive

(1) Remind them to be subject to rulers and authorities, to be obedient, prepared for any good work, (2) not to blaspheme anyone, to avoid quarreling, to be gentle, and to show perfect courtesy toward all people.

(3) For we ourselves were once foolish, disobedient, led astray, slaves to various passions and pleasures, passing our days in malice and envy, despicable and hating one another.

(4) But when the generosity and loving kindness of God _our Savior_ appeared, (5) —not because of the works of **righteousness** we had done, but out of his own mercy—he _saved_ us by the washing that brings rebirth and renewal in the Holy Spirit, (6) which he poured out upon us richly through Jesus Christ _our Savior,_ (7) in

order that—made **righteous** by his grace—we might become heirs in hope of eternal life.

COMMENT

Verse 1: In 1 Tim. 2:1–2 "Paul" had urged the community to pray for their rulers, and thereby to ensure a quiet and peaceful life. Here the author "reminds" this congregation of the command to obey rulers without indicating the purpose of such a command. Submission in the sphere of politics corresponds to submission in the area of religion.

Verse 2: Compare with the remarks on 2 Tim. 2:24–26.

Verse 3: Using a catalog of vices,[161] the author reflects upon the pre-Christian time.

Verses 4–7: The author contrasts the past with the Christian present. This reflects a known pattern of primitive Christian preaching. Verse 4 echoes 2:11.[162] The terms "generosity" and "loving kindness" derive from "the language of the Emperor-cult and may actually have been copied from an inscription in honor of Caligula and Nero."[163] The insertion of parts of verse 5 and verse 7 adds a Pauline flavor to the text and once again shows that the author envisions himself as an heir of Paul. (See further 2:11–14 on this point.) Verses 4–7 (minus the insertions) contain a baptismal hymn that designates baptism of rebirth and renewal. The vocabulary[164] and rhythm of the hymn show it to have been a preexistent unit that the author commented upon and inserted into the letter.

3:8–11: Final Warning against Heretics

(8) The word stands firm. I desire you to insist on these things, so that those who have believed in God may be careful to apply themselves to good works; these things are excellent and **profitable** to everyone.

(9) But stupid controversies, genealogies, dissensions, and quarrels over the law you must avoid, for they are **unprofitable** and futile.

(10) As for a heretic, after admonishing him once or twice, shun him, (11) knowing that such a person is perverted and sinful; he is self-condemned.

COMMENT

"The Epistle is summarized; the purpose of sound teaching is to lead men away from harmful speculation and into good conduct."[165]

Verse 8: For the formula of affirmation see above, p. 118, on 1 Tim. 1:15.

Verse 9: The author describes "heresy" as the antithesis of "true" Christianity. For a similar evaluation see Titus 1:10–16.

Verse 10: The following rules[166] apply to relations with "heretics." First, they should be admonished, but if that fails, they must be rebuffed. Of course, the author does not really expect any positive result from the admonition. The rejection seems to be a sort of excommunication. Interestingly enough, the use of the term "heretic" in this context may have a technical meaning. Not only is the person in question causing controversy and divisiveness, but also the group formally declares him heretic by dissociating itself from him.

In this matter the discussion in the Pastorals is not very different from what the historical Paul has to say on the subject.

Rom. 16:17–20

(17) I appeal to you, brothers, to take note of those who create **dissensions** and difficulties, in opposition to the doctrine that you have been taught; **turn away from** them. (18) For such persons do not serve our Lord Christ, but their own appetites, and by **smooth talk** and **flattery** they deceive the hearts of the simple-minded. (19) For while the report of your obedience **has reached** everyone, so that I rejoice over you, I would have you wise as to what is good, but guileless as to what is evil; (20) then the God of peace will **soon crush** Satan under your feet. The grace of our Lord Jesus Christ be with you.

COMMENT

Because of the harshness of the content, the partly non-Pauline language (I have set in boldface the traditional elements), and the literary break between this passage and the greeting list of the preceding section (Rom. 16:1–16), some scholars doubt the genuineness of the text.[167]

Against this must be pointed out both the general attestation of this text as part of Romans and Paul's occasional practice of including at the end of his letters material that stands in notable contrast to what he had earlier written.[168] Besides, the call to share a "holy kiss" immediately preceding this section (Rom. 16:16) may have reminded Paul of the beginning of the Lord's Supper, when the "holy kiss"[169] and the curse upon those who do not love the Lord[170] have a traditional place.[171] For all these reasons we are eminently justified in assuming the genuineness of Rom. 16:17–20. Let me hasten to add that this text is a sample of how powerful an effect an antiheretical statement by the historical Paul has had in the history of interpretation. In this passage, at least, the author of the Pastorals is a true heir of Paul.

Verse 11: The rejection of the heretic carries out the condemnation that the heretic has brought on himself, for according to the author of the Pastorals he is perverted and sinful.

3:12–15: Personal Assignments and Final Greetings

(12) When I send Artemas or Tychicus to you, <u>make every effort</u> to come to me at Nicopolis, for I have decided to spend the winter there. (13) <u>Make every effort</u> to set Zenas the lawyer and Apollos on their way, and see that they lack nothing. (14) And let our people learn to apply themselves to good works in order to provide the necessities of life and live productive lives.

(15a) All who are with me send greetings to you. Greet those who love us in the faith.

(15b) Grace be with you all.

COMMENT

Verses 12–15: The personal messages and statements about the current situation with which the letter concludes bear a great similarity to those in 2 Timothy.[172]

5. INTOLERANCE AND THE GOSPEL IN THE PASTORAL EPISTLES

The Historical Situation

The detailed treatment of widows[173] in the Pastorals is particularly striking, as we see in the prohibition against women teaching in 1 Tim. 2:12–13: "I permit no woman to teach or to have authority over a man; she is to keep silent. For Adam was formed first, then Eve." This has a parallel in the secondary passage in 1 Cor. 14:33b–35.[174] Another striking observation is that women who, "burdened with sins and swayed by various impulses, will listen to anyone and can never arrive at a knowledge of the truth."[175] They are said to be especially vulnerable because certain people whom the author condemns have wormed their way into the houses of these women and captured them.[176] These are "people of corrupt mind and counterfeit faith; but they will not get very far, for their folly will be plain to all."[177] What kind of malefactors is the author attacking?

As regards the verb "to worm their way in,"[178] Ulrich B. Müller thinks that itinerant teachers had invaded the communities of the Pastorals from outside and caused confusion among the women there.[179] Yet an internal origin of the heresy is eminently more probable. Observe that 1 Tim. 1:19 speaks of those who have suffered shipwreck in the faith, and 1:20 continues in a deliberately stylized way, "Among them Hymenaeus and Alexander, whom I have delivered to Satan that they may learn not to blaspheme."[180] To be sure, the historical basis for this is the exclusion from the community of the two persons mentioned, but that ostracism may not have prevented certain others from gaining influence over people, including the women who are referred to. The author seems to have this in mind when at another point he issues the warning "Avoid such godless chatter, for it will lead people into more and more ungodliness, and their talk will eat its way like gangrene."[181] Note further that in connection with this the author again mentions two people: "Among them are Hymenaeus and Philetus, who have swerved from the truth."[182] That means, of course, that Hymenaeus, Philetus, and Alexander were originally members of the same Pauline group as the author of Pastorals, but at present are carrying on their own activity outside this association of communities. Yet this activity was meant to promote Pauline ideas, since these renegades teach that "the resurrection has already taken place."[183]

And while this thesis does not exactly accord with Paul's teaching, the author of the Pastorals must have been familiar with it in the context of baptism[184] and so interprets it. But Paul's immediate disciples[185] as well as numerous second-century Gnostics adopted the concept and developed it further. At this point it can be most plausibly understood as a doctrinal slogan promoted by nonconformist followers of Paul within the Pauline community—and one that proved to be a contributory cause of the breakup of this community.

If we further note that the activity of the opponents in the Pastorals is often described as "teaching,"[186] it is reasonable to assume that they are to be included among such second-century teachers as the Gnostics Valentinus, Ptolemy, and Marcus, as well as the Apologists Justin and Tatian. The opponents targeted by the Pastorals were people concerned with cultivating and developing the legacy of Paul, and they have remarkable similarities with Ephesians and those under attack in 2 Thessalonians.[187]

The Specific Nature of the Intolerance of the Gospel in the Pastorals

The prospect of the prophesied battle against the heretics in the end-time[188] calls for an uncompromising posture of defense and exclusion. The characteristics of the struggle are neither dialogue nor dispute but a programmatic expulsion[189] of "heretics" that does not shrink even from slander.[190]

This kind of intolerance squares with relationship to "heretics" displayed by Bishop Polycarp.[191] Note carefully the report of Bishop Irenaeus of Lyons concerning Polycarp's account of a confrontation between the "heretic" Cerinth and the disciple John in a bathhouse in Ephesus, for it will support the conclusion that Polycarp later appropriated John's strategy of separation. Irenaeus writes:

Against All Heresies 3.3.4

There are also those who heard from him that John, the disciple of the Lord, going to bathe at Ephesus, and perceiving Cerinthus within, rushed out of the bath-house without bathing, exclaiming, "Let us fly, lest even the bath-house fall down, because Cerinthus, the enemy of the truth, is within."

And immediately after the above report, Irenaeus tells about an encounter between Polycarp and the heterodox teacher Marcion.

Against All Heresies 3.3.4

When Marcion once met Polycarp and said to him, "Recognize us," Polycarp answered, "I do, I recognize the firstborn of Satan."

Like all legends that portray hatred, this tradition practically vibrates with intensity, but behind it stands the indisputable fact that Polycarp of Smyrna saw in Marcion a dangerous reformer and therefore a bitter enemy.

Following the above two reports Irenaeus writes, "Such was the horror which the apostles and their disciples had against holding even verbal communication with any corrupters of the truth" (*Against All Heresies 3.3.4*). After that he quotes Titus 3:10–11: "As for a heretic, after admonishing him once or twice, shun him, knowing that such a person is perverted and sinful; he is self-condemned." Thus from very early times the Pastorals served as a model of how to deal with "heretics," and the approved form of such encounters depended chiefly on avoidance, disciplinary action, or slander and damnation. What we see clearly represented has been aptly termed "a whole culture of subordination."[192]

NOTES

1. Bernhard Lang, "Segregation and Intolerance," in Morton Smith and R. Joseph Hoffmann, eds., *What the Bible Really Says* (Amherst, NY: Prometheus Books, 1989), p. 133.

2. For the following see my *Heretics: The Other Side of Early Christianity* (Louisville, KY: Westminster John Knox Press, 1996), pp. 135–42.

3. For a renewed convincing defense of this date see Joseph Verheyden, "The Canon Muratori: A Matter of Dispute," in *The Biblical Canons*, ed. J.-M. Auwers and H. J. de Jonge (Löwen: University Press, 2003), pp. 487–556.

4. Among many examples note the division of Moses' life into three forty-year periods in the Pentateuch (cf. Acts 7:23, 30, 36); three measures—an ephah—of meal designating divine presence (Gen. 18:6, and cf. Matt. 13:33 par.); Jonah's sojourn in the fish's maw; and Jesus' period of entombment.

5. See Colossians, Ephesians, and the Letter to Rheginos as well as the analyses in my *Heretics*, pp. 120–35.

6. Acts 20:17–38.

7. 1 Tim. 2–3; 5:1–6:2; Titus 1:5–3:2.

8. 1 Tim 4; 6:3–10; 2 Tim. 2:14–3:9; Titus 3:8–11.

9. In passing let me note that in too many cases contemporary research no longer seriously considers these two possibilities. The widely used commentary by Jouette M. Bassler, *1 Timothy, 2 Timothy, Titus* (Nashville, TN: Abingdon Press, 1996) is but one example. On Marcion's relationship to the Pastorals she writes: "[A]ttempts by early investigators to link the 'contradictions' [Gk. *antitheseis*] mentioned here (in 1 Tim. 6:20) with a known work (*Antitheses*) by the late-second-century heretic Marcion were surely wrong (see Introduction)" (p. 122). Yet in the introduction (pp. 17–34) she fails to mention Marcion or *The Antitheses*; and just for the record, Marcion was not a "late-second-century heretic" but clearly belongs to the first part of the second century. Bassler seems similarly confused about Polycarp; on the one hand she writes, "Polycarp . . . seems to quote several passages from the (Pastoral) letters" (p. 18), on the other, we read, "If Polycarp did in fact, know and quote the Pastorals (see above)—and there is no firm consensus on this point—they must have been written before the middle of the second century (p. 20). All this is said without a single analysis of the relevant texts. It is quite frustrating to see how many New Testament exegetes have, for whatever reason, blithely neglected to take into account nonbiblical sources.

10. In Greek, *antitheseis*.

11. In Greek, *gnôsis*.

12. With one exception: Heb. 12:13. See above in the text.

13. In Greek, *parathêkê*.

14. In Greek, *ektrepesthai*.

15. In Greek, *bebêloi kenophoniai*.

16. In Greek, *apostochein*.

17. 1 Tim. 2:4; 2 Tim. 2:25; 3:7; Titus 1:1.

18. In Greek, *pseudônymos*.

19. Gal. 2:4.

20. 2 Cor. 11:13.

21. 1 Cor. 15:15.

22. Note that "to profess" in 1 Tim. 2:10 suggests belonging to a specific group.

23. See 2 Tim. 1:15; 2:17.

24. See further below, pp. 244–46.

25. Hans von Campenhausen, *Polycarp von Smyrna und die Pastoralbriefe* (Heidelberg: Carl Winter Universitätsverlag, 1951).

26. Ibid., pp. 25–26. The four hapax legomena are *mataiologia* (2:2), *enkratês* (5:2), *diabolos* (5:2), and *dilochos* (5:2).

27. Polycarp *Phil.* 5:2; 9:2.

28. 1 Tim. 6:17; 2 Tim. 4:10; Titus 2:12.

29. Campenhausen, *Polycarp von Smyrna*, p. 26.

30. See ibid., p. 28.

31. Ibid., p. 29.

32. 1 Tim. 1:15; 3:1; 4:9; 2 Tim. 2:11; Titus 3:8.

33. Hans von Campenhausen, *The Formation of the Christian Bible* (Philadelphia: Fortress Press, 1972), p. 181.

34. The Latin infinitive *decessisse* requires an active and not a passive ("was removed") translation.

35. Tertullian *On Baptism* 17.5 quoting 1 Cor. 14:35 at the end. For a slightly different translation see *New Testament Apocrypha*, revised edition of the Collection initiated by Edgar Hennecke and edited by Wilhelm Schneemelcher, English translation ed. R. McL. Wilson, vol. 2, *Writings Related to the Apostles, Apocalypses, and Related Subjects* (Louisville, KY: Westminster John Knox Press, 1992), p. 214 (with an incorrect translation of the Latin *decessisse*).

36. Cf. Willy Rordorf, *Lex Orandi—Lex Credendi* (Freiburg and Schweiz: Universitätsverlag, 1993), pp. 449–50. See ibid., p. 449n2, on the correct rendering of *decessisse*.

37. See 2 Bar. 78:2: "Thus speaks Baruch, the son of Neriah, to the brothers who were carried away in captivity: Grace and peace with you."

38. Num. 6:24–26: "Yahweh bless you and keep you. (25) Yahweh make his face shine upon you, and be gracious to you. (26) Yahweh lift up his countenance upon you, and give you peace."

39. Rev. 1:4–5a: "John to the seven churches that are in Asia. 'Grace to you and peace from him who is and who was and who is to come, and from the seven spirits that are before his throne (5a) and from Jesus Christ the faithful witness, the firstborn of the dead, and the ruler of kings on earth.'"

40. Acts 15:23: "The apostles and the elders, (your) brothers, send greetings to the brothers who are of the Gentiles in Antioch and Syria and Cilicia"; 23:26: "Claudius Lysias, to his Excellency the governor Felix, greetings!"

41. James 1:1: "James, servant of God and of the Lord Jesus Christ, sends greetings to the twelve tribes in the dispersion."

42. For example, the use of the oriental prescript in the Pauline letters and Revelation may suggest that the author of the latter knew the Pauline letters.

43. Cf. 1 Tim. 3:14; 4:13.

44. Cf. 1 Cor. 16:8.

45. In Greek, *heterodidaskalein*.

46. 1 Tim. 4:7; 2 Tim. 4:4; Titus 1:14.

47. See the "Hypostasis of the Archons" (NHC II.4) and "On the Origin of the World" (NHC II.5). See further below, pp. 213–28.

48. E.g., understanding myth as a carrier of meaning that can be expressed only in the language of myth.

49. Cf. 1 Tim. 6:3–4.

50. Compare the genealogy in Matt. 1:1–17 with its three periods of fourteen (2x7) generations, and the 21 (3x7) virtues listed in Wisd. of Sol. 7:22–23.

51. 1 Tim. 1:9; 2 Tim. 4:3; Titus 1:13.

52. 1 Tim. 6:3; 2 Tim. 1:13; Titus 2:8.

53. Titus 1:13; 2:2.

54. Burton Scott Easton, *The Pastoral Epistles: Introduction, Translation, Commentary and Word Studies* (New York: Charles Scribner's Sons, 1947), p. 111.

55. Gal. 1:13–15.

56. Gal. 1:23.

57. Gal. 1:14.

58. 1 Tim. 3:1; 4:9; 2 Tim. 2:11; Titus 3:8.

59. See Rom. 11:13.

60. Cf. Acts 13:2.

61. 1 Tim. 6:11–12.

62. Cf. 1 Tim. 4:12–16; 6:11–16; 2 Tim. 1:6.

63. See above, pp. 44–45.

64. In Greek, *epignôsis alêtheias.*

65. See 2 Tim. 2:25; 3:7; Titus 1:1 (cf. Heb. 10:26).

66. See 1 Tim. 6:15; Titus 1:3.

67. See below, p. 166 n174.

68. Cf. Genesis 2 and 3.

69. Bassler, *1 Timothy, 2 Timothy, Titus,* p. 61.

70. Cf. "suffer[ing] shipwreck in the faith," 1 Tim. 1:19.

71. For the texts see my *The Resurrection of Christ: A Historical Inquiry* (Amherst, NY: Prometheus Books, 2004), pp. 213–25. See also Karen King, *The Gospel of Mary of Magdala* (Santa Rosa, CA: Polebridge Press, 2003), esp. pp. 87–90.

72. See Norbert Brox, *Die Pastoralbriefe* (Regensburg: Friedrich Pustet, 1969), p. 142.

73. Cf. 2 Tim. 2:2–6.

74. See the remarks of the historical Paul: 1 Cor. 10:32; 1 Thess. 4:12. Cf. Col. 4:5; 1 Tim. 5:14; 6:1; Titus 2:5, 8, 10; 1 Pet. 2:12, 15; 3:1, 16.

75. Cf. 1 Cor. 2:7; 4:1; 13:2; 14:2; 15:51.

76. See Martin Dibelius and Hans Conzelmann, *The Pastoral Epistles: A Commentary on the Pastoral Epistles* (Philadelphia: Fortress Press, 1972), p. 59.

77. The plan to come for a visit is often found in Paul's genuine letters, 1 Thess. 2:17; 3:6; Rom. 1:11, 13.

78. See Philipp Vielhauer, *Geschichte der urchristlichen Literatur* (Berlin: Walter de Gruyter, 1975), p. 42.

79. Cf. Mark 13:5-6, 22; Acts 20:29-30; 2 Thess. 2:3-4, 8-10; Jude 17-18; 2 Pet. 2:1-3; 1 John 2:18.

80. See 1 Cor. 11:19.

81. 2 Cor. 4:4; 11:3, 13-14.

82. 2 Cor. 12:7.

83. 1 Tim. 1:18; 3:14-15; 5:21.

84. In Greek, *paraiteisthai.*

85. 2 Tim. 2:23; Titus 3:10.

86. See 1 Tim. 2:2; 3:16; 4:7, 8; 6:3, 5, 6, 11; 2 Tim. 3:5; Titus 1:1.

87. 2 Pet. 1:3, 6, 7; 3:11.

88. Acts 3:12.

89. Cf. Ignatius *To the Magnesians* 3:1: "But it is not right for you to take advantage of your bishop because of his age. You should render him all due respect according to the power of God the Father, just as I have learned that even your holy presbyters have not exploited his seemingly youthful appearance."

90. Cf. 2 Tim. 3:15-17; 2 Cor. 7:8; 1 Thess. 5:27.

91. For public reading in a Christian service, cf. 2 Clem. 9:1.

92. See the parallels in wisdom literature (Prov. 15:28; 30:11-12; Sir. 3:8; 8:6) and in Plato's *Republic* 463c.

93. Cf. Rev. 2:13.

94. The first comes from Deut. 25:4 (cf. 1 Cor. 9:9a). We know the second from Luke 10:7 and Matt. 10:10 as a saying of Jesus. However, it appears that "Jesus is appealing to a recognized saying from Scripture, i.e. that such a saying is ascribed to him" (Dibelius and Conzelmann, *Pastoral Epistles*, p. 79). The most likely of several possible passages are Lev. 19:13 and Deut. 24:15 (but cf. Jer. 22:13; Mal. 3:5; Sir. 7:20, 34:23; Tob. 4:14). Thus it may well be the *source* of Luke 10:7 that the author of the Pastorals here refers to as scripture.

95. See Deut. 19:15 (cf. Matt. 18:16).

96. In passing let me quote a perceptive comment on this aspect by Morton Smith, "Slavery," in Smith and Hoffmann, *What the Bible Really Says*, p. 145: The "picture of the entire world as an estate in which all the inhabitants are the slaves of God, the owner, had appeared already in Leviticus, 25:55, where Yahweh, prohibiting the Israelites to sell in perpetuity their ancestral landholdings, justified the prohibition by claiming that the land belonged to him, 'For all the Israelites are my slaves. They are my slaves because I brought them out of Egypt.' The conqueror owns the spoils. By Paul's times the notion was moving toward legal implementation in the Roman Empire; the emperors were beginning to take the title *dominus* proper to the head of a household and owner of its slaves. The triumph of Christianity did much to strengthen the

trend, and, among the elements of Christianity, Paul's habitual designation of himself as 'Paul, the slave of Christ' (Rom. 1:1; Gal. 1:10; Phil. 1:1; imitated in Titus 1:1) was particularly influential. . . . Another important factor in shaping the picture of men as slaves and God as slaveowner was of course the Gospels; the parables often use the relation of a slave to master as an example of the relation of a man to God. . . . With all these clear passages, there is no reasonable doubt that the New Testament, like the Old, not only tolerated chattel slavery (the form prevalent in the Greco-Roman world at Paul's time) but helped to perpetuate it by making the slaves' obedience to their masters a religious duty."

97. On verse 7 cf. Job 1:21; on verse 8 cf. Prov. 30:8; on verse 9 cf. Prov. 23:4; 28:22.

98. Philo *Special Laws* 4:65; Diogenes Laertius 6:50.

99. Cf. 1 Tim. 1:19.

100. Cf. 2 Tim. 3:17

101. See further 2 Tim. 4:1; Titus 2:13.

102. For details see my *Heretics*, pp. 162–64.

103. Rom. 1:1–7.

104. 1 Cor. 1:1–3.

105. 2 Tim. 3:15.

106. "Savior" in the Pastorals is used interchangeably for God (1 Tim. 1:1; 2:3; 4:10; Titus 1:3; 2:10; 3:4) and Christ (2 Tim. 1:10; Titus 1:4; 2:13; 3:6. The noun "appearance" (in Greek, *epiphaneia*) is a favorite word of the Pastoral author and is employed in the New Testament outside the Pastorals only at 2 Thess. 2:8. With one exception in the present verse 10 when it signifies Jesus' first coming, it always means Jesus' Second Coming at the end of time (2 Tim. 4:1, 8; Titus 2:13 [along with "savior"]).

107. Cf. Easton, *Pastoral Epistles*, p. 38.

108. See Eph. 3:4–5, 9–11; Rom. 16:25–26; 1 Pet. 1:20.

109. See further on 1 Tim. 2:7.

110. In Greek, *kēryx*.

111. Cf. 1 Tim. 6:20.

112. Cf. Rom. 8:11.

113. See Georg Strecker, *Theology of the New Testament* (New York: Walter de Gruyter, 2000), pp. 66–69.

114. Cf. only Deut. 4:37.

115. See, for example, Rom. 8:33 and the comments in my *Paul: The Founder of Christianity* (Amherst, NY: Prometheus Books, 2002), p. 80.

116. On verse 12a cf. Rev. 20:4–6; on verse 12b cf. Matt. 10:32–33/Luke 12:8–9.

117. See further Matt. 19:28; 1 Cor. 6:2–3; Rev. 21:7.

118. Cf. Rom. 3:3–4 with reference to God.

119. This has an affinity with John's "realized eschatology."

120. Cf. 1 Cor. 1:2.

121. 1 Tim. 1:4; cf. Titus 3:9.

122. Cf. Titus 2:2.

123. 2 Tim. 3:7.

124. Cf. 1 Clem. 7:4; Barn. 16:9; Hermas, Sim. 8.6.1–2.

125. See 1 Tim. 2:4.

126. On the "snare of the devil" compare the "trap of the devil" (1 Tim. 3:7) and the turning to spirits of deceit (1 Tim. 4:1), which is connected with the doctrine of demons.

127. For the Pastorals cf. 1 Tim. 1:9–10; 6:4–5; Titus 1:7; 3:3.

128. See Mark 7:21–22; Gal. 5:19–21.

129. Cf. 2 Tim. 2:19–20.

130. In Greek, *endynein.*

131. On the status of women in Gnostic communities see above, pp. 121–22, on 1 Tim. 2:15.

132. In Exod. 7:8–12 the Egyptian magicians opposed to Moses and Aaron are not given names.

133. Cf. Exod. 7:12: "Each one (of the sorcerers) threw down his staff, and they became snakes; but Aaron's staff swallowed up theirs" (NRSV).

134. In Greek, *prokoptein.*

135. Cf. 2 Pet. 1:19–21.

136. Cf. Luke 10:7; Lev. 19:13; Jer. 22:13; Tob. 4:14.

137. On the details of the admonition see 1 Tim. 5:20; Titus 1:9, 13.

138. See 1 Tim. 1:18; 6:12; 2 Tim. 2:5.

139. 2 Tim. 1:4.

140. 2 Tim. 1:15.

141. On the "elect" as a self-designation of Christians cf. Mark 13:20, 22; Rom. 8:33; Col. 3:12; 1 Tim. 5:21; 2 Tim. 2:10.

142. In Greek, *apseudês.*

143. See Clementine Homilies 2.43.1, and appendices 1 and 4 in this book.

144. Plato *Politeia* 2.382e.

145. See above, pp. 122–23, the comments on 1 Tim. 3:2–13.

146. In Greek, *epistomizein,* which literally means "to stop the mouth."

147. "But that the Pastor attributed the verse to Epimenides can scarcely be doubted, for the Cretans had exalted their poet to mythical heights" (Easton, *Pastoral Epistles,* p. 88).

148. Titus 1:5.

149. In Greek, *elegchein.*

150. Seneca *Epist.* 98.16.3 has the negative form, "The bad man makes all things bad."

151. Easton, *Pastoral Epistles,* p. 89.

152. Ibid., p. 90.

153. On the demand that wives should withdraw to their houses and obey their husbands see 1 Tim. 5:14.

154. The church officials who receive special instructions in the Pastorals are bishops (1 Tim. 3:2–7), deacons (1 Tim. 3:8–12), and elders and bishops (Titus 1:5–9).

155. 2 Tim. 1:10.

156. John 20:28; Heb. 1:8–9; 2 Pet. 1:1.

157. See Pliny *Letters* 10.97.6: The Christians "sing to Christ as their God;" Ignatius *To the Ephesians* Inscriptio: "Ignatius, who is also called God-bearer, to the church that is blessed with greatness by the fullness of God the Father, a church foreordained from eternity past to obtain a constant glory which is enduring and unchanging, a church that has been unified and chosen in true suffering by the will of the Father and of Jesus Christ, our God; to the church in Ephesus and Asia, which is worthy of all good fortune. Warmest greetings in Jesus Christ and in blameless joy."

158. Compare the introduction of a hymn by the relative pronoun *hos* in 1 Tim. 3:16; Col. 1:15–20; Phil. 2:6–11.

159. Raymond F. Collins, *1 & 2 Timothy and Titus: A Commentary* (Louisville, KY: Westminster John Knox Press, 2002), p. 353.

160. Cf. 2 Tim. 2:21; 3:17; Titus 2:7; 3:1.

161. Cf. 2 Tim. 3:2–4.

162. Cf. Gal. 4:4.

163. Easton, *Pastoral Epistles*, p. 99.

164. The words "washing," "rebirth," "renewal," "pour out," "richly," and "heir" are not used anywhere else in the Pastorals. "Mercy" does not appear elsewhere in Titus.

165. Easton, *Pastoral Epistles*, p. 101.

166. Cf. 2 Tim. 2:23–26.

167. Cf. only Robert Jewett, *Christian Tolerance: Paul's Message to the Modern Church* (Philadelphia: Westminster Press, 1982), pp. 17–22, whose interest in the nonauthenticity of the passage in question is evident in the subtitle of his book.

168. Cf. Gal. 6:11–16.

169. 1 Cor. 16:20; 1 Thess. 5:26.

170. 1 Cor. 16:22.

171. Thus the use of traditional language in Rom. 16:17–20 may be accounted for.

172. On verse 12 compare the literal correspondence with 2 Tim. 4:9, and on the whole section see 2 Tim. 4:9–18.

173. 1 Tim. 5:3–16.

174. 1 Cor. 14:33b–35—along with verse 36—is to be seen as an addition by later "orthodox" disciples of Paul who have redacted 1 Corinthians by inserting views appropriate to their times. For one thing, verse 33b is clearly intrusive, inasmuch as verse 37 returns to the subject of prophecy found in verses 29–33a. For another, this total subordination of women stands in con-

siderable tension with 1 Cor. 11:5, which explicitly portrays women participating in worship, both praying and prophesying. On 1 Cor. 11:2–16 see my *Paul*, pp. 144–46.

175. 2 Tim. 3:6b–7.

176. 2 Tim. 3:6a.

177. 2 Tim. 3:8–9.

178. In Greek, *endynein*.

179. Ulrich B. Müller, *Zur frühchristlichen Theologiegeschichte* (Gütersloh: Gerd Mohn, 1975), p. 62.

180. Cf. 1 Cor. 5:5.

181. 2 Tim. 2:16.

182. 2 Tim. 2:17–18.

183. 2 Tim. 2:18.

184. Rom. 6:4.

185. Col. 3:1; Eph. 2:6.

186. 1 Tim. 1:3, 7; 4:1; 6.3; 2 Tim. 4:3; Titus 1:11.

187. See above, p. 75.

188. 1 Tim. 4:1; 2 Tim. 3:1.

189. Cf. the use of the verb "to shun" (in Greek, *paraiteisthai*) in 1 Tim. 4:7; 2 Tim. 2:23; Titus 3:10.

190. Cf. 2 Tim. 3:5; Titus 1:16.

191. See the demonstration above, pp. 112–13, that the Pastorals derive from the circle around Polycarp or from the bishop himself.

192. Frances M. Young, *The Theology of the Pastoral Letters* (Cambridge: Cambridge University Press, 1994), p. 147.

Chapter V

THE LETTER OF JUDE AND THE SECOND LETTER OF PETER

> *The earliest doubt on historical record was twenty-six hundred years ago, which makes doubt older than most faiths. Faith can be a wonderful thing, but it is not the only wonderful thing. Doubt has been just as vibrant in its prescriptions for a good life, and just as passionate for the truth. By many standards it has had tremendous success.*[1]
>
> —Jennifer Michael Hecht

1. INTRODUCTION

Jude

Properly speaking, the epistle of Jude is neither a letter nor a treatise, for its author has no personal relationship to the recipients and it contains no didactic elements. It is rather a polemical tractate in the form of a letter that serves a specific function in a specific situation. Most of it "is simply filled with invective and name-calling."[2] The communities represented by Jude tried to spread the writing to as many congregations as possible.

Whoever wrote it demonstrates an effective and indeed polished command of Greek.[3] Noteworthy in this regard is the powerful rhetorical effect of the phrase "these are the ones" used in verses 8, 10, 12, 16, and 19. A play on the word "keeping" runs through the epistle like a scarlet thread: God has provided Christ's safekeeping for the addressees (verse 1). The penalty meted out to wicked angels who did not keep their place was to be kept in chains (verse 6). Similarly, the nether darkness is being kept in reserve for present and future rebels (verse 13). And readers are enjoined to keep themselves in the love of God (verse 21). Finally, it is God alone who can keep his people from falling.

According to verse 4, "opponents" had invaded communities from outside, and had even become members of these communities (verse 12). In all likelihood they originated in Pauline circles. Thus in verse 4b the author of Jude picks up a central Pauline term—"grace"[4]—and turns the claim of these disciples of Paul against them by assailing them for perverting "grace" into its opposite.[5] Furthermore, in verse 19 "Jude" pictures the opponents as "psychics" deprived of the Spirit. This move is reminiscent of debates between the historical Paul and his pupils in Corinth over the dualism of the psychic and spiritual man[6] and their clash over the relationship of Christians to angels.[7] The Pauline tradition shows a strong antipathy to powers independent of Christ,[8] and in an ancient hymn used in the Pauline sphere Jesus triumphs over the powers.[9] The author of Colossians warns his readers against worshiping angels.[10] Not only that, but at least some of Paul's followers in Corinth rejected the earthly Jesus, and indeed even cursed him.[11] All these elements may bear some relation to the opponents' denial of Jesus Christ adduced in verse 4b.

As Jude and 2 Peter are closely related, we may surmise that Paul's letters evoked in the circle around Jude a reception as critical as that visible at 2 Pet. 3:15–16. The opponents of Jude, then, have a specific interpretation of Paul, whereas the author of Jude, finding himself on the defensive, does not even mention Paul but attacks his pupils instead. If this is correct, the clearly false ascription of the letter to Jude, the brother of James, takes on special importance, because that means the author of Jude seeks to gain the support of the branch of early Christian tradition loyal to James, the brother of Jesus—an important coalition that is critical of Paul.[12]

Another but less likely possibility is that "the name [Jude] may have been chosen in view of the claim of Gnostic circles to the authority of Judas Thomas . . . who was also known as the brother of Jesus. The author of this pseudonymous epistle may have chosen Jude/Judas in order to denigrate the Gnostics' claim to this name, and 'brother of James' was meant to deflate their boast that their tradition was authorized by Jesus' very brother."[13]

Be all that as it may, we must reject the notion that the writer of this letter is the historical Jude, the brother of Jesus, who is mentioned at Mark 6:3.[14] For one thing, in verse 17 the author looks back to the apostles as bearers of the tradition and in verse 18 ascribes to them a message about the last times. Such a view is necessarily characteristic of later generations. For another, the author had an excellent command of literary as well as a broad familiarity with apocryphal literature. Jesus' brother Jude, on the other hand, was an uneducated, Aramaic-speaking peasant. Second-century sources attest that down to the third generation Jude's family consisted of uneducated peasant farmers.[15]

2 Peter

Addressed to all the faithful, this letter purports to be from the pen of Peter, now approaching death; it is a polemical antiheretical writing, which, like Jude, consists mainly of damning judgments.

In 2 Pet. 3:1 the author refers to 1 Peter and designates his text as a "second letter." Pretending to be a close disciple of Jesus, he includes personal reminiscences of the master, feigns to be an eyewitness of the transfiguration,[16] and claims that his imminent death as a martyr had been prophesied by Jesus.[17] By the phrase "our beloved brother Paul" he identifies himself as a contemporary of the apostle to the Gentiles, although he admits that portions of the latter's epistles are puzzling and all too easily distorted.[18]

2 Peter almost fully incorporates Jude[19]—so much so that the use of Jude by 2 Peter (and not vice versa) is beyond doubt. For one thing, the author of 2 Peter places Jude's statements about present false teachers in the future in order to have Peter appear to prophesy their appearance.[20] For another, he changes details about the conduct of the false teachers and even more than Jude 12a reviles their participation in the common meal.[21] And finally, the author of 2 Peter deletes Jude's quotation of the book of Enoch (Jude 14–15a) because as a defender of proto-orthodoxy he cannot allow Peter to quote a noncanonical writing.

The main purpose of his writing is to defend the expectation of Jesus' future coming,[22] a defense necessitated by such questions and objections as "Where is the promise of his coming? For ever since the fathers fell asleep, all things have continued as they were from the beginning of creation."[23] In early Christian texts the problem of the delay of the Parousia is at times alluded to, but only occasionally made an explicit issue.[24] Yet in view of specific texts[25] we must assume the very real existence of the predicament.[26] Those skeptical about the Parousia rely on a collection of Paul's letters and "other scriptures"—under which heading they no doubt included portions of what later came to be called "the Old Testament" and such early Christian writings as the Gospels.[27] Note that Paul's collected letters have the same authority as the "other scriptures," and that not only Paul's letters but also the other scriptures received a specific interpretation by the opponents.[28] In response, the author of 2 Peter rejects any interpretation of scripture "by human will."[29] As a counterbalance against the reference to scriptures and Paul's letters he introduces the authority of Peter supposedly documented in these two letters of his.[30]

2 Peter defends the traditional apocalyptic eschatology and emphasizes that the suddenness of its arrival will mark the end of the world. Yet, "it does not proclaim that expectation as a hope and consolation . . . rather, it tries to defend it as theological dogma."[31] In defense of this dogma 2 Peter introduces three arguments (without being too concerned about whether they are mutually consistent). First, our understanding of time is not sufficient to comprehend God's actions;[32] second, we deal not with delay here, but with forbearance;[33] and third, believers ought to hasten the coming of the Parousia by leading holy lives.[34]

Of equal importance to his defense of the Parousia hope is the author's concern to attach the community not only to the earliest faith but also to its transmitters, the apostles. Indeed, for him the apostolic tradition is the primary bulwark against false teaching. The doctrine of the faith that was "once for all delivered to the saints"[35] corresponds to what the author of 2 Peter calls "the truth that you have,"[36] "the holy commandment delivered to them,"[37] and "the commandment of the Lord and Savior through your apostles."[38] As one of these apostles, "Peter" emerges in the course of the writing as the preeminent guarantor of the tradition. And thus the false attribution to Peter in effect bridges the gap between past and present. It is a deliberately untrue ascription and not, as some would have it, a "*transparent* fiction, a literary convention which the author expected his readers to recognize as such"[39]—because in that case the author would have been more careful not to bridge the gap between past and present.[40]

2. TRANSLATION AND ANALYSIS OF JUDE

Verses 1–2: Prescript

(1) Jude, a servant of Jesus Christ, and brother of James, to those who are called, <u>beloved</u> in God the Father, and kept for Jesus Christ: (2) May mercy, peace, and <u>love</u> be multiplied to you.

COMMENT

The prescript in two parts matches the so-called oriental form that we find in the Pauline letters and generally in Primitive Christianity and its areas of influence.[41]

Verse 1: Jude's authority derives both from his status as "servant of Jesus Christ" and from association with James, who in this case must be the Lord's brother. Beginning in the early forties of the first century CE, James was the leader of the Jerusalem community, and accordingly exerted a strong influence over the earliest church.[42]

In the letter's opening the author introduces topics that he will develop in the main body and repeat in the closing. One example of this is the motif of "keeping." God is called upon to keep the addressees safe for Jesus Christ (verses 1, 24), and they are exhorted to reciprocate by keeping themselves in God's love until the Parousia (verse 21). Set in sharp contrast to this he will offer the tragic example of the angels who failed to keep their assigned place in the divine scheme by indulging in sexual relations with women,[43] and who are now kept in chains and darkness until the day of judgment (verse 6)—a fate that likewise awaits those who are false teachers (verse 13). This development of the topic assures the recipients of their favorable standing with God, instructs them in resisting the wiles of heretics, and warns of the consequences to be suffered by those who do not remain steadfast.

Verse 2: The greeting anticipates the admonition near the end of the epistle, verse 21: "Keep yourselves in the love of God; wait for the mercy of our Lord Jesus Christ unto eternal life." The triad "mercy, peace, love" reflects what was current church usage; similar formulae from the time of Jude are "grace, mercy, peace,"[44] "grace, peace,"[45] and "grace, mercy, peace in truth and love."[46]

Verses 3–4: The Reason for the Letter

(3) Beloved, being very eager to write to you about our common salvation, I found it necessary to write and exhort you to contend for the faith handed on once and for all to the saints. (4a) For some people long ago marked down for condemnation have infiltrated your ranks, godless persons (4b) who pervert the grace of our God into licentiousness and deny our only Master and Lord, Jesus Christ.

COMMENT

Verse 3: "The faith"—"handed on once and for all to the saints"— appears here and at verse 20 as the fundamental ingredient of sound doctrine, namely the tradition that was transmitted to the "saints"[47] at the time of the foundation of the church. Such an understanding of tradition excludes any idea of development. Later generations of Christians can only keep and fight for this tradition thus understood—or join in Satan's efforts to destroy it. The historical Paul was acquainted with such "objective" understanding of faith,[48] yet he does not limit the content of faith by describing it as "once and for all" (in Greek, *hapax*). "Jude" thus bestows on the tradition a greater emphasis and fixity than did Paul, who often quotes traditions and interprets them by additions. In doing so, however, the author equates traditions and his own theological viewpoints.[49] "In the Pastorals these credal statements are often introduced in such a way as to promote their authority."[50] See 1 Tim. 2:5–6a; 3:16; 2 Tim. 2:11–13; Titus 3:4–7 for other creedal statements in the Pastorals.

Verse 4a: On the people who have "infiltrated" compare with the "false brothers" whom the historical Paul in Gal. 2:4 accuses of having "slipped in." Both groups are understood to play a negative role and both have invaded territories where according to "Jude" and Paul they do not belong. Yet it is misleading to say that these "intruders" were outsiders to the community Jude addresses. That is, of course, the theological point that "Jude" wishes to make, but it has little to do with the historical situation. The author emphasizes that the intruders will be condemned at the final judgment[51] as predicted in sacred scriptures (the Old Testament, 1 Enoch, etc.; cf. verses 14–15). Contrary to their own self-understanding, the author of Jude designates the intruders as "godless." No other writing of the New Testament uses the term "godless"[52] as often as Jude (five times), although the entire text contains only twenty-five verses.

Verse 4b: The author accuses the opponents first, of perversion of "the grace of our God into licentiousness" and second, of denial of "our only Master and Lord, Jesus Christ." The first charge is polemical. In Rom. 3:8 Paul reports that he himself was the target of such a charge (which he terms a slander): Jewish Christians accused him of encouraging other Christians to do evil in order that good might result. As for the second charge, one may reasonably ask precisely who was denied and what words or actions constituted the "denial." In this context "Lord"[53] refers to Christ, although other Primitive Christian texts use the term in referring to God.[54] In favor of the reference being to Christ in the present verse, one may well point to line 2 of verse 4b where the second part mentions Christ[55]—an excellent reason to see him as the referent in the first part of the half verse. The specifics of the denial, then, could involve either distancing oneself from Christ in the context of persecution[56] or expressing doubt of the full humanity of Christ in favor of a Docetic attitude.[57] In view of the overall thrust and purpose of Jude, the latter situation is likelier, the more so since the expression "only Master and Lord" has a distinctly anti-Gnostic flavor.[58]

Verses 5–7: Three Biblical Examples of Punishment

(5) Now I desire to remind you—though you already know all about it—that the Lord who once and for all delivered the people out of the land of Egypt afterward destroyed those who did not believe.

(6) The angels who did not *keep* to their own domain but abandoned their proper sphere he *kept* for judgment on the great day in **eternal** chains in the darkness of the underworld.

(7) Likewise Sodom and Gomorrah and the surrounding cities that indulged in fornication and unnatural lust in the same way as these serve as an example by having suffered the punishment of **eternal** fire.

COMMENT

The list of punishments by God has an indelibly Old Testament and/or Jewish background.[59]

Verse 5: This is an admonition in the form of a remembrance[60] with reference to Old Testament examples.[61] The adverbial "once and for all" picks up the same word in verse 3 and thus emphasizes the uniqueness of God's act of salvation at the time of both the old and new covenants. In both cases the issue is faith. The adverb "afterward" (in Greek, *deuteron*) stands in contrast with "once and for all" (in Greek, *hapax*) and thus stresses that God's grace may be lost if not accepted at the first time.

Verse 6: Note the wordplay with the verb "to keep."[62] On the sexual union of angels with women see Gen. 6:1–4.[63] The fallen angels are punished by being chained in the underworld until the judgment. This "reflects Jude's familiarity with the book known as *1 Enoch* or *aethiopic Enoch*, a familiarity that is confirmed by the direct quotation of 1 Enoch 1:9 in Jude 14–15."[64]

Verse 7: The author underscores the correspondence ("eternal punishment") between those of the environs of Sodom and Gomorrah and the angels mentioned in the previous verse. It should be noted that many Gnostics identified themselves with the people of Sodom.[65]

Verses 8–10: Application to the Present

(8a) Yet in like manner **THESE** in their dreamings defile the flesh, (8b) reject authority, (8c) and *blaspheme* the glorious ones. (9) But when the archangel Michael contended with the devil in a dispute over the body of Moses, he did not dare to condemn him for *blasphemy*, but said, "The Lord rebuke you." (10a) But **THESE**,

(10b) <u>Whatever</u> they do not know, they *blaspheme*,

(10c) And by <u>whatever</u> they do understand—though only like animals, without reason—they are destroyed.

COMMENT

Verse 8: For other references to "these" in Jude see verses 10, 12, 16, and 19. The "intruders" of verse 4 are supposed to have caused the crisis in the churches. Because of the stereotypical character of the polemic, biblical scholars sometimes deny the possibility of specifying the position of the opponents.[66] Yet all three charges match what we know about Gnostics. Verse 8a may allude to visionary experiences,[67] while verses 8b–c likely reflect Gnostic teachings about angels as the representatives of a hostile power that is related to creation. Gnostic polemics from other sources illustrate this. They range from cursing the earthly Jesus[68] to blaspheming Old Testament heroes.[69] Moreover, verse 8b is an echo of verse 4b in that the refusal to accept authority corresponds to the denial of Christ.

Verse 9: This verse mirrors Jewish traditions about Moses.[70] They stem from the implication in Deuteronomy[71] that God himself buried Moses' body and tell of a struggle between the archangel Michael and the devil over the corpse of Moses. The author's point in this verse is to emphasize that even Michael is reluctant to call down a curse on the devil because it is always God who has the last say.

Verse 10: Here the attack on the opponents reaches its climax. The charge in verse 10b echoes that in verse 8c. The keyword is "to blaspheme." Likening the self-destructive conduct of the dissidents to that of brute animals caps this bitter polemic against them.

Verses 11–13: Three Types of Irredeemable Sinners

(11a) Woe to them!

(11b) For they walk in the way of Cain.

(11c) They abandon themselves to Balaam's error for the sake of gain.

(11d) They perish in Korah's rebellion.

(12a) **THESE** are a blot on your love feasts,

(12b) where they brazenly eat and drink without reverence;

(12c) they are waterless clouds, carried along by winds;

(12d) fruitless trees in late autumn, twice dead, uprooted;

(13a) wild waves of the sea, casting up the foam of their own shame;

(13b) wandering stars for which the deepest darkness has been reserved forever.

COMMENT

Verse 11: The author relates the opponents to three infamous persons in the Old Testament: Cain,[72] Balaam,[73] and Korah.[74] The statement "they perished" takes its cue from the phrase "they are destroyed" in the previous verse and rhetorically seals the common fate of the godless blasphemers.

Verse 12: This verse is unique in the New Testament in testifying to the Greek word *agapê*[75] as a technical term for the common Christian meal as it was practiced by the early church.[76] It goes without saying that the presence of the opponents at this common meal showed that the community had welcomed them. Verse 12b condemns both the hypocrisy and the irreverence of their "brazen" behavior. In verse 12c "carried along by winds" adds a suggestion of aimlessness to the uselessness of "waterless clouds." Verse 12d invokes the image of the fruitless tree.[77]

Verse 13: Using Old Testament images (as before in verse 12) the author paints a grim picture of the opponents and their fate.[78]

Verses 14–16: A Prophecy of Judgment

(14a) It was of **THESE** also that Enoch in the seventh generation from Adam prophesied, saying, (14b) "Look, the Lord came with his holy myriads, (15) to execute judgment on _all_, and to convict _all_ the **godless** of _all_ their deeds of **godlessness** that they have committed in such a **godless** way, and of _all_ the harsh things that **godless** sinners have spoken against him."

(16) **THESE** are grumblers, malcontents, following their own passions, loud-mouthed boasters, flattering people to their own advantage.

COMMENT

Verses 14–15: To the writer of Jude the book of Enoch and its putative author have canonical rank. As a prophet (our author opines) Enoch has predicted the chastisement of the godless antagonists in Jude's community together with the punishment of the godless in general. With slight variations verses 14b–15 quote 1 Enoch 1:9.

Verse 16: This application of the Enoch text to the present situation asserts, with the addition of standard polemic, that the opponents who participate in the common meals are morally deficient. The pronoun "these" picks up the same word in verses 12a and 14a.

Verses 17–21: Exhortation of the True Believers

(17) <u>But you</u> must remember, <u>BELOVED</u>, the predictions of the apostles *<u>of our Lord Jesus Christ</u>*. (18) They said to you, "In the last time there will be scoffers, following their own godless passions."

(19) It is these worldly people, devoid of the SPIRIT, who are causing divisions.

(20) <u>But you</u>, BELOVED, build yourselves up on your most **holy** faith; pray in the **Holy** SPIRIT; (21) keep yourselves in the LOVE of GOD; wait for the mercy *<u>of our Lord Jesus Christ</u>* that leads to eternal life.

COMMENT

Verse 17: Like Enoch the apostles have made predictions—which, as we will learn from the next verse, concern the final phase of world history. The readers and hearers of Jude are exhorted to remember the words of these people, who belong to a much older generation than the author and his congregations. See the earlier comment on verse 3. The fixed entity of "faith handed on once and for all" invoked in verse 3 corresponds to the stability of "the circle of the apostles."

Verse 18: The writer summarizes the content of the apostolic teaching about the end-time. This is not a quotation, and what verse 18 attributes to the apostles appears in no known apostolic text. Rather, we have here a generic statement of our author and other Christians from the third or fourth generation—a formula they believed to be apostolic preaching.[79]

Verse 19: For polemical reasons the author ascribes to the opponents the move to separate from the community, and he turns their claim to be bearers of the Spirit[80] against them by branding them as psychics.[81]

Verses 20–21: These two verses with their four admonitions form a unit. The first admonition looks back to the original establishment of the faith. The demand to build up refers to the faith that has been handed on, which verse 3 describes as a literal acceptance of doctrinal sentences. In this way, our author insists, the community is and will remain safe from false teachers. The second admonition follows Paul[82] in considering the Holy Spirit to be an agent of prayer, while the third enjoins believers to love God.[83] The fourth and last admonition looks forward to its fulfillment in eternal life. The promise of the Lord's mercy, though, is peculiar to Jude.

Verses 22–23: Rules of Conduct toward Endangered and Fallen Community Members

(22) And have <u>mercy</u> on **some**, those who are in doubt.

(23a) Save **some**, by snatching them out of the fire.

(23b) And let your <u>mercy</u> on **some** be tinged with fear, hating even the garments stained by their flesh.[84]

COMMENT

Verses 22–23: In order to separate the addressees from the "heretics" the author distinguishes three different groups of community members: (a) those who waver in doubt (verse 22), (b) those who are almost lost to heretical beliefs (verse 23a), and (c) those who despite a prior history of hateful sins of the flesh (verse 23b) may be accorded cautious and ever-watchful mercy.

(a) The first group deserves nothing but mercy—after the model of the promised mercy of Christ to which "Jude" referred in verse 21. According to my overall reading of Jude, this means that one should separate these people from the dangerous influence of the false teachers and rebuild their faith on the basis of traditional apostolic doctrine.

(b) The situation of the members of the second group is different. Although their rescue may be possible, it will require overcoming the imminent threat of hellfire.[85] One possible analogy is the case of the incestuous Christian in Corinth whom Paul consigns to Satan for the destruction of the flesh in order that his spirit may be saved at the Day of Judgment.[86] Remember also the baptism for the dead practiced in Corinth that Paul mentions[87] without condemnation. Its likely purpose was to save deceased relatives and friends of Corinthian Christians from the fire of the final judgment.

(c) With respect to the third group—apparently members of the community *stained*[88] by sexual impurity—the author advises a circumspect or even skeptical[89] acceptance of their salvageable status. It is possible to hate what they have done, yet offer them conditional mercy and reserve final judgment. "Mercy" echoes the same noun in verses 21 and 22, and its emphasis by repetition may be intended to suggest a way of bridging a present gulf with an eye to future solidarity.[90]

Other early Christian texts provide analogies for the different measures of separation that the author of Jude commands:

> In 2 John 9–10 the Elder urges his community not to greet, let alone welcome, certain Christians who deny the full humanity of Christ.

See further the measures taken by Bishop Ignatius.

To the Smyrnaeans 4:1

> I watch over you to guard you from wild beasts in the form of men, whom you must refuse not only to receive, but, if possible, not even meet. Only pray for them, if perhaps they may repent. Though this is difficult, yet Jesus Christ, our true Life, has power to effect it.

The community rule which Christians put into Jesus' mouth displays how discipline was enforced.

Matt. 18:15–17

(15) "And **if** your brother sins against you, go to him and tell him, the two of you alone. If he *listens* to you, you have gained your brother.

(16) But **if** he does not *listen*, take one or two others along with you, that every word may be confirmed by the evidence of two or three witnesses.

(17) And **if** *he refuses* to *listen* to them, tell (it) to the community. And **if** *he refuses* to *listen* to the community, let him be to you as a Gentile and a tax collector."

See further how in the oldest gospel "Jesus" distinguishes between various sins:

Mark 3:28–29

(28) "Truly, I say to you, Everything will be <u>forgiven</u> the sons of men, the *sins* and the **blasphemies**, however much they **blaspheme**. (29) But whoever **blasphemes** against the Holy Spirit will have no <u>forgiveness</u> in eternity, but is guilty of the eternal *sin*."

Like the injunctions in Jude, these words of the post-Easter Christ presuppose clear rules with respect to specific transgressions, for otherwise the community's responses, which run the full gamut from forgiveness to eternal damnation,[91] could become dangerously arbitrary.

Verses 24–25: Doxology

(24) Now to him who is able to keep you from falling and to present you without blemish before the presence of his glory with rejoicing—(25) to the only God, our Savior through Jesus Christ our Lord—be glory, majesty, dominion, and authority, before all time and now and for ever. Amen.

COMMENT

Verses 24–25: The concluding doxology leads back to the beginning of the letter in that verse 24 picks up the verb "to keep" in verse 1. Furthermore, the invocation of "the only God" in verse 25 may be a polemic against the opponents' denial of the "only Master and Lord, Jesus Christ" at verse 4. The doxology has many analogies in Jewish and Christian literature.[92] Calling on "the only God" and referring to him as "savior" seem especially in keeping with Jewish tradition. The lack of any personal remarks at the end of the work shows that Jude is not a real letter, but an antiheretical tract addressed to Christian communities in danger of doctrinal subversion. A formula affirming divine omnipotence in all ages concludes the discourse.

3. TRANSLATION AND ANALYSIS OF 2 PETER

1:1–2: Prescript

(1) Simeon Peter, a servant and apostle of Jesus Christ, to those who have received a faith as precious as ours in the righteousness of our GOD and Savior Jesus Christ. (2) May grace and peace be multiplied to you in the knowledge of GOD and of Jesus our Lord.

COMMENT

Verse 1: "Simeon" is the Semitic form of Simon[93] and Peter comes from the Greek translation (*petros*) of his Aramaic nickname, "Cephas" (rock).[94] The archaic form Simeon was probably used to create an illusion of authenticity. "Servant" seems to be taken over from Jude 1. The lack of an article before "savior" in the Greek text renders it likely that Jesus is being identified with "God."[95]

Verse 2: The phrase "God and Jesus" in the benediction is traditional.[96] Therefore it involves no real contradiction to the equation of Jesus with God in verse 1.

1:3–11: Proem: Christian Life

(3) His divine power has BESTOWED ON us all things necessary for life and **_godliness_**, through the **knowledge** of him who called us to his own glory and excellence, (4) by which he has BESTOWED ON us his most precious promises, that through these you may escape from the corruption that is in the world because of lust, and become partakers of the divine nature.

(5) For this vital reason make every effort to supplement
your **FAITH** with virtue,
and virtue with **knowledge**,
(6) and **knowledge** with self-control,
and self-control with steadfastness,
and steadfastness with **_godliness_**,
(7) and **_godliness_** with brotherly affection,
and brotherly affection with **LOVE**.
(8) For if these things are yours in increasing measure, they keep

you from being ineffective or unfruitful in the **knowledge** *of our Lord Jesus Christ*. (9) But whoever lacks these things is blind and short-sighted and has forgotten that he was cleansed from his past sins.

(10) Therefore, brothers, be the more zealous to confirm your call and election, for if you do this you will never fall, (11) and you will be richly provided with an entrance into the eternal kingdom *of our Lord* and Savior *Jesus Christ*.

COMMENT

Verse 3: The adjective "divine" is widely used in Christian literature of the second century.[97] "Divine power" as an attribute of "Jesus, our Lord" (verse 2) has bestowed on Christians "all things necessary for life and godliness." This must be accepted through "the knowledge of the one (= Jesus) who has called us."

Verse 4: Here the author introduces a basic topic of Greek piety: the presupposition that human beings are capable of taking part in God's nature. It is noteworthy that here this remains part of the promise and bears no connection with later statements about the Second Coming at 3:1–13. According to "Peter," it is lust—being seduced to sin—that causes the moral corruption that leads at last to destruction.[98] The formulation of verse 4 may have been inspired by the author's familiarity with baptismal instruction, which usually included the idea of overcoming the corruption inherited from Adam's fall.[99]

Verses 5–7: The author adds a list of eight virtues, beginning with faith and ending with love, and organized in the form of an interlocking chain.[100] They are the specific virtues that enable the Christian to claim the reward described in verses 3–4. For the relation of the context to the specific virtues, note the special fonts and other features used in the translation.

Verse 8: The more that addressees strive to fulfill these virtues, the more their knowledge of Jesus Christ will increase.

Verse 9: The author warns against neglecting these virtuous behaviors: slackers will all too soon forget the blessing of having been cleansed of past sins.

Verse 10: The introductory "therefore," the address "brothers," and the term "call" (which picks up the same term in verse 3) all show that the author is consciously employing a rhetorical formula in summing up what he has written.

Verse 11: The author's introductory exhortation culminates in the assurance of a positive result: the entrance into the eternal kingdom of Christ. "Savior" echoes the same word at verse 1; "of our Lord . . . Jesus Christ" takes up the same phrase at verse 8.

1:12–15: The Present Letter as the Testament of Peter

(12) Therefore I intend to keep **reminding** you of these matters, though you already know them and are established in the truth that has come to you. (13) But as long as I am still in this tent [= body], I think it only right to stimulate you with an occasional **reminder**, (14) since I know that the putting off of my tent [body] is not far off, as our Lord Jesus Christ made clear to me. (15) And I will see to it that after my departure you will be able at any time to **keep in mind** these matters.

COMMENT

The writer "Peter" has a role much like that of the speaker "Paul" of Acts;[101] he creates a sense of the presence of things past by recalling them. Indeed, one could well term this letter a testament, inasmuch as according to verse 14 "Christ" has informed "Peter" of his imminent death.

Verse 12: In 1 Thessalonians the historical Paul similarly tells the members of his community that they do not need any instruction about the details of the end-time and then proceeds to give precisely that instruction.[102] Clearly we are dealing with rhetoric here.[103]

Verses 13–14: "Peter" offers the solemn affirmation that he is writing shortly before his death in order to emphasize that the readers must hold fast to the truth they have been given. Verse 14a is an allusion to Peter's martyrdom and verse 14b contains a strong echo of John 21:18–19. As in 2 Cor. 5:1–4, "tent" is an image of the human body that the soul casts off at death.

Verse 15: The "intention" of verse 12 has become a commitment; "Peter" will "see to it" that his legacy lives on.

1:16–21: Apostolic Eyewitness and the Role of the Prophets

(16) For we did not follow subtly concocted myths when we made known to you the power and coming of our Lord Jesus Christ, but we were eyewitnesses of his majesty. (17) For when he received honor and _glory_ from God the Father and there CAME to him the VOICE of the Majestic _Glory_ saying,

"This is my beloved Son, with whom I am well pleased,"

(18) we heard this VOICE that CAME from heaven, for we were with him on the holy mountain.

(19) And we have the **prophetic** word more fully confirmed. You will do well to pay attention to this as to a lamp shining in a dark place, until the day dawns and the morning star rises in your hearts.

(20) First of all you must understand that no scriptural **prophecy** is the result of someone's individual interpretation, (21) because no **prophecy** ever CAME by way of human will, but rather through human beings moved by the Holy Spirit who spoke from GOD.

COMMENT

The author offers two arguments to support his contentions about the call and the election of the community. First, he was an eyewitness to Jesus' adoption (verses 16–18); second, the prophetic word is reliable (verses 19–21).

Verse 16: "Peter" distinguishes his message from rival teachings. Unlike them it is not a myth,[104] for he was an eyewitness[105] of Christ's "majesty." This claim is clarified in the two next verses, which allude to Jesus' transfiguration.[106] By pointing out his own role in the event, "Peter" both enhances his own authority and sets forth in summary form the message of the whole letter, which is a discourse based on the opposition between "myths" and "reports of eyewitnesses." The preface to Luke-Acts[107] belongs to the same rhetorical category, for its author claims eyewitness sources[108] and later includes himself among the "we" who are companions of Paul.[109] The apostolic message about Jesus Christ is thus trustworthy because it is founded on factual history rather than speculative myths. Actually, 2 Peter is not the only early Christian writing to distinguish between the two. The Pastorals, which date from around the same time as 2 Peter, do the same (see above, p. 116). "The power and coming" as the object of the author's preaching refers to the life and return of Jesus Christ. On the latter see below, p. 194, on 3:4 and 3:12a.

Verse 17: The first part of the verse provides an advance summary of the last part.[110] Jesus' glory results from his proclamation as the Son of God in front of his disciples; note that verse 16 has carefully attested to the presence of the disciples during this solemn event.

Verse 18: The author underscores yet again that the apostles were present on the mountain during Jesus' transfiguration and that they heard "the voice that came from heaven."

Verse 19: At the core of his message is the prophetic word whose reliability the author stresses by comparing its power to that of the sun and metaphorically relating that morning star to both the rising (resurrection) of Jesus and his rising influence in the hearts of his followers.

Verses 20–21: For the content, see 2 Tim. 3:16. Stressing the special character of the prophetic word, the author urges his readers not to understand scriptural prophecy as a human phenomenon, for it was the Holy Spirit who moved human beings. This seems to be directed at the opponents who later will be directly attacked (3:4) for having doubted that the prophecies had anything to do with the Second Coming. Against this "Peter" stresses that when human beings utter authentic prophecies, they function as instruments of the Holy Spirit upon God's command. Prophecy, then, is not subject to human doubt, but a matter of divine inspiration. Note that "Peter" through deliberate triple use of "came" (printed in capitals) draws a parallel between the report of the transfiguration and his own statements about authentic prophecy.

2:1–3: The Coming of the False Prophets

(1) But **false** prophets also arose among the people, just as there will be **false** teachers among you, who will secretly bring in heresies of *destruction*, even denying the Master who bought them, bringing upon themselves swift *destruction*. (2) And many will follow their licentiousness, and because of them the path of truth will be reviled, (3) and in their greed they will seek to deceive you with fabrications. But their condemnation was pronounced in ancient times, and certain *destruction* awaits them.

COMMENT

The section contains a damning judgment on the dissidents. They will suffer destruction. Note that the word "destruction"[111] is used three times.

Verse 1: "False *prophets*" is a keyword connection to the end of the previous chapter: "prophetic" in verse 19 and "prophecy" in verses 20–21. The author thus sets true and false prophecy in opposition. By using the expression "false prophets" he not only denies the validity and authority of his opponents, but also denounces them. In the present context the verb "to deny" is either suggestive of persecutions[112] or—more likely—is an allusion to Docetism.[113]

Verse 2: "Truth" picks up by antithesis the "false teachers" and "false prophets" of verse 1. "Path of truth" is a common metonymy for being a Christian.[114] The theme of revilement[115] in this context has Old Testament overtones.[116] The wicked behavior of the opponents leads people to vilify Christianity.

Verse 3: The charge of "greed" has many parallels in attacks on religious or philosophical rivals in the Greco-Roman world[117] and is repeated in 2 Pet. 2:14. "Fabrications" corresponds to "subtly concocted myths" in 1:16. "Peter" makes clear that it is not we but they—the false teachers—who have followed and promoted fraudulent doctrines. Since these have no basis in scripture, it is apparent that the opponents are seeking to "buy" you. But scripture promises that destruction is in store for them.

2:4–10a: The Judgment against the Opponents— Based on Scripture

(4) For **if** God *did not spare* the angels when they sinned, but held them captive in hell and committed them to chains of darkness to be kept until the JUDGMENT;

(5) **if** he *did not spare* the ancient world, but preserved Noah, a herald of righteousness, with seven other persons, when he brought a flood upon the world of the GODLESS;

(6) **if** by turning the cities of Sodom and Gomorrah to ashes he condemned them to extinction and made them an example for what will happen to the GODLESS; and

(7) **if** he rescued **RIGHTEOUS** Lot, greatly distressed by the

licentiousness of the <u>lawless</u> (8)—for by what that **RIGHTEOUS** man saw and heard as he lived among them, he was vexed in his **RIGHTEOUS** soul day after day with their <u>lawless</u> deeds—,

(9) then the Lord knows how to rescue the pious from trial, and to keep the **UNRIGHTEOUS** under punishment until the day of *JUDGMENT,* (10a) especially those who indulge in lustful passion and those who despise [God's] authority and power.

COMMENT

In the present section the author again is heavily dependent on Jude (see the listings in note 19). Examples of the history of Israel support the conclusion that judgment is inevitable. Later in 3:5–7 the author will return to the present section—a sign of how important the issue of judgment is for him.

Verse 4: See further on Jude 6. The underworld is the prison to which the demonic powers have been condemned.[118]

Verse 5: Cf. Gen. 8:18.

Verse 6: See further on Jude 7.

Verses 7–8: This puts a positive spin on the story of Lot's rescue[119] by creating a clearly apologetic description of his situation. Its aim is to persuade the readers of this letter to regard Lot as a model, and to disregard the false teachers who, by focusing on the lawless elements in the story, show themselves to be lawless.

Verses 9–10a: These verses sum up the section by their assurance that the Lord will save the pious from temptation and condemn the false teachers (verse 10a) to a judgment similar to that assigned to the unjust (verse 9b). On the meaning of "despise God's authority and power," see above, pp. 176–77, on Jude 8. Contrary to many a recent interpreter, it should be evident that verse 10a reveals not the libertinism of the opponents but the author's proclivity for polemic.[120]

2:10b–22: Attack on the Opponents for Mental and Moral Corruption

(10b) Bold and willful, they are not afraid to **blaspheme** the glorious ones, (11) whereas angels, though greater in might and power, do not pronounce a **blaspheming** judgment upon them before the Lord.

(12) But **THESE, blaspheming** in matters of which they are ignorant, are like irrational animals, creatures of instinct born to be caught and killed, and will be in like manner destroyed, (13a) thereby suffering wrong for their wrongdoing.

(13b) They count it pleasure to revel in the daytime. They are stains and blemishes on your community, reveling in their dissipation when they join in your meals.

(14) They have eyes full of adultery, insatiable for sin. They entice unsteady souls. They have hearts trained in greed. Accursed children!

(15) Forsaking the right path, they have gone astray; they have followed the path of Balaam, the son of Beor, who loved gain from wrongdoing, (16) but was rebuked for his own transgression; a mute ass spoke with human voice and restrained the prophet's madness.

(17) **THESE** are waterless springs and mists driven by a storm; for them the nether gloom of darkness has been reserved.

(18) For, uttering loud boasts of folly, they entice with licentious passions of the flesh people who have barely **escaped** from those who live in error.

(19a) They promise them freedom, but they themselves are slaves of corruption; (19b) for whatever overcomes someone, to that he or she is enslaved.

(20) For if, after they have **escaped** the defilements of the world through the _knowledge_ of our Lord and Savior Jesus Christ, they are again entangled in them and overpowered, the last state has become worse for them than the first. (21) For it would have been better for them never to have _known_ the path of righteousness than after _knowing_ it to turn back from the holy commandment handed on to them. (22) It has happened to them according to the true proverb: The dog turns back to his own vomit, and the sow is washed only to wallow in the mire.

COMMENT

Verses 10b–11: The author shortens the text of Jude 8–9 and as a result describes angels differently.

Verses 12–13: On verse 12 see Jude 10; on verse 13 see Jude 12. In contrast with Jude, "Peter" no longer speaks of meals—that is, community "love feasts" (in Greek, *agapais*)—but of the deceptions (in Greek, *apatais*) perpetrated by "these people." By changing two Greek letters the author has cleverly directed another stinging polemic against the opponents.

Verse 14: To the list in Jude "Peter" adds two points of moral attack: enticement and greed. The first charge adduces the destructive effects of immoral example on the weaker members of the congregation; the second reiterates the allegation of greed in 2 Pet. 2:3.

Verses 15–16: Building on the supposed avarice of the opponents the author blames them for "following the path of Balaam . . . who loved gain from wrongdoing." By way of explanation he offers a much-abridged retelling of the fanciful story of Balaam (Numbers 22–25) and so slants it as to serve his purpose of contrasting the wisdom of an irrational animal (Balaam's recalcitrant donkey) with the greedy prophet's moral and spiritual blindness. The muted irony of juxtaposing a human and an ass is an effective complement to the author's polemic.

Verse 17: See further on Jude 12–13.

Verse 18: See further on Jude 16. This verse amounts to nothing more than shrill denunciation. That polemical elements have been added to the diatribe found in Jude displays the author's concern over the number of members of the congregation who are attracted by the false teachers.

Verse 19: The attack in verse 19a—that the opponents promise freedom, yet remain slaves of corruption—finds echoes in the statements of the historical Paul.[121] This may suggest that pupils of Paul are the target of the polemic, especially since later at 3:15–16 the author addresses their "false" interpretation of Paul's letters. Verse 19b is a proverb[122] that strengthens the point made by verse 19a.

Verses 20–21: "Defilements" points back to "stains" in verse 13b. The author emphasizes the former Christian status of the opponents. For one thing, they had escaped the pollutions of this world through the knowledge of the Lord and savior Jesus Christ; for another, they had known the path of righteousness. The holy commandment had been handed on to them.

Verse 22: The climax of "Peter's" denunciation of the false teachers comes in the form of a proverb that charges them with backsliding into the corruption of immorality after their sins were washed away. Like animals, he says, they are attracted by filth. In the author's world dogs and pigs, being especially despised, were often proverbial symbols of

Gentile immorality.[123] "Peter" has borrowed an image from Prov. 26:11 for the first of his offensive caricatures; the second insult is drawn from traditional lore. Duane F. Watson is very charitable in this matter:

> The author's denunciation of other Christians . . . may seem harsh and unchristian to us . . . [but] [i]t was the practice to associate one's opponents with all kinds of negative images in order to destroy their reputation and thus to lessen the proclivity of others to accept their doctrine and practice. We still must speak out against aberrations of doctrine in our day, but we must be sure to do so in ways that are effective in our culture.[124]

Watson, it would seem, assigns a cynic's criterion to good manners: petulant and vulgar name-calling can be approved on tactical grounds. But this overlooks the general recognition that polemic comes in varying degrees from mild to malevolent, and that in any form of discourse it is better to be objective than objectionable. Paul, at least, quotes or paraphrases what his opponents say and represents them more or less fairly. But "Peter" casts accuracy to the winds when, for example, he charges his opponents with libertinism—and Watson uncritically accepts this slander. Perhaps in a commentary that pastors may use in sermon preparation he is loath to call into question the complete accuracy of any text that someone sixteen centuries ago decided to insert in the canon.

3:1–13: Rebuttals of Objections to Jesus' Second Coming

(1) This is now the second letter that I write to you, beloved, and in both of them I try to stimulate you in serious thinking by reminding you of things you already know: (2) the predictions of the holy prophets and the commandment of the <u>**Lord**</u> and Savior through your apostles.

(3) First of all you must understand this: that in the last days scoffers will come, people who care only for their own ease and pleasure, and they will mock you, (4) saying,

"Where is the **promise** of his **COMING**? For ever since the fathers fell asleep, all things have continued as they were from the beginning of creation."

(5) They deliberately ignore that the <u>*heavens and the earth*</u>

existed long ago as ordained by the *word* of GOD, the earth formed out of <u>water</u> and by means of <u>water</u>, (6) by which the world that then existed was deluged with <u>water</u> and perished. (7) But by the same *word* the *<u>heavens and the earth</u>* that now exist are in store for burning, and are presently being preserved only until the day of judgment and destruction of godless persons.

(8) But do not ignore this one fact, beloved, that with ***<u>the Lord</u>*** one day is as a thousand years, and a thousand years as one day.

(9) ***<u>The Lord</u>*** is not slow about his **promise** as some count slowness, but is forbearing toward you, not wishing that any should perish, but rather that all should reach repentance.

(10) But the day of ***<u>the Lord</u>*** will come like a thief, and then the heavens will pass away with a loud noise, and the elements will be dissolved with fire, and the earth and the works that are upon it will be burned up.

(11) Since everything is thus to be destroyed, what sort of persons ought you to be? You should lead lives of holiness and piety, (12) waiting for and hastening the **COMING** of the day of GOD, when the heavens will be kindled and dissolved, and the elements will melt with fire. (13) Nonetheless, because of his **promise** we wait for new heavens and a new earth in which righteousness dwells.

COMMENT

Verse 1: Here the author makes such an unambiguous claim to authenticity that it is no longer possible to consider 2 Peter as a work of open or avowed pseudepigraphy. Gerd Theissen, however, sees it otherwise:

> In the case of Peter we could have a false attribution of authorship which the contemporary reader would see through—an open pseudepigraphy with no intent to deceive. It is too plain that Peter is on the one hand warning against false teachers after him and on the other acting as if he is contemporaneous with them. These false teachers say that the fathers are dead—yet Peter himself is one of them (2 Peter 3.4).[125]

Rebuttal: The argument would be more convincing if the author (i.e., "Peter") had said that the fathers were dead or if he had not included the anachronistic references to "your apostles" and "last days" noted in the comments on verses 2 and 3 below. It is likewise noteworthy that "Peter" nowhere implies that he is a contemporary of the opponents.

The reference to 1 Peter indicates that both the author and addressees are familiar with it. Yet the two writings have little in common except that both claim a desire to stir their readers to serious reflection; indeed, they show great differences in both intended purpose and viewpoint.

Verse 2: The "serious thinking" of the addressees is to focus on their "remembering the predictions of the holy prophets and the commandment of the Lord and Savior through your apostles." "Your apostles" reflects the relatively late time of composition of 2 Peter (cf. also Jude 17). "*Holy* prophets" echoes "*holy* commandment delivered to them" in 2:21.

Verse 3: Another subject for serious thought is the knowledge that in the last days scoffers will step forward. The author has thus advanced his time line to the present. From the very beginning he has discredited the opponents by portraying them as selfish people who jeer at everyone else.

Verse 4: "Peter" is quoting a teaching of the opponents. We do not know how precise the citation is.[126]

Verses 5–7: This section contains the first argument against the statements of the "scoffers." Its content matches 2:5–10a, where "Peter" draws a parallel between the judgment against Noah's generation and the judgment against the opponents.

Verse 8: The second argument, that with the Lord one day is as a thousand years and a thousand years as one day, derives from scripture.[127]

Verse 9: The third argument relies on the idea of God's forbearance, which can be found in scriptural[128] and other Jewish texts.[129]

Verse 10: The fourth argument stresses that the day of the Lord will come unannounced, like a thief.[130]

Verse 11: For the necessity of inward piety in order to escape the final judgment see 2 Pet. 1:3–4, 7–8.

Verses 12–13: The eschatological admonition that concludes the section employs scriptural motifs.[131] "Day of God" apparently means the same as "coming of Christ" in 1:16; 3:4a.

3:14–18: Concluding Remarks with an Appendix on Paul's Letters

(14) Therefore, *beloved*, since you wait for these things, be zealous to be found by him without stain or blemish, and at peace. (15a) And count the forbearance **OF OUR LORD** as salvation.

(15b) So also our *beloved* brother Paul wrote to you according to the wisdom given him, (16) speaking of this as he does in all his letters. Some things in them are hard to understand, and the ignorant and **unstable** twist these to their own destruction, as they do the other scriptures.

(17) You therefore, *beloved*, knowing this beforehand, beware lest you be carried away by the errors of lawless people and lose your own **stability**.

(18) But grow in the grace and knowledge **OF OUR LORD** and Savior Jesus Christ. To him be the glory both now and to the day of eternity. Amen.

COMMENT

The end of the letter shows that the problem of the delay of the Second Coming was related to a controversy over Paul. The author necessarily had to refer to Paul, who by that time had gained general recognition in the church catholic. This situation was quite different from what had obtained at the time Jude was written. Furthermore, 1 Clement 5 had had a tremendous impact by making of the two apostles Peter and Paul a symbol of unity for the Roman church.[132]

Verse 14: The catchword phrase "without stain" indicates that this verse is a deliberate antithesis to 2:13b ("they are stains and blemishes").

Verses 15–16: "Forbearance" in verse 15a takes up "forbearing" in verse 9. In verses 15b–16 the author's abrupt turn to Paul is noteworthy on several counts. First, "Peter" has a positive view of Paul. Second, a collection of Paul's letters already existed, and they were understood to be addressed to the whole church ("you"). Third, the author considers all of Paul's letters to have dealt with the message of God's forbearance. Fourth, not only does this "forbearance" refer to the eschatological statements in Paul's letters, that is, his view of the future, but the author ascribes to Paul his own view of the future as depicted in verses 3–10. Fifth, even more important is the author's reference in verse 16 to things in Paul's letters, which are "hard to understand," and that "the ignorant and unstable twist them to their own destruction." This suggests that in appealing to Paul the opponents of 2 Peter had a special way of dealing with these passages.

Verse 17: "Peter" speaks to the members of the community about the teachers mentioned in the previous verse and calls them "lawless people." Note that in 2:7 he had used the same word with respect to Lot's opponents. Christians are warned against this threat to their spiritual stability and reminded that they had previously been forewarned of it.

Verse 18: Note that the term "knowledge" from the beginning of the letter (1:2, 3, 8) is here used again. The concluding praise is addressed not to God but to Jesus Christ. This does not happen often in the New Testament; elsewhere it occurs only in 2 Tim. 4:18 and Rev. 1:5, 6.

4. INTOLERANCE AND THE GOSPEL IN JUDE AND 2 PETER

The Historical Situation of Jude and 2 Peter with Special Attention to the Other Six Selected New Testament Texts

In order to understand Jude historically we must recognize its close relationship to 2 Peter, a fact that naturally leads to the thesis that both writings belong to the same place and cannot be far apart chronologically.[133] My further suggestion is to apply all that can be safely said about 2 Peter to the interpretation of Jude. In this regard, we would have to assume (a) the existence of a collection of Paul's letters, (b) the presence of teachers who offered a special interpretation of Paul's letters and of other writings, and (c) the rejection of the Second Coming as a future historical event.

Jude sheds light on a period in Primitive Christian history when independently and at several different places a number of teachers began to develop interpretations of Christian faith that differed from traditional doctrine. Similarities to the situation discernible in Jude can be ascertained in the communities that gave rise to the Pastorals, Luke-Acts,[134] 2 and 3 John, and probably 2 Thessalonians. Outside the New

Testament one can observe similar phenomena in the letters of Ignatius of Antioch and Polycarp of Smyrna, and a generation later in Irenaeus's antiheretical work.

The opponents' teaching in the aforementioned texts can properly be said to have a "Gnostic" basis. Gnosticism,[135] whose very existence is clearly attested at the beginning of the second century, marked with its indelible stamp the further development of Primitive Christian thought. Its negative result is the denial of the incarnation of Jesus and his Second Coming to judge the world. On the positive side, Gnosticism meant that a greater emphasis was placed on the individual experience of the "believer." Consequently, the hierarchical structure of the church catholic was dealt a considerable blow, the more so since egalitarian tendencies of Paul's preaching were further developed.

The Intolerance of the Gospel in Jude and 2 Peter as a Characteristic Feature of the Church in the New Testament

In all the cases we know of, the reactions of church officials led to a separation of Christian communities from the Gnostic teachers without any real attempt at compromise or conjunction. In the most favorable case (Jude), the heretics were left to God's mercy, a resolution that in view of the bitter attacks against them meant very little. If the polemics, excoriations, and vile slanders against the opponents show us anything, it is that damnations of others constituted a large part of the identity of the proto-orthodox churches of the New Testament. Yet the price for enforcing orthodoxy in such a way—by slander and lie—was quite high. For a long time such ideas as religious freedom, tolerance, and truth remained foreign to the Christian churches.

The shared theology of the writings we have examined displays the following features: exclusive monotheism, preservation of God's honor, election, incarnation of the Son of God, and his return to judge the world. Furthermore, all the texts presuppose a restitution theory with regard to Israel as well as a "hostile" takeover of Israel's scripture—henceforth to be known as the "Old Testament." (The New Testament as a collection of normative texts was just coming into existence around the time when the latest of the above writings was composed.)[136]

With the exception of Diotrephes (3 John), those under attack seem to have been more inclined to tolerance than the proto-orthodox

bishops and church functionaries, particularly in view of their willingness to develop the deposit of faith in order to meet the challenges of
changing experience and critical thought. Thus their sophistication
appears to have been of a higher order than that of their contemptuous
proto-orthodox attackers.

Still, what can have been the underlying issue that prompted such
a bitter attack by one group against the other? Perhaps a fundamental
motivation may be discerned in the nontheological aspects of the situation: the almost democratic character of the Gnostic Christian communities aroused suspicion,[137] for the central issue was power and
authority, perquisites that the bishops were clearly unwilling to share.

NOTES

1. Jennifer Michael Hecht, *Doubt: A History: The Great Doubters and Their
Legacy of Innovation, from Socrates and Jesus to Thomas Jefferson and Emily Dick-
inson* (San Francisco: HarperSanFrancisco, 2003), p. xxi.

2. Bart Ehrman, *The New Testament: A Historical Introduction to the Early
Christian Writings*, 3rd ed. (New York: Oxford University Press, 2004), p. 456.

3. For details see Duane Frederick Watson, *Invention, Arrangement, and
Style: Rhetorical Criticism of Jude and 2 Peter* (Atlanta, GA: Scholars Press, 1988),
pp. 29–79, 194.

4. See only Rom. 1:5; 3:24; 5:2.

5. Cf. the similar reversal in James 3:13–16.

6. Cf. 1 Cor. 2:14–15; 15:44, etc.

7. 1 Cor. 6:3; 13:1.

8. Therefore the Pauline disciple who wrote Colossians is emphatic: "In
him (Jesus Christ) all things in heaven and on earth were created, things visible
and invisible, whether thrones or dominions or rulers or powers—all things
have been created through him and for him." (Col. 1:16)

9. Col. 1:15–20.

10. Col. 2:18.

11. 1 Cor. 12:3. On the cursing of Jesus see further my *Primitive Christianity: A Survey of Recent Studies and Some New Proposals* (London: T & T Clark,
2003), pp. 156–57.

12. An offshoot of this trajectory is the Palestinian Christian Hegesippus.
For details see my *Opposition to Paul in Early Christianity* (Minneapolis, MN:
Fortress Press, 1989), pp. 155–68.

13. Helmut Koester, *Introduction to the New Testament*, 2 vols., 2nd ed.
(New York: Walter de Gruyter, 1995–2000), 2:252.

14. Against Richard Bauckham, *Jude and the Relatives of Jesus in the Early Church* (Edinburgh: T & T Clark, 1990), esp. pp. 171–78; Bauckham, *Jude, 2 Peter: Word Biblical Themes* (Dallas, TX: Word Publishing, 1990), pp. 3–4. See his remark "The special interest of the letter of Jude is that it is one of the very few surviving documents of early Palestinian Jewish Christianity—the original movement from which the whole of the rest of the early Christian movement derived. It offers us a glimpse of the convictions about Jesus and the Gospel which were preached by the earliest Christian missionaries in Palestine" (Bauckham, *Jude, 2 Peter*, p. 4).

15. See my *Opposition to Paul in Early Christianity*, pp. 119–28.

16. 2 Pet. 1:16–18.

17. 2 Pet. 1:14. Cf. John 21:18–19.

18. See 2 Pet. 3:15–16.

19. Cf. Jude 2/2 Pet. 1:2; Jude 3/2 Pet. 1:5; Jude 4/2 Pet. 2:1–3; Jude 5/2 Pet.1:12; Jude 6/2 Pet. 2:4; Jude 7/2 Pet. 2:6 (cf. 3:3), Jude 8/2 Pet. 2:10; Jude 9/2 Pet. 2:11; Jude 10/2 Pet. 2:12; Jude 11/2 Pet. 2:15; Jude 12–13/2 Pet. 2:17; Jude 16/2 Pet. 2:18; Jude 17/2 Pet. 3:2; Jude 18/2 Pet. 3:3; Jude 23–24/2 Pet. 3:14 (cf. 3:17); Jude 25/2 Pet. 3:18.

20. Cf. Jude 4 and 2 Pet. 2:1–3.

21. 2 Pet. 2:13.

22. In Greek, *Parousia*.

23. 2 Pet. 3:4.

24. See 1 Clem. 23:2–5; 2 Clem. 11:2.

25. See especially Mark 9:1; John 21:23; 1 Thess. 4:13–17 and the comments in my *Paul, Apostle of the Gentiles: Studies in Chronology* (Philadelphia: Fortress Press, 1984), pp. 201–44.

26. Georg Strecker, *Theology of the New Testament* (New York: Walter de Gruyter, 2000), pp. 327–36.

27. See 2 Pet. 1:20–21.

28. 2 Pet. 3:16.

29. 2 Pet. 1:20–21.

30. On this point see especially 1 Pet. 5:12b.

31. Koester, *Introduction to the New Testament*, 2:298.

32. 2 Pet. 3:8.

33. 2 Pet. 3:9.

34. 2 Pet. 3:11–12.

35. Jude 3.

36. 2 Pet. 1:12.

37. 2 Pet. 2:21.

38. 2 Pet. 3:2.

39. Bauckham, *Jude, 2 Peter*, p. 44.

40. See more above, pp. 193–94, on the theory—in my view all too apologetic—of "open pseudepigraphy."

41. See above, p. 86.

42. See Gal. 1:19; 2:9, 12; Acts 21:18.

43. See Gen. 6:1–4.

44. 1 Tim. 1:2; 2 Tim. 1:2.

45. Titus 1:4.

46. 2 John 3.

47. "Saints" (in Greek, *hagioi*) is one of the honorific titles of the members of the earliest Christian communities. See Rom. 15:26, etc.

48. Rom. 6:17; 16:17; Gal. 1:23; 3:23, etc.

49. See Rom. 1:3–4; 3:25–26; Phil. 2:6–11, etc. See the literature in my *The Resurrection of Christ*, p. 37n2.

50. Daniel J. Harrington, "Jude and 2 Peter," in Donald P. Senior and Daniel J. Harrington, *1 Peter, Jude, and 2 Peter* (Collegeville, MN: Liturgical Press, 2003), p. 192.

51. Duane F. Watson, "The Letter of Jude," in *The New Interpreter's Bible*, vol. 12 (Nashville, TN: Abingdon, 1998), p. 477, suggests that verse 4 refers to the letter of Jude as condemnation (in Greek, *krima*). This thesis results from overindulgence in rhetorical criticism without looking at the content and context of Jude.

52. In Greek, *asebês*.

53. In Greek, *despotês*.

54. See Luke 2:29; Rev. 6:10; Barnabas 1:7; 4:3; 1 Clem. 59:4; 60:3; 61:7.

55. Besides, 2 Pet. 2:1 uses "Master" as an appellation for Christ (following Jude 4).

56. Cf. Luke 12:9 and the comments on it in my *Jesus After 2000 Years: What He Really Said and Did* (Amherst, NY: Prometheus Books, 2001), pp. 343–44.

57. For details see below, pp. 222–24.

58. See below, pp. 213–28.

59. See Sir. 16:7–10: (7) "He did not forgive the leaders of old who rebelled long ago in their might. (8) He did not spare the neighbors of Lot whom he detested for their pride. (9) Nor did he spare the doomed people who were uprooted because of their sin; (10) nor the six hundred thousand foot soldiers who perished for the impiety of their hearts."

60. Cf. 2 Tim. 2:14; Titus 3:1; 2 Pet. 1:12.

61. For details see Num. 14:29–37. Cf. also 1 Cor. 10:5

62. In Greek, *têrein*.

63. Cf. 1 Enoch 6:1–2; 7:1. See also the masterful and first ever written commentary by George W. E. Nickelsburg, *1 Enoch 1: A Commentary on the Book of 1 Enoch, Chapters 1–36; 81–106* (Minneapolis, MN: Fortress Press, 2001).

64. Harrington, "Jude and 2 Peter," p. 203.

65. See below, pp. 219, 245.

66. Cf. only Henning Paulsen, *Der Zweite Petrusbrief und der Judasbrief* (Göttingen: Vandenhoeck & Ruprecht, 1992), p. 47.

67. Note, however, that visionary experiences are not limited to Gnostics.

68. 1 Cor. 12:3.

69. See further below, pp. 216–17.

70. See the survey by Harrington, "Jude and 2 Peter," pp. 207–209.

71. Deut. 34:6.

72. Gen. 4:1–16. "The biblical example (of Cain) suggests that the intruders are effectively committing spiritual murder against their Christian brothers and sisters" (Harrington, "Jude and 2 Peter," p. 199).

73. Numbers 31. Yet in Numbers 22–24 Balaam receives a positive treatment.

74. Num. 16:1–35.

75. The basic meaning of *agapē* is love. From that root it developed the meaning "meal of love."

76. Cf. 1 Cor. 11:25: ". . . after the supper " (in Greek, *meta to deipnēsai*).

77. Wisd. of Sol. 4:3–5; Matt. 3:10.

78. Cf. Isa. 57:20; Wisd. of Sol. 14:1.

79. See Acts 20:29–30; 1 Tim. 4:1–3; 2 Tim. 3:1–5; 4:3; Didache 16:3. Cf. Mark 13:22; Matt. 24:14.

80. See further 1 Cor. 2:14–16; 15:44–49; Gal. 5:17; James 3:15.

81. Against Frederik Wisse, "The Epistle of Jude in the History of Heresiology," in *Essays on the Nag Hammadi Texts in Honour of Alexander Böhlig*, ed. Martin Krause (Leiden: Brill, 1972), p. 142: "Paul's use of *psychikoi* in 1 Cor. 2:13–3:3 adequately explains their occurrence in Jude. The author had already made the same point about the opponents in vs. 10." Yet there is no reason why the author should favor a Pauline phrase unless he wants to defeat the "intruders" with their own weapons, namely Paul's letters.

82. Rom. 8:26–27.

83. "Love of God" (i.e., love *for* God) could also be translated by "love that God gives." Yet, in view of the fourth admonition, which speaks of the Lord's mercy, this seems unlikely.

84. It should be pointed out that Jude 22–23 is one of the greatest text-critical problems in the New Testament. Following the 27th edition of the Nestle-Aland text (and, among others, NRSV), I see three groups reflected in the text. For other possibilities and a description of the problem see Harrington, "Jude and 2 Peter," pp. 220–25.

85. Cf. Amos 4:11; Zech. 3:2; 1 Cor. 3:13.

86. 1 Cor. 5:1–5.

87. 1 Cor. 15:29.

88. On the motif of defilement of the garment see Rev. 3:4.

89. Cf. verse 12a with verse 23b.

90. Cf. Didache 2:7.

91. See the statement on the deadly sin in 1 John 5:16 (on this text see above, pp. 102–103).

92. See Rom. 16:25–27; Eph. 3:20; Phil. 4:20; 1 Thess. 5:23–24; 1 Tim. 1:17; 6:15; 1 Pet. 4:11; 1 Clem. 65:7; Martyrdom of Polycarp 20:2.

93. The form *Simeon* is also used at Acts 15:14.

94. See John 1:42b: "Jesus looked at him and said: 'You are Simon the son of John, you will be called Cephas,' which is translated Peter."

95. Cf. John 1:1; 20:28; Heb. 1:8; Titus 2:13; and Jude 25a (see above, p. 182).

96. See Rom. 1:7; 1 Cor. 1:3; 2 Cor. 1:2; Eph. 1:2; Phil. 1:2; 2 Thess. 1:2.

97. But at only one other place in the New Testament, Acts 17:29.

98. Cf. Rom. 7:7.

99. See Rom. 5:12–6:11.

100. Bishop Ignatius of Antioch *To the Ephesians* 14:1 speaks of faith and love as the beginning and end of life.

101. Acts 20:31–35 is a particularly apposite example.

102. See how 1 Thess. 5:2 leads into the very thing that the preceding verse declared unnecessary.

103. *Praeteritio.*

104. Note that it is "Peter" who charges his opponents with devising myths, and not the other way around. This must be stressed against Duane F. Watson, "The Second Letter of Peter," in *The New Interpreter's Bible*, vol. 12 (Nashville, TN: Abingdon Press, 1998), p. 342: "The false teachers charged that the apostolic proclamation of the 'power and coming' or 'coming in power' of Christ (parousia) was based on 'cleverly devised myths' (NRSV) or 'cleverly invented stories' (NIV)." Bauckham, *Jude, 2 Peter*, p. 80, as well as Harrington, "Jude and 2 Peter," p. 258, offer the same erroneous argument.

105. In Greek, *epoptēs*, which mostly means "overseer." The author wants to emphasize the miraculous character of the event.

106. Mark 9:2–13 parr.

107. Luke 1:1–4.

108. In Greek, *autoptai* (Luke 1:2).

109. Acts 16:10–17; 20:5–15; 21:1–18; 27:1–28:16.

110. Similarly the historical Paul at 1 Thess. 4:15 summarizes the subsequent proclamation, 1 Thess. 4:16–17.

111. In Greek, *apôleia.*

112. See Matt. 10:32–33.

113. See above on Jude 4.

114. See, for example, the explanation of "path of truth" in 1 Clem. 35:5: "[We receive the gift that God has promised] when our understanding is faithfully fixed on God, when we seek after what is pleasing and acceptable to him, when we accomplish what accords with his perfect will and follow in the path of truth, casting from ourselves all injustice and lawlessness, greed, strife, malice and deceit, gossip and slander, hatred of God, haughtiness and arrogance, vanity and inhospitality."

115. In Greek, *blasphēmia.*

116. See Ps. 119:30 ("path of truth"); Isa. 52:5 ("revilement").

117. See Harrington, "Jude and 2 Peter," p. 262.

118. See Rev. 11:7. *Tartarôsas*, Tartarus (actually a verb, "to send to Tartarus"), is a hapax legomenon: this is the only time in the New Testament that the word is used. The word in Revelation is *abyssos*, the abyss, which itself occurs only twice outside Revelation (it is used seven times in Revelation). In the Gospels, Jesus is never recorded as using either word; he says *geenna*, Gehenna (mainly in Matthew) and, less frequently, *hadês*, Hades.

119. Gen. 19:1–25.

120. Note, for example, Watson, "The Second Letter of Peter," p. 348. It is puzzling to me that an author who has spent so much time on the rhetoric of 2 Peter takes its statements about the opponents at historical face value.

121. See Rom. 8:12–17, 21 with the special coloring of "corruption" (in Greek, *pthora*).

122. Cf. Rom. 6:16; John 8:34.

123. Matt. 7:6; Rev. 22:15.

124. Watson, "The Second Letter of Peter," p. 353.

125. Gerd Theissen, *Fortress Introduction to the New Testament* (Minneapolis, MN: Fortress Press, 2003), p. 141. Similarly Anton Vögtle, *Der Judasbrief / Der 2. Petrusbrief* (Freiburg: Herder, 1994), p. 127. For rebuttals see Martina Janssen, *Unter falschem Namen: Eine kritische Forschungsbilanz urchristlicher Pseudepigraphie* (Frankfurt: Peter Lang, 2003), pp. 182–85, and above, p. 186.

126. In passing I note that to Bauckham, *Jude, 2 Peter*, p. 85, "the whole objection, as formulated in 2 Pet. 3:4, sounds remarkably similar to a famous statement of the modern theologian Rudolf Bultmann, explaining one reason why he was convinced that the message of the New Testament needed to be 'demythologized' in order to be made intelligible to modern people." That is clearly an anachronism that should not be pursued.

127. See Ps. 90:4.

128. Exod. 34:6–7; Ps. 103:8.

129. Syriac Baruch 21:20–21.

130. The Second Coming of Christ will be like a thief in the night: 1 Thess. 5:2; Matt. 24:44; Luke 12:40; Rev. 3:3; 16:15.

131. See Isa. 34:4; 65:17; 66:22.

132. On 1 Clem. 5:4–7 see my *The Acts of the Apostles: What Really Happened in the Earliest Days of the Church* (Amherst, NY: Prometheus Books, 2005), p. 348.

133. A different view appears in Koester, *Introduction to the New Testament*, 2:56 (on 2 Peter), 2:251–53 (on Jude). See also Harrington, "Jude and 2 Peter," p. 161, where he proposes that 2 Peter was written in Rome while Jude was composed in the Holy Land, Syria, or Asia Minor. My suggestion pays more attention to the many literary overlaps in both writings and the probability that both texts attack Paul's pupils.

134. Acts 20:29–30.

135. On Gnosticism see in detail my *Primitive Christianity*, pp. 147–62, 200–203, and appendix 1 in this book, pp. 213–28.

136. See my *Heretics: The Other Side of Christianity* (Louisville, KY: Westminster John Knox Press, 1996), pp. 193–208.

137. See Tertullian *Prescription against Heretics* 41:1–4, 8: (1) "I must not omit an account of the conduct also of the heretics—how frivolous it is, how worldly, how merely human, without seriousness, without authority, without discipline, as suits their creed. (2) To begin with, it is doubtful who is a catechumen, and who a believer; they have all access alike, they hear alike, they pray alike—even heathens, if any such happen to come among them. 'That which is holy they will cast to the dogs, and their pearls,' although (to be sure) they are not real ones, 'they will fling to the swine.' (3) Simplicity they will have to consist in the overthrow of discipline, attention to which on our part they call brothelry Peace also they huddle up anyhow with all comers; (4) for it matters not to them, however different be their treatment of subjects, provided only they can conspire together to storm the citadel of the one only Truth. All are puffed up, all offer you knowledge. Their catechumens are perfect before they are fully taught. The very women of these heretics, how wanton they are! For they are bold enough to teach, to dispute, to enact exorcisms, to undertake cures—it may be even to baptize. Their ordinations are carelessly administered, capricious, changeable. At one time they put novices in office; at another time, men who are bound to some secular employment; at another, persons who have apostatized from us, to bind them by vainglory, since they cannot by the truth. Nowhere is promotion easier than in the camp of rebels, where the mere fact of being there is a foremost service. . . . (8) And so it comes to pass that today one man is their bishop, tomorrow another; today he is a deacon who tomorrow is a reader; today he is a presbyter who tomorrow is a layman. For even on laymen do they impose the functions of priesthood."

Epilogue

INTOLERANCE, GOSPEL, CHURCH

Whoever believes and is baptized will be saved; but whoever does not believe will be condemned.[1]

—"Jesus"

At the Consummation of the World Christ will appear for judgment and will raise up all the dead. He will give to the godly and elect eternal life and everlasting joys, but ungodly men and the devils He will condemn to be tormented without end. They condemn the Anabaptists, who think that there will be an end to the punishments of condemned men and devils.

—Augsburg Confession (1530), Article XVII:
Of Christ's Return to Judgment

THE RESULT OF THE EXEGETICAL INVESTIGATIONS AND VAIN ATTEMPTS AT RELATIVIZING THEM

The authors of the writings examined in the foregoing—presumably leaders of churches between 80 and 140 CE—were shaped by the intolerance of the First Commandment: "I am Yahweh your God, you shall have no other gods beside me." Their conviction of having been specially elected by this god inclined them to a way of thinking that was distinguished from most other faiths by its radical dualism: for them the world was divided into such irreconcilable opposites as truth and lie, light and darkness, good and evil. Accordingly, they were unwilling or unable to accept the inherent right of others to accept, promote, and live by other belief systems. At a time of crisis—approximately between 80 and 140 CE, when the first apostolic generation had vanished with no authority left behind—these people made a desperate attempt to defend their own supposedly intact and holy world. In the process of self-assertion and self-definition they demonized members of their own communities, forbade dialogue with "apostates," falsified writings in the name of what they mistakenly took for a higher purpose, and built walls against the rational search for enlightenment.[2] The author of the Pastorals was especially guilty of equating "correct" belief with obedience, projecting onto the screen of heaven a social fabric based on subordination, and creating a culture of suppression.[3] Above all, the strong bond of exclusive monotheism bound these writers together in a brotherhood they proclaimed but whose destructive spirit they failed to understand: they were indeed the true heirs of Israel.[4] Like their pious Jewish precursors, the sects they represented imbibed from their monolatric faith a fanatical persistence that kept them aloof from the realities of this world and enabled the Christian church to survive until the present day. The intolerance of their gospel yielded for both good and ill a payoff that they could never have imagined.

In view of the negative impression that these writings present to critical readers, progressive theologians often favor what might be termed an in-house criticism (*Sachkritik*). In effect, they attempt to create a cosmetic effect by comparing pseudonymous statements about slaves or women or God—to mention only a few embarrassing points—with the equivalent Pauline texts in order to mitigate or even justify them. Yet such an attempt is not only dishonest, but also doomed to failure from the outset, for Paul had a similarly patriarchal image of God, and when conflict arose his exclusive monotheism likewise culminated in theological totalitarianism. "As a Jewish teacher schooled in the law, Paul could not resist appropriating deuteronomistic policies of segregation and intolerance."[5] Indeed, for him faith was not a free decision, but a matter of foreordained obedience. Unfortunately, as history shows all too clearly, belief in an exclusive monotheistic God produced hierarchic structures that led to destructive effects on the individual and crippling deterrents to any form of democratic government. Like the author of the Pastorals, the apostle was not really concerned about the political freedom of slaves[6] and made no efforts to promote the equality of men and women.[7] He treated his opponents with as much intolerance as the authors we have studied treated theirs. He labels them "false apostles," "deceitful workmen," "servants of Satan," who disguise themselves as servants of righteousness[8]—he even reviles them as "dogs."[9] "No doubt, even Paul the convert would have been capable of violently persecuting such foes, and the apostates too, as enemies of God, if he had only had the power."[10]

Moreover, Paul's sharp rejection of supposedly heretical Christians in his letter to the Romans[11] did much to define the protracted and ruinous witch-hunt directed against heresy.[12] He does not show himself naturally inclined to compassion and forgiveness. At the beginning of Galatians[13] the apostle pronounces against his opponents a conditional curse that, he opines, would destroy them both physically and mentally should it take effect. For a sexual transgression he remands a Christian to Satan to be killed in order that the person's spirit may find salvation in the future world.[14] Indeed, Paul's behavior was for the most part authoritarian.[15] "His status in his own communities was . . . that of a master. He was accustomed to carry out his own will and force it upon others; he laid claim to the authority of an apostle, was always right, and always ready to show his rough side to the less docile members."[16] Occasionally, his attitude was more open than those of the authors of the documents we have examined, but overall one can discern little difference. The upshot of all this is that an in-house criticism of these texts amounts to little more than a whitewash.[17]

THE IMPOSSIBILITY OF BRINGING TOLERANCE INTO HARMONY WITH THE GOSPEL

Having despaired of finding in the New Testament a solid foundation on which to construct a positive relationship between tolerance and gospel, we may be less than surprised to find that the same must be said about the Reformers of the sixteenth century. Contrary to the popular thesis that their understanding of freedom entailed tolerance and freedom of religion, I hasten to remind the reader of their inability to endure other viewpoints, whether religious or nonreligious. Indeed, the idea of tolerance is essentially alien to Luther, Calvin, and the other reformers. Instead, religious tolerance developed among the Humanists[18] and the left-leaning exponents of Reform.[19] Both groups sought to establish a common devotion to tolerance on such New Testament passages as the parable of the weeds and their interpretation of it,[20] but without success. When centuries of ecclesiastical dominion were at last succeeded by the grant of religious freedom, this enactment had to be enforced against the bitter opposition of both the Catholic and the Reformed churches.

It is a sad commentary on the church that after three centuries of promoting religious freedom in the face of persecution,[21] Christian theologians celebrated the church's establishment as the official state religion by denying all others freedom of religion and initiating persecutions that far exceeded what Christians had suffered in the first three centuries. The zeal of the orthodox bishops to destroy paganism found deadly expression in the passion to annihilate heretics inside and outside their own parishes.

Thus, tolerance and intolerance are not directly related to power: it is not necessarily the case that a powerful majority becomes intolerant and those in the minority favor tolerance. Rather, the phenomenon we have seen seems to reflect the nature and structure of the Christian faith. I suggest that the intolerant spirit of the faith, latent in its inherited monotheism, was aggravated and focused by exclusivist claims about Jesus Christ. Surely, intolerance seems to be a characteristic of all religions that proclaim the unity of God, whereas tolerance is mostly at home among polytheistic religions. As Arthur Schopenhauer insightfully observed,

> Indeed, intolerance is essential only to monotheism; an only God is by nature a jealous God who will not allow another to live. On the other hand, polytheistic gods are naturally tolerant; they live and let live. In the first place, they gladly tolerate their colleagues, the gods of the same religion, and this tolerance is afterwards extended even to foreign gods who are, accordingly, hospitably received and later admitted, in some cases, to an equality of rights. An instance of this is seen in the Romans who willingly admitted and respected Phrygian, Egyptian, and other foreign gods. Thus it is only the monotheistic religions that furnish us with the spectacle of religious wars, religious persecutions, courts for trying heretics, and also with that of iconoclasm, the destruction of the images of foreign gods, the demolition of Indian temples and Egyptian colossi that had looked at the sun for

three thousand years; all this because their jealous God had said: "Thou shalt make no graven image," and so on.[22]

Christianity's aggressive proclivity is further attested by the many religiously inspired wars fought by Christian Europeans in total disregard of the exaltation of peace that is a central theme in the New Testament. How, then, can that promised gift of peace ever come to pass? In the twenty-first century we cannot help finding the New Testament answer as unpalatable as it is unambiguous: Jesus Christ will wield the cosmic power implicit in his resurrection by returning from heaven and *forcibly* establishing "the peace of God" on Earth. And that conflicted promise of peace imposed by a supernatural power has misled Christians into claiming the sacred duty to deploy that power against any who so much as express a different understanding of the Gospel they consider a shared gift. Such intolerance must reflect either an innate flaw in human nature or some inherent perverseness of the Christian religion. Since some faith traditions show few if any indications of this self-promoting intolerance, one cannot help but suspect the latter to be the source of the problem. The noted theologian Karl Barth says it quite openly:

> No sentence is more dangerous or revolutionary than that God is One and there is no other like Him. . . . Let this sentence be uttered in such a way that it is heard and grasped, and at once 450 prophets of Baal are always in fear of their lives. There is no more room now for what the recent past called toleration. Beside God there are only His creatures or false gods, and beside faith in Him there are religions only as religions of superstition, error and finally irreligion.[23]

Despite the pious proclamations of some of its champions, the Christian message has not proved to be a source document for freedom, religious or otherwise. Quite the contrary: the tradition that calls its titular founder "the Prince of Peace" has from its inception refused to countenance divergence of opinion. And despite the protestations of ecclesiarchs who covet the good opinion of secular leaders, this is often as true today as it ever was.

In reality, a good deal of latent hypocrisy must infuse any claim of Christian theology or the church to stand in the forefront of those who love freedom. For true tolerance prohibits attaching such speculative criteria as belief in God—let alone a specific creedal formulation—as preconditions for granting freedom and dignity to all human beings; but the jealous Yahweh of the Bible cannot be a party to such creedal liberalism. Acknowledging religious and nonreligious people as partners in an open dialogue whose outcome is equally open cannot be countenanced by a religion whose very essence is the claim to possess an exclusive franchise for the dispensation of salvation and truth.

The counterproposal of this epilogue is modest, but more amenable to the spirit of the present world and eminently more conducive to a safe future for humankind than the absolutist claims of traditional Christianity. Gotthold Ephraim Lessing neatly epitomizes it in what has been called "the most famous of all his sayings":[24]

> Individual worth as a human being does not consist in the truth one possesses, but in the efforts expended to attain that truth; for our powers are amplified not by the possession of truth, but through the search for it. In this pursuit alone does people's ever-growing perfection consist; possession makes us lazy, indolent, and proud.
>   If God held all truth in his right hand and in his left the everlasting striving after truth—even with the proviso that I should always and everlastingly be mistaken—and said to me, "Choose," with humility I would select the left hand and say, "Father, grant me this; absolute truth is for you alone."[25]

NOTES

1. Mark 16:16.
2. "Throughout primitive Christianity there is no trace of any enthusiasm for culture; learning and culture are, fundamentally, without significance for the faith" (Hans von Campenhausen, *Tradition and Life in the Church: Essays and Lectures in Church History* [London: Collins, 1968), p. 29).
3. In passing let me remind the reader that "[t]his biblical morality was one of the great handicaps that the emancipation movement in the United States had to overcome. The opponents of abolition had clear biblical evidence on their side when they argued. As one said in 1857: 'Slavery is of God' (F. Ross, *Slavery Ordained of God* [Philadelphia, 1857], p. 5)" (Morton Smith, "Slavery," in *What the Bible Really Says,* ed. Morton Smith and R. Joseph Hoffmann [Amherst, NY: Prometheus Books, 1989], pp. 145–46).
4. For a fascinating study of the Hebrew Bible's monotheism and its pro-

clivity to violence see Regina M. Schwartz, *The Curse of Cain: The Violent Legacy of Monotheism* (Chicago and London: University of Chicago Press, 1997).

5. Bernhard Lang, "Segregation and Intolerance," in Smith and Hoffmann, *What the Bible Really Says*, p. 133.

6. 1 Cor. 7:21.

7. 1 Cor. 11:2–16.

8. Cf. 2 Cor. 11:13–15.

9. Phil. 3:2.

10. William Wrede, *Paul* (Boston: American Unitarian Association, 1908), p. 32.

11. Rom. 16:17–20.

12. For an Old Testament precursor of witch-hunt see Deuteronomy 13. Yet modern theologians find a way even to adapt to such a text. See Timo Veijola, "Wahrheit und Intoleranz nach Deuteronomium 13," *Zeitschrift für Theologie und Kirche* 92 (1995): 287–314. According to Veijola, "the truth claim of Deut. 13 does not exclude tolerance toward other religions, world-views and their adherents" (p. 314). But since it neither includes nor even fosters such tolerance, I am led to question the truth of Veijola's claim. Would he argue that a person who abstains from hatred thereby demonstrates love?

13. Gal. 1:6, 9.

14. 1 Cor. 5:1–5.

15. 1 Cor. 11:16b.

16. Wrede, *Paul*, pp. 37–38.

17. In passing, let me register my serious doubt as to whether, despite its scholarly respectability, recourse to the historical Jesus can help us to define Christianity anew. For the reasons, see my *Jesus After 2000 Years: What He Really Said and Did* (Amherst, NY: Prometheus Books, 2001), passim and pp. 686–93; and my *The Great Deception* (Amherst, NY: Prometheus Books, 1999), pp. 1–9 ("A Letter to Jesus").

18. See Roland H. Bainton, ed., *Concerning Heretics: Whether they are to be persecuted and How they are to be treated: A Collection of the opinions of learned men both ancient and modern: An anonymous work attributed to Sebastian Castellio* (New York: Columbia: University Press, 1935), with ample documentation.

19. Sebastian Franck (1499–1542) is one of many examples. See, for example, his *280 Paradoxes or Wondrous Sayings*, translated and introduced by E. J. Furcha (Lewiston, NY: Edwin Mellen Press, 1986). He writes, "Everyone without question can be pious by himself, wherever he is, yet no one should run hither and yon to look for, start or seek a special sect, baptism and church in a particular cluster. Nor should he, to please his following, feign faith, piety and servitude" (ibid., p. 9). Franck demanded tolerance not only for all varieties of Christians but also for Jews, Turks, and Gentiles. See Meinulf Barbers, *Toleranz bei Sebastian Franck* (Bonn: Ludwig Röhrscheid Verlag, 1964), pp. 145–56. See also Franck's remark about the heretics in the apostolic age quoted above, p. 26n45.

20. Matt. 13:24–30, 36–43.

21. See Tertullian *To Scapula* 2: "It is a fundamental human right, a privilege of nature, that every man should worship according to his own convictions (in Latin, *humani iuris et naturalis potestatis est unicuique quod putaverit colere*): one man's religion neither harms nor helps another man. It is assuredly no part of religion to compel religion—to which free will and not force should lead us."

22. Arthur Schopenhauer, *Parerga and Paralipomena: Short Philosophical Essays*, vol. 2 (Oxford and New York: Oxford University Press, 1974), pp. 358–59.

23. Karl Barth, *Church Dogmatics*, vol. 2, pt. 1 (Edinburgh: T. & T. Clark, 1957), p. 444.

24. Henry Chadwick, *Lessing's Theological Writings: Selections in Translation with an Introductory Essay* (Stanford, CA: Stanford University Press, 1957), p. 42.

25. Gotthold Ephraim Lessing, "Eine Duplik" (A Rejoinder) (1778). For the English translation I have consulted Gotthold Ephraim Lessing, *Philosophical and Theological Writings*, trans. and ed. H. B. Nisbet (Cambridge and New York: Cambridge University Press, 2005), p. 98, and Chadwick, *Lessing's Theological Writings*, pp. 42–43.

Appendix 1

GNOSTIC EXCERPTS AS A FRAME OF REFERENCE FOR NEW TESTAMENT POLEMICS

All great truths were initially heresies.

—George Bernard Shaw

The analyses of selected New Testament texts that constituted the greater portion of this book focused on the authors' purposes. I sought to discover their intention by precisely tracing their train of thought. Since I dealt for the most part with polemical texts, determining an author's intent necessitated reconstructing the position of those being attacked despite the absence of extant sources. Such a situation is, of course, less than satisfactory. This appendix attempts to make up in part for this deficiency by presenting several original Gnostic texts.[1] To be sure, these documents do not derive directly from those we find under attack in the selected New Testament texts; nevertheless, the topics they address reflect the thinking of the epistle writers' opponents. Moreover, since most of these Gnostic texts come from the second century, they are in close chronological proximity to the New Testament writings under study. And although their authors remain unknown, and in some cases we cannot certify the Christian basis of their teaching, the texts can be related to circles similar to those attacked by our pseudepigraphical writers. Therefore these documents offer a useful window into the world of these "heretics" and a better understanding of the selected New Testament writings.

The primary message of the original Gnostic documents contains two interrelated elements:

On the positive side, the redeemer and the members of the human fellowship who profess him ("those who know") are more powerful than any of the pseudogods or heroes of the Bible—figures who deserve nothing but scorn. Indeed, they even surpass the highest God of the Bible, variously called Jaldabaoth, Samael, or Archigenitor. That deity is guilty of arrogance and blindness, unable, of course, to compete with the Father of the All to whom the Gnostics give praise. Conversely, such scripturally accursed persons as the Sodomites receive all the more honor. In the interpretation of the selected New Testament texts, we encountered this side of Gnosticism in such words as "blaspheme," "godlessness," "denial," "only god," and "unique god."

On the negative side, the Gnostic redeemer—who bears more than one name—has remained undiscovered by the forces of darkness and has not really died. In studying the texts, we encountered this phenomenon under the label "Docetism." This "negative" feature had the paradoxical effect of giving the redeemer and his knowing flock additional strength, for henceforth they are no longer subject, but rather superior to the rule of the creator god and his heavenly entourage, and so effectively able to destroy the hostile powers. Moreover, having spiritually distanced themselves from the material aspects of creation, the Gnostics abstain from certain foods and in many cases from procreation in order to overcome any tendency toward physical regeneration that might redound to the benefit of the creator god.

I have assembled the texts to illustrate each of the aspects mentioned. In order to foster a better comprehension of the texts I have used underlinings, italics, capitals, and boldfaced type.[2] Note that some of the texts seem to have a poetic structure. I have tried to take that into account by printing each verse or stanza in different lines.

POSITIVE ASPECTS OF THE MESSAGE OF GNOSTIC DOCUMENTS

(a) *The good unknown Father of the All is indescribable and surpasses everything*

Letter of Eugnostos[3]

The one who exists is indescribable.
No force knew him,
    nor power,
    nor subjection,
    nor any creature from the foundation of the world,
Except he alone.

That one is immortal, he is eternal, he has no birth.
    <u>For everyone who has a birth will die.</u>
He is unbegotten, he has no beginning.
    <u>For everyone who has a beginning has an end.</u>
No one rules over him. He has no name;
    <u>For whoever has a name is the creation of another.</u>
He is nameless. He has no human form.
    <u>For whoever has human form is the creation of another.</u>

He has his own semblance,
Not like the semblance we have received and seen,
But a strange semblance that surpasses all things and is better than
    the allnesses.
It looks to every side and sees itself from itself.
He is infinite.
He is incomprehensible.
He is one who is ever imperishable.
He is one who does not have his like.
He is unchangeably good.
He is without defect.
He is one who is everlasting.
He is blessed.

He is unknowable, whereas he is accustomed to know himself.
He is immeasurable.
He is undiscoverable.
He is perfect, because he has no defect.
He is imperishably blessed.
He is called "Father of the All."

(b) The heroes of scripture deserve nothing but ridicule, and the Gnostics are superior to them

The Second Treatise of the Great Seth[4]

("Seth" alias "Christ" says:)

For **AN OBJECT OF RIDICULE** was ADAM, and he was created from the image of a pattern of a man *by the Hebdomad* (= Jaldabaoth),[5] as though he had become stronger than me and my brothers. *We are innocent with respect to him, since we did not sin.*

And **OBJECTS OF RIDICULE** were ABRAHAM, and ISAAC and JACOB, since they were given a name *by the Hebdomad*, namely the fathers from the image, as though he had become stronger than me and my brothers. *We are innocent with respect to him, since we did not sin.*

AN OBJECT OF RIDICULE was DAVID, since his son was named the Son of Man,[6] having been activated *by the Hebdomad*, as though he had become stronger than me and the friends of my race. But *we are innocent with respect to him; we did not sin.*

AN OBJECT OF RIDICULE was SOLOMON, since he thought that he was Christ, having become arrogant *through the Hebdomad*, as though he had become stronger than me and my brothers. But *we are innocent with respect to him. I did not sin.*

OBJECTS OF RIDICULE were THE TWELVE PROPHETS, since they have come forth as imitations of the true prophets. They came into being from the image *through the Hebdomad*, as though he had become stronger than me and my brothers. But *we are innocent with respect to him, since we did not sin.*

AN OBJECT OF RIDICULE was MOSES, "a faithful servant,"[7] being named "the friend."[8]

They bore witness concerning him in iniquity, since he never *knew* me.

Neither he nor those before him, from Adam to Moses and John the Baptist, none of them *knew* me, nor my brothers. For a doctrine of angels is what arose through them to keep dietary rules and bitter slavery. They never *knew* truth, nor will they *know* it. For there is a great cloud of deception upon their soul, and they have no ability to find a mind of freedom ever, in order to *know* him, until they come to *know* the Son of Man.

But concerning my Father, I am the one whom the world did not *know*, and on this account, it rose up against me and my brothers.[9]

But we are innocent with respect to him; we did not sin.

AN OBJECT OF RIDICULE was the RULER because he said, "I am God, and there is none greater than me. I alone am the Father, the Lord, and there is no other beside me.[10] I am a jealous God, who brings the sins of the fathers upon the children for three and four generations,"[11] as though he had become stronger than I and my brothers!

But we are innocent with respect to him, for we did not sin.

Though we mastered his *doctrine* in this way, he lives *in conceit, and he does not agree with our Father*. And thus through our friendship we prevailed over his *doctrine*, since he is arrogant *in conceit and he does not agree with our Father*. For he was **AN OBJECT OF RIDICULE** with (his) judgment and false prophecy.

(c) The supreme God of the Bible is blind and arrogant

The Hypostasis of the Archons[12]

Their chief is blind; because of his power and his ignorance and his arrogance he said, with his power, "It is I who am God; there is none apart from me."[13]

When he said this, he sinned against the entirety. And this speech ascended to Incorruptibility; then there was a voice that came forth from Incorruptibility, saying, "You are mistaken, Samael"[14]—which is, "god of the blind."

His thoughts became blind and he expelled his power—that is, the blasphemy he had spoken.

On the Origin of the World[15]

Now when the heavens had consolidated themselves along with their forces and all their administration, the prime parent became insolent. And he was honored by all the army of angels. And all the gods and their angels gave blessing and honor to him. And for his part, he was delighted and continually boasted, saying to them, "I have no need of anyone." He said, "It is I who am God, and there is no other one that exists apart from me."[16]

And when he said this, he sinned against all the immortal beings who gave answer. And they laid it to his charge.

Then when Pistis[17] saw the impiety of the chief ruler, she was filled with anger. She was invisible. She said, "You are mistaken, Samael,"—that is, "blind god." "There is an immortal man of light who has been in existence before you. . . ."

Now when Sabaoth, the son of Yaldabaoth, heard the voice of Pistis, he sang praises to her, and he condemned the father.

Testimony of Truth[18]

But of what sort is this God? First he envied Adam that he should eat from the tree of knowledge. And secondly he said, "Adam, where are you?"[19] And God does not have foreknowledge, since he did not know from the beginning.

And afterward, he said, "Let us cast him out of this place, lest he eat of the tree of life and live forever."[20] Surely he has shown himself to be a malicious envier.

What kind of a God is this? For great is the blindness of those who read, and they did not know it. And he said, "I am the jealous God; I will bring the sins of the fathers upon the children until three (and) four generations."[21] And he said, "I will make their heart thick, and I will cause their mind to become blind, that they might not know nor comprehend the things that are said."[22] But these things he has said to those who believe in him and serve him!

(d) The people of Sodom have a pure heart and a good conscience

The Paraphrase of Shem[23]

(The savior and revealer Derdekeas speaks:)
I shall appear to those who will acquire the thought of the light of the Spirit. For because of them my **Majesty**[24] <u>appeared</u>. When he will have appeared, O Shem, upon the earth, in the place which will be called <u>Sodom</u>, safeguard the insight which I shall give you. For those whose **heart was pure** will congregate to you, because of the word that you will reveal. For when you <u>appear</u> in creation, dark Nature will shake against you, together with the winds and a demon, that they may destroy the insight. But you, proclaim quickly to the <u>Sodomites</u> your universal teaching, for they are your members.

For the demon of human form will part from that place by my will, since he is ignorant. He will guard this utterance. But the <u>Sodomites</u>, according to the will of the **MAJESTY**, will bear witness to the universal testimony. They will rest with a **pure conscience** in the place of their repose, which is the unbegotten Spirit. And as these things will happen, <u>Sodom</u> will be burned unjustly by a wicked Nature. For the evil will not cease in order that your **MAJESTY** may appear there.

NEGATIVE ASPECTS OF THE MESSAGE OF GNOSTIC DOCUMENTS

(a) The savior remained unknown while subjecting all hostile powers[25]

Paraphrase of Shem[26]

(The heavenly redeemer Derdekeas says:)
It is I who opened the eternal gates that are shut from the beginning.

—To those who long for the height of life, and those who are worthy of the repose he revealed them.—
I granted perception to those who are perceptive.
I disclosed to them all the thoughts and the teaching of the righteous ones.
And I did not become their enemy at all.
But I—having endured the <u>wrath</u> of the world—was victorious.

There was not one of them who knew me.
The gates of fire and endless smoke opened against me.
All the winds *rose up against me*.
The thunderings and the lightning-flashes for a time will *rise up against me*.
And they will bring their <u>wrath</u> upon me.
And on account of me, as far as the flesh is concerned, they will rule over each tribe of them.

Apocalypse of Adam[27]

Then the god of the powers will be disturbed, saying, "What is the power of this man who is higher than we?" Then he will arouse a great wrath against that man. And the glory will withdraw and dwell in holy houses that it has chosen for itself. And the powers will not see it with their eyes nor will they see the Illuminator either. Then they will punish the flesh of the man upon whom the Holy Spirit has come.

Apocryphon of John[28]

I, therefore, the perfect Pronoia[29] of the All, changed myself into my seed, For I was (present) first, and went on every way.

For I am the richness of the light, I am the thought of the pleroma.[30]
And I went into the realm of darkness and I endured,
Until *I entered the MIDDLE of* the *prison*.
<u>And the foundations of chaos were shaken.</u>
And I, I hid myself from them because of their wickedness,
And they did not recognize me.

Again I returned for the second time.

I went,

I came forth from those who belong to the light.

—That is what I am: the thought of the Pronoia.—

I went *into the* **MIDDLE** *of darkness and into the inside of the underworld.*

I wanted (to accomplish) my task.

And the foundations of chaos were shaken,

In order to fall down upon those who are in chaos and *destroy* them.

And again I ran up to my root of light, lest they be *destroyed* before the time.

Furthermore, for the third time I went

—I am the light which exists in the light, I am the thought of the Pronoia— In order to enter *into the* **MIDDLE** *of darkness and the inside of the underworld.*

And I filled my face with the light of the completion of their aeon.

And *I entered the* **MIDDLE** *of* the **prison**,

Which is the prison of the body.

Trimorphic Protennoia[31]

But now I have come down and reached down to Chaos. And I was with my own who were in that place. I am hidden within them, empowering them, giving them shape. And from the first day until the day when I will grant mighty glory to those who are mine, I will reveal myself to those who have heard my mysteries, that is, the Sons of the Light.

I am their Father, and I shall tell you a mystery, ineffable and unutterable by any mouth:

Every bond I loosed from you,

And the chains of the demons of the underworld I broke,

—these things which are bound on my members, restraining them—

And the high walls of darkness I overthrew,

And the secure gates of those pitiless ones I broke,

And I smashed their bars,

the evil force,

the one who beats you,
the one who hinders you,
the tyrant,
the adversary,
the one who is King,
the present enemy.

Indeed all these (matters) I explained to those who are mine, who are the Sons of the Light, in order that they might nullify them all, and be saved from all those bonds, and enter into the place where they were at first.

(b) The savior did not really die

Second Treatise of the Great Seth[32]

I was in the jaws of lions.
The plan that they devised about me (led) to the dissolving of **their deception** and their lack of understanding.
I did not give myself up to them as they had planned.
I was not disturbed in any way, although they tormented me.
I did not really die but only in semblance,
So that they would (not) put me to shame through them because these are a part of me.
I was removed from any shame,
I was not anxious in the face of what had happened to me through them.
I was only apparently to become a slave of fear,
But I suffered pain (only) in their sight and thought, so that a word will never be found to speak about them.

For my death, which they think occurred, (happened spiritually) rather to them in **their deception** and their blindness, when they nailed their man unto their death.
For their minds did not see me.
For they were deaf and blind.
And in doing this, they condemned themselves.
Yes, they saw me; they punished me.

It was another, their father, who drank the gall and the vinegar; it was not I.

They struck me with the reed.

It was another who bore the cross on his shoulder, Simon.

It was another upon whose head they placed the crown of thorns.

But I was high above them, rejoicing
> in the (apparent) wealth of the rulers
> and the seed of their deception,
> and their vain glory.

And I was laughing at their ignorance.

And I set at naught all their powers.

For when I came downward, no one saw me.

For I was altering my shapes, changing from one appearance to an(other) appearance.

And therefore, when I was at their gates, I assumed their likeness.

And I passed them by quietly, and I saw the places, and I did not fear and was not ashamed, for I was undefiled.

And I was speaking with them, mingling with them through those who are mine, and I trod on those who out of envy were harsh to them.

And I quenched the fire.

And I did all these things in my determination to accomplish what I desired by the will of the Father above.

Apocalypse of Peter[33]

The Savior said to me, "The one whom you see above alongside the cross, joyful and laughing, is the living Jesus. But the one into whose hands and feet nails are driven is his bodily part, which is the substitute. *They put to shame* this one, which came into being in his likeness. But look at him and me."

And after I had looked, I said, "Lord, no one sees you. Let us flee from this place."

But he said to me, "I have told you that they are blind. Depart from them. And see, they do not know what they are saying. For the son of their glory *they have put to shame* instead of my servant."

And I saw how someone was about to approach us, who resembled him, and how the one who was by the cross laughed. And he was *full* of the Holy Spirit, and he is (was) the Savior. And there was a great, *ineffable* light around them, and the multitude of *ineffable* and invisible angels _praising_ them. And it was I who saw when he was revealed as the one to whom _praise_ was given.

(c) The Gnostics distance themselves from creation and procreation

Testimony of Truth[34]

I will speak to those who know to hear not with the ears of the body but with the ears of the mind.

For many have sought after the **TRUTH** and have not been able to find it; because there has taken hold of them the old leaven of the Pharisees and the scribes of the Law. And the leaven is the errant desire of the angels and the demons and the stars. The Pharisees and the scribes are those who belong to the Rulers who have authority over them. For no one who is under the Law[35] will be able to look up to the **TRUTH**, for they wil
l not be able to serve two masters.[36]

For the **defilement** of the Law is manifest; but **undefilement** belongs to the _light_. The Law commands (one) to take a husband (or) to take a wife, and to beget, to multiply (and become) like the sand of the seashore.[37] But passion, which is a delight to them, constrains the souls of those who are begotten in this place, those who **defile** and those who are **defiled**, in order that the Law might be fulfilled through them.

And they (the passions) show that they are assisting the world; and they turn away from the _light,_ who are unable to pass by the Ruler of darkness until they pay the last penny.[38]

But the Son of Man came forth from Imperishability, being alien to **defilement**. He came to the world by the _Jordan_ River, and immediately the _Jordan_ turned back. And John bore witness to the descent of Jesus.[39] For he is the one who saw the power which came down upon the _Jordan_ River;[40] for he knew that the dominion of carnal procreation had come to an end. The Jordan River is the power of the body, that is, the senses of pleasures. The water of the *Jordan* is the desire for sexual intercourse. John is the Ruler of the womb.

And this is what the Son of Man reveals to us: It is fitting for you (pl.) to receive the word of **TRUTH**, if one will receive it perfectly.

NOTES

1. On the term "Gnosticism," the usefulness of which as a descriptive category has been recently questioned, see my *Primitive Christianity: A Survey of Recent Studies and Some New Proposals* (London: T & T Clark, 2003), pp. 147–62, 200–203 ("On the Problem of Pre-Christian Gnosticism"). There and in this appendix I use the term not to delineate a movement but to designate a specific myth (see also above, p. 197). Unfortunately some commentators—even those who should know better—have adduced that the book by Carsten Colpe, *Die religionsgeschichtliche Schule. Darstellung und Kritik ihres Bildes vom gnostischen Erlösermythos* (Göttingen: Vandenhoeck & Ruprecht, 1961), quite contrary to his intentions, challenges the existence of a pre-Christian Gnosticism. Consider the following two examples, each coming from a master in the field. (a) Christoph Markschies, *Gnosis: An Introduction* (London: T & T Clark, 2003), writes that Colpe in his book has refuted the classical theses of the "history-of-religions-school" (p. 134). Yet as indicated by Colpe's subtitle—*A Description and Critique of Its Image of a Gnostic Redeemer Myth* (Darstellung und Kritik ihres Bildes vom gnostischen Erlösermythos)—he dealt with one specific issue. Moreover, Colpe rejects the thesis that Gnosticism included the redeemer figure only as a result of Christian influence (p. 207) and speaks highly of the achievement of the "history-of-religions-school" in research on Gnosticism. (b) A whole section on Colpe's book appears in Karen L. King, *What Is Gnosticism?* (Cambridge: Harvard University Press, 2003), pp. 141–47. King skillfully describes Colpe's reasons for rejecting Richard Reitzenstein's construction of a Gnostic redeemer myth based on Iranian texts that subsequently made its way to the West. Colpe's successful refutation of Reitzenstein leads her to claim, "Credit for the final demise of the pre-Christian redeemer myth belongs primarily to the German history of religions scholar Carsten Colpe. . . . Colpe brought the results of recent scholarship in Iranian studies to bear on the work of Reitzenstein, Bousset, and others. The results proved to be devastating" (p. 141).—I hasten to add that the linguistic foundations of the Iranian part of Colpe's book received a devastating critique by Geo Widengren, in *Orientalistische Literaturzeitung* 58 (1963): 533–48, and he never completed the two additional volumes to which he repeatedly referred. Volume 2 is, for example, more

than sixty times quoted. Be that as it may, a more balanced reference to Colpe's famous but virtually unread book from 1961 is called for. In this regard see Carsten Colpe, *Iranier—Aramäer—Hebräer—Hellenen: Iranische Religionen und ihre Westbeziehungen. Einzelstudien und Versuch einer Zusammenschau* (Tübingen: J. C. B. Mohr/ Paul Siebeck, 2003). In future discussions of "gnosticism"— which ought to focus more on texts than on definitions—we would do well to heed Jacob Burckhardt's observation: "History is actually the most unscientific of all the sciences, although it communicates so much that is worth knowing. Clear-cut concepts belong to logic, not history, where everything is in a state of flux, of perpetual transition and combination. Philosophical and historical ideas differ in essence and origin; the former must be as firm and exclusive as possible, the latter as fluid and open" (Jacob Burckhardt, *Reflections on History* [London: George Allen & Unwin, 1943], p. 74).—See now Antti Marjanen, ed., *Was There a Gnostic Religion?* (Helsinki: Finnish Exegetical Society, 2005).

2. In order to facilitate a smooth reading of the texts, I have not indicated where words have been inserted to compensate for lacunae in the manuscript. For one thing, the Coptic originals of the various texts are in relatively good shape. For another, painstaking use of linguistic and contextual clues has enabled scholars to provide highly likely reconstructions of the original Coptic text.

3. NHC III, 70:1–90:12. Translation after Gerd Lüdemann and Martina Janssen, *Suppressed Prayers: Gnostic Spirituality in Early Christianity* (Harrisburg, PA: Trinity Press International, 1998), p. 18. Under the heading "The Unknown Father" in chapter 1 of that book (pp. 17–38) and in the section "Additional Material" (pp. 124–28) more Gnostic texts on the same or a similar topic are collected.

4. NHC VII, 62:27–65:1. Translation, for the most part, after Gregory Riley, in *Nag Hammadi Codex VII*, ed. Birger A. Pearson (Leiden: Brill, 1996), pp. 181–87. Following Kurt Rudolph, *Gnosis: The Nature and History of Gnosticism* (San Francisco: Harper & Row, 1983), pp. 147–48, I have imitated the Coptic syntax by always leaving "an object of ridicule" (or, "a laughingstock") at the beginning of each section.

5. See Irenaeus *Against All Heresies* 1.30 where Irenaeus gives a detailed account of the cosmogony of the group in which the text printed above had its origin. The date of the composition of Irenaeus's work—180 CE—is the terminus ad quem of the texts from this group of Gnostics.

6. See the specification of Jesus as "Son of David" (Mark 12:35; Matt. 1:1) and "Son of Man" (Mark 2:28, etc.).

7. Heb. 3:5.

8. James 2:23.

9. The indented section is clearly secondary. The attestation of innocence ("But we are innocent with respect to him. We have not sinned") picks up the traditional piece again.

10. Isa. 45:5.

11. Exod. 20:5; 34:7.

12. NHC II, 86:27–87:7. Translation after Bentley Layton, in *Nag Hammadi Codex II,2–7*, vol. 1, ed. Bentley Layton (Leiden: Brill, 1989), pp. 234–37.

13. Isa. 45:5.

14. A Jewish name for the devil.

15. NHC II, 103:3–34. Translation after Hans-Gebhard Bethge, Bentley Layton, and the Societas Coptica Hierosolymitana, in Layton, *Nag Hammadi Codex II,2–7*, vol. 2 , pp. 40–43.

16. Cf. Isa. 45:5.

17. In the mythological system of the Sethians "Pistis" or "Sophia" is the mother of Jaldabaoth.

18. NHC IX, 47:14–48:15. Translation after S. Giversen and Birger A. Pearson, in, ed., *Nag Hammadi Codices IX and X*, ed. Birger A. Pearson (Leiden: Brill, 1981), pp. 162–67.

19. Gen. 3:9.

20. Gen. 3:22.

21. Exod. 20:5.

22. Isa. 6:10.

23. NHC VII, 28:31–29:33. Translation after Frederik Wisse, in *Nag Hammadi Codex VII*, ed. Birger A. Pearson (Leiden: Brill, 1996), pp. 84–87.

24. This is a description of God. The Coptic translation uses the Greek noun *megethos* (in English, "greatness") as a loan word.

25. In passing let me emphasize that the first two texts—from the *Paraphrase of Shem* and the *Apocalypse of Adam*—reflect a Gnosticism that shows no Christian influence. While thus witnessing to the existence of a pre-Christian Gnostic myth, the texts themselves do not necessarily predate the beginnings of Christianity; but this, of course, cannot be adduced as evidence that Gnosticism is chronologically younger than Christianity. Bluntly put, unless one can show that Christian elements were removed from these and other texts at a later stage, they attest the existence of a pre-Christian Gnostic myth.

26. NHC VII, 36:2–24. Translation after Frederik Wisse, in Pearson, *Nag Hammadi Codex VII*, pp. 99–101. I have indicated by the textual format that the passage is poetical and must be divided into two parts. See also the underlining and italics in the text. Line two is a parenthesis possibly added by a later reader of the document.

27. NHC V, 77:4–18. Translation after George MacRae, in *Nag Hammadi Codices V, 2–5 and VI with Papyrus Berolinensis 8502, 1 and 4*, ed. Douglas M. Parrott (Leiden: Brill, 1979), pp. 177–79. On the *Apocalypse of Adam* see especially Birger A. Pearson, *The Emergence of the Christian Religion: Essays on Early Christianity* (Harrisburg, PA: Trinity Press International, 1997), pp. 135–44.

28. NHC II, 30.11–31.4. Translation after Lüdemann and Janssen, *Suppressed Prayers*, pp. 59–60.

29. The Coptic uses the Greek word *pronoia*, which means "forethought" or "providence."

30. Pleroma (from the Greek, *plêrôma*)—literally, "fullness"—is the designation of the heavenly world.

31. NHC XIII, 40.29–41.19. Translation after John D. Turner, in *Nag Hammadi Codices XI, XII, XIII*, ed. Charles W. Hedrick (Leiden: Brill, 1990), pp. 412–15.

32. NHC VII, 55.9–57.7 Translation Lüdemann and Janssen, *Suppressed Prayers*, pp. 72–73. See further Klaus Koschorke, *Die Polemik der Gnostiker gegen das kirchliche Christentum* (Leiden: Brill, 1978), pp. 44–48 ("Gnostische Polemik gegen die Verkündigung des Gekreuzigten").

33. NHC VII, 81.15–82.16. Translation after Lüdemann and Janssen, *Suppressed Prayers*, p. 160.

34. NHC IX, 29:6–31:10. Translation after Giversen and Pearson, in Pearson, *Nag Hammadi Codices IX and X*, pp. 122–27.

35. See Rom. 6:14; 1 Cor. 9:20; Gal. 4:4, 5, 21.

36. See Matt. 6:24.

37. See Gen. 1:28; 8:17; 9:1; 13:16, etc.

38. Cf. Matt. 5:26.

39. Cf. John 1:7,15, 32, 34.

40. Cf. Matt. 3:13–17.

Appendix 2

LUSTING AFTER MARTYRDOM:
BISHOP IGNATIUS OF ANTIOCH

INTRODUCTION

As he was being transported to Rome early in the second century
CE, Bishop Ignatius of Antioch wrote seven letters to various
congregations. While serving as bishop of the church of Antioch, he
had been imprisoned and sentenced to death. Yet neither his own community nor any of the Asian congregations with which he had contact
during his journey to Rome were molested by Roman authorities. The
apparent reason for his imprisonment and sentence was the confession
by which the bishop "handed himself over to death,"[1] a document that
may have referred generally to his preaching or specifically to his inter-
rogation before a Roman officer.

One of his letters is directed to the church in Rome. In it Ignatius
writes about the martyrdom that he intensely longs for and his ardent
desire to attain God and/or Jesus Christ soon. Although this is typical
of the mentality of early Christians in a situation of imminent martyrdom,[2] Ignatius does not make his attitude a norm for every Christian. Above all, this letter helps us understand the quandary facing
Roman governors who, though far from eager to execute Christians,
had to deal with people like Ignatius who would do everything to attain
death.[3]

Below I have selected Ignatius's most telling remarks about the martyrdom he yearned for. Walter Bauer may have had a point in urging us
to be circumspect in evaluating the bishop's protestations, for Ignatius

"in his exuberance time and again loses all sense of proportion."[4] Yet, the texts presented below speak for themselves and need only a few explanations. Their formal and somewhat convoluted rhetoric must not obscure the fact that they are the words of a person who is eager for a bloody martyrdom. One ought not to explain this away by saying that Ignatius's only desire was to fulfill God's will,[5] for he mentions his wish to suffer martyrdom as often as he invokes the will of God. Besides, there is no contradiction here. Obviously the Christian who wants to die as a martyr considers this to be God's will, and only in such a way will he or she receive the heavenly reward. In short, "the charge of fanaticism is not entirely without foundation in the case of Ignatius."[6]

SELECTED TEXTS ON IGNATIUS'S PASSION FOR MARTYRDOM[7]

Ignatius writes to the Christian community of Rome:

(1:1) By my prayer to God I have *attained* my wish to see your God-pleasing faces—as indeed I have asked to receive even more. For as a prisoner in Christ Jesus I hope to greet you, if it be the will of the one who has judged me worthy until the end. (1:2) For the beginning is auspicious if I *attain* the grace to obtain my lot unimpeded. For I fear your love precisely lest it may do me harm. For it is easy for you to do what you want, but it is hard for me **to *attain* GOD**, if you do not spare me.

(2:1) For I do not want you to please people but to please God, as indeed you are doing. For I shall never have such an opportunity **to *attain* GOD**, nor can you, if you keep silent, be credited with a better work. For if you remain silent and let me be, I shall be a word of God; but if you love my flesh, I shall again be a mere noise. (2:2) Grant me nothing more than to be poured out as a libation for God while an altar is still at hand, that by becoming a chorus in love, you may sing to the Father in Jesus Christ because God judged the bishop of Syria worthy to be found at the sun's setting having sent him from where it rises. It is good to set off from the world to God, that I may rise up to him.

COMMENT

Ignatius must fear lest the love of the Roman church may do him harm by purchasing or otherwise arranging for his release from imprisonment (1:2). He wishes at all costs to avoid that eventuality, for he lusts for martyrdom in order to attain God and Jesus Christ.

(4:1) I write to all the churches, and give instructions to all that I die willingly for God unless you hinder me. I exhort you: do not become an untimely kindness for me; let me be the food for the wild beasts; through them it is possible **to *attain* God.** I am the wheat of God and I am ground by the teeth of wild beasts in order that I may be found the pure bread of Christ. (4:2) Rather, coax the wild beasts that they may become my tomb and leave behind no part of my body that I, falling asleep, may burden no one. Then I shall truly be a disciple of Jesus Christ, when the world will not even see my body. Petition Christ on behalf of me that through these instruments of God I may be found a sacrifice of God (...)

(5:1) From Syria to Rome I am fighting the wild beasts, through land and sea, night and day, bound to ten leopards—that is, a company of soldiers—who when treated well become worse. By their mistreatment I become more of a disciple, but "not for that reason I am justified."[8] (5:2) May I have the full pleasure of the wild beasts prepared for me; I pray they will be found ready for me. Indeed, I will coax them to devour me quickly—not as with some whom they were too timid to touch; and should they not consent voluntarily, I shall force them.[9] (5:3) Grant this to me; I know what is to my advantage: Now I am beginning to be a disciple. May nothing of things visible and invisible envy me, in order that **I *attain* Jesus Christ.** Fire and cross, and packs of wild beasts, the wrenching of bones, the mangling of limbs, the grinding of my whole body, evil punishments of the devil—let them come on me, only in order that **I *attain* Jesus Christ.**[10]

(6:1) Neither the ends of the world nor the kingdoms of this age are of profit to me. It is better for me to die in Jesus Christ[11] than to rule the ends of the earth. I seek him who died for us. I want him who arose for our sake. The pains of birth[12] are on me. (6:2) Indulge me, brothers: do not prevent me from living,[13] do not want me to die,[14] do not give to the world one who wants to be God's, nor deceive him by what is material. Allow me to receive the pure light—when I am there, I shall be a human being (. . .)

NOTES

1. Ignatius *To the Smyrneans* 4.2.

2. According to earliest Christian traditions all true disciples—in freely accepting suffering or martyrdom—participate in the future glory of Christ: Mark 10:37–40; Rom. 8:17; 2 Tim. 2:12a; 1 Pet. 4:13; 5:1; Rev. 20:4, 6.

3. See above, pp. 50–51.

4. Walter Bauer, *Orthodoxy and Heresy in Earliest Christianity* (Philadelphia: Fortress Press, 1971), p. 61.

5. Thus Christel Butterweck, *"Martyriumssucht" in der Alten Kirche?* (Tübingen: J. C. B. Mohr/Paul Siebeck, 1995), p. 16.

6. William R. Schoedel, *Ignatius of Antioch: A Commentary on the Letters of Ignatius of Antioch* (Philadelphia: Fortress Press, 1985), p. xii.

7. For the translations I have consulted Schoedel, *Ignatius of Antioch*, passim, and Bart D. Ehrman, ed., *The Apostolic Fathers I*, Loeb Classical Library, vol. 24 (Cambridge, MA: Harvard University Press, 2003), pp. 201–321.

8. 1 Cor. 4:4.

9. Eusebius *Ecclesiastical History* 5.1.42 notes a refusal by the animals to kill a victim.

10. For the structure of the sentence cf. Rom. 8:38–39.

11. Cf. Phil. 1:21–23.

12. "The pains of birth" here means to start the process of dying.

13. "Living" here means to suffer martyrdom.

14. "To die" here means *not* to suffer execution.

Appendix 3

THE PROBLEM OF FALSE ATTRIBUTIONS IN NEW TESTAMENT WRITINGS

As a young student attending a series of lectures by a celebrated liberal Old Testament theologian, I learned that Moses had not written Deuteronomy, the so-called Fifth Book of Moses. Although it claims throughout to have been spoken and indeed been written down by the great lawgiver, it was in fact composed some seven centuries later to serve a contemporary and quite specific purpose. Since I came from a strictly orthodox Lutheran family, I was deeply moved and not a little troubled by what I heard, in particular because it was entirely persuasive. Accordingly, that same day I sought out my teacher during his office hours, and in the course of discussion let slip the question, "So is the Fifth Book of Moses what might be called a forgery?" His answer was, "For God's sake! It may well be, but you can't say things like that."[1]

—Friedrich Delitzsch

THE STATE OF RESEARCH

It was not until thirty years ago that the investigation of pseudepigraphy (false attribution) in the ancient world became a serious pursuit of critical scholars. Milestones in this effort were the anthology by Kurt von Fritz[2] and the thesaurus by Wolfgang Speyer.[3] In addition, several volumes by Norbert Brox[4] have summarized and applied to ancient Christian texts the conclusions thus far arrived at, and Martina Janssen[5] has recently published a comprehensive history of research, a work that provides a reliable basis for further investigation.

233

ON THE CONSCIOUSNESS OF INTELLECTUAL PROPERTY IN THE GRECO-ROMAN WORLD

The net impact of this considerable research on the present study is of central importance, for it demonstrates beyond cavil that ancient authors were far from indifferent to matters involving intellectual deception and falsification. Moreover, those of the Greek and Roman intelligentsia, though lacking the sophistication of modern critics, had developed clear criteria by which to uncover fraud. Let me first offer the example of the great physician Galen of Pergamum, and after that two further citations. All three will demonstrate that if writers of literary works intended for an educated audience knowingly employed false attribution or deliberately falsified a text, they were considered guilty of a malfeasance.[6]

In *My Own Books* Galen reports the following incident:

> I was recently in the Sandalarium (= sandal-makers' street), the area of Rome with the largest concentration of booksellers, where I witnessed a dispute as to whether a certain book for sale was by me or someone else. The book bore the title: *Galen the doctor*. Someone had bought the book under the impression that it was one of mine, someone else—a man of letters—struck by the odd form of the title, desired to know the book's subject. On reading the first two lines he immediately tore up the inscription, saying simply: "This is not Galen's language—the title is false." Now, the man in question had received only the basic education that Greek children were always given by teachers of grammar and rhetoric.[7]

A little later Galen complains:

> My books have been subject to all sorts of mutilations, whereby people in different countries publish (literally, "read") different texts under their own names, with all sorts of cuts, additions, and alterations.[8]

COMMENT

Concerning false attributions Galen's report allows us to draw three conclusions:

(a) People of even moderate education learned enough of what we would call style-criticism to enable them to distinguish genuine from false writings.

(b) Plagiarism, that is, spreading someone else's ideas under one's own name, was considered wrong.

(c) Pseudepigraphy, that is, publishing one's own ideas under someone else's name, was not acceptable.

Two episodes from *The Lives of Eminent Philosophers* by the Greek writer Diogenes Laertius in the third century CE shed further light on the general disapprobation of false attribution and plagiarism.

Lives of Eminent Philosophers 5.92–93

Aristoxenus the musician asserts that Heraclides also composed tragedies, inscribing upon them the name of Thespis. Chamaeleon complains that Heraclides' treatise on the work of Homer and Hesiod was plagiarized from his own. Furthermore, Autodorus the Epicurean criticizes him in a polemic against his tract *Of Justice*. Again, Dionysius the Renegade, or, as some people call him, the "Spark," when he wrote the *Parthenopaeus*, entitled it a play of Sophocles; and Heraclides, such was his credulity, in one of his own works drew upon this forged play as Sophoclean evidence. Dionysius, on perceiving this, confessed what he had done; and . . . the other denied the fact and would not believe him.[9]

The examination of both the authenticity and completeness of writings was a daily task for the librarians of such great libraries of antiquity as Pergamum and Alexandria, to mention only these two. Athenodor, the head librarian of the library of Pergamum, got himself into trouble by altering Stoic writings. Diogenes Laertius gives this report:

Lives of Eminent Philosophers 7.34

Isidore of Pergamum . . . likewise affirms that the passages disproved by the school were expunged from his works by Athenodorus the Stoic, who was in charge of the Pergamene library; and that afterward, when Athenodorus was detected and compromised, they were replaced.[10]

ON THE PROBLEM OF INTELLECTUAL PROPERTY IN THE OLD TESTAMENT AND THE JEWISH SPHERE

When we compare it to the literary meticulousness of the Greco-Roman world, Hebrew literature shows a lack of development in awareness of intellectual property, commitment to historical truth, and sense of authorial individuality. In fact, the literature of what later became the Old Testament was for the most part tradition-literature rather than author-literature. Even the books of the prophets were constantly reworked by their disciples and by later theological schools.[11] And not only is the same true for the panoramic history that stretches from 1 Samuel to 2 Kings,[12] but the Chronicler's account is ultimately a further commentary on those narratives,[13] for he is engaged in the same task as that of his prophetic and historical predecessors: rewriting earlier proclamations or accounts to suit the needs of the present generation.[14] To be sure, it sometimes appears that when the reworking of earlier accounts produced contradictions too obvious to overlook, the author-redactor felt obliged to observe some elementary literary scruples. That suspicion gains credence especially if, as is widely accepted, the original text of Deuteronomy (= Ur-Deuteronomy)[15] was discovered in the Temple as the report in 2 Kings 22–23 suggests. For that can mean only that priests had written it and then either staged or simply claimed its discovery before handing it on to King Josiah.[16] In this same vein, one may reasonably wonder why this particular piece of Old Testament literature repeats the so-called "canon formula" of Deut. 4:2a at 13:1,[17] which resurfaces in Rev. 22:18–19 with its dire threats against any who add to or subtract from the received words (of God). Obviously two canons of truth, the religious and the intellectual, collide here. Yet most parts of the Old Testament and many Jewish sources recognize only one of these principles and remain oblivious to or unaware of the other. That basic fact makes it extremely difficult for the critical scholar to relate to these writings, let alone establish meaningful dialogue with people who take seriously the historical accuracy of these "holy" texts.

Be that as it may, the necessity of arriving at interpretive conclusions concerning falsely attributed documents cannot be avoided, even when their authors may be lacking in historical reliability or truthfulness. This is especially the case because many of these very authors are in the habit of asserting their own truthfulness while warning against the forgeries of others. Thus their reliability is doubly undermined, for they not only show themselves untrustworthy, but also hypocritically proclaim the untrustworthiness of others who are playing the same game.

THE RELEVANCE OF THE PROBLEM OF BIBLICAL PSEUDEPIGRAPHY AND AN EXAMPLE OF THEOLOGICAL EVASION

In this book I have used the tools of the historical-critical method to examine each of the selected pseudepigraphic New Testament writings separately, and thereby have tried to determine their historical settings and their aims. But of course a rigorous application of this methodology is subject to the theological objection that these writings should be examined differently from noncanonical texts. And even if the criterion of canonicity is rejected as false or irrelevant, and historical criticism is considered to be an indispensable tool for examining Holy Scripture, the canonical texts are almost inevitably accorded special status. Indeed, theologians who feel obliged to remain loyal to the confessions of their church are often unwilling to address forthrightly the phenomenon of false attributions in the New Testament. I consider it worthwhile to demonstrate this by looking at a highly regarded continental *Introduction to the New Testament*[18]—a book whose appearance in English Hans Dieter Betz of the University of Chicago hailed on the back cover as a "wonderful introduction by one of the best young continental scholars."

Udo Schnelle writes,

> New Testament pseudepigraphy was . . . related to a very particular historical situation, and must be seen as a successful attempt of the third Christian generation's struggle to overcome its central problems. The goal of New Testament pseudepigraphy consisted not only in establishing the continuity of the apostolic tradition in the time after the death of the apostles. Rather the authority of the apostle was above all to be brought to bear in new words and language for the present. By appealing to the origins of the tradition, the authors grounded their claim to the binding authority of their new interpretations directed to the new problems that had arisen in the present. The sec-

ondary attribution to authors of the past thus always testifies to the significance of the primary authors![19]

Rebuttal: While I agree that various New Testament writings successfully used pseudepigraphy as a means of dealing with local problems, Schnelle does not pay enough attention to the fact that the "opponents" attacked in these writings used the same means unsuccessfully.[20] Thus pseudepigraphy was not always effective in overcoming problems faced by Christian groups at the end of the first century precisely because, formally speaking, the "opponents" used pseudepigraphy with the same aim as the New Testament authors! Moreover, the phenomenon of pseudepigraphy can hardly be limited to the third Christian generation. 2 Peter clearly belongs to the fourth or fifth generation, and we have "orthodox" pseudepigraphic writings from an even later time (3 Corinthians; on it see appendix 4).

At this point one may ask how Schnelle deals with the admitted falsity of attribution we find in pseudepigraphic writings. On this he writes,

> A theological evaluation of the phenomenon of pseudepigraphy may not have as its starting point the ethical categories of deceit and fraud, but must take into consideration the internal connection between the historical situation and the phenomenon of New Testament pseudepigraphy. In the last third of the first century, the literary form of pseudepigraphy was the most effective means of addressing and resolving the problems that had newly arisen as the authors of the pseudepigraphical documents interpreted them from the point of view of the past authorities they claimed to represent. The ethical category of "fraud" is therefore inappropriate as a way of grasping the phenomenon of [New Testament] pseudepigraphy. It is better to speak of "adopted authorial designations" in which the apostolic authority steps forward as a guarantor for the validity of what is said. New Testament pseudepigrapha must be seen as the theologically legitimate and ecclesiologically necessary attempt to preserve the apostolic tradition in a changed situation, at the same time giving the necessary response to new situations and questions. This is why the characteristic perspective of the pseudepigraphical writings is that of the whole church, for they originated out of a sense of ecumenical responsibility.[21]

Rebuttal: Here Schnelle's protestations are basically similar to those in the previous quotation, but this time he introduces the category "theological" at the very outset, thereby possibly implying that other kinds of evaluation might be used—and that they might produce a different result. In a further assault on simple logic, he claims that what the authors of the pseudepigraphic texts did was theologically justified (for it served an ecumenical purpose), but he fails to explain why the similarly intended attempts of the Pauline opponents were not equally legitimate. In other words, Schnelle's transparent purpose is to justify the status quo of the New Testament writings in question. Thus what his book most clearly demonstrates is that a "theologically" oriented approach does not lead to any new results. Theology in his case means simply conservatism on the basis of the canon. By a preemptive exclusion of the categories of deceit and fraud he determines in advance what conclusions a theologian is or is not allowed to reach. For example, Schnelle summarily excludes the thesis earlier examined[22] that the author of 2 Thessalonians intended to paint 1 Thessalonians as a forgery, and his only "proof" is the indignant quip, "This is an action [with] which a New Testament author ought not to be charged!"[23] Nowhere does his theological prejudice show more clearly than when in the first of the above quotations he argues, in effect, that fraud was effective and its effectiveness justified its use.[24]

RESULT

A theological approach to the study of pseudepigraphical texts offers little if any insight into the problems they pose, and no new knowledge.

NOTES

1. Friedrich Delitzsch, *Die grosse Täuschung. Kritische Betrachtungen zu den alttestamentlichen Berichten über Israels Eindringen in Kanaan, die Gottesoffenbarungen vom Sinai und die Wirksamkeit der Propheten* (Stuttgart: Deutsche Verlagsanstalt, 1920), pp. 5–6. On Delitzsch's anti-Semitism, which is not the issue here, see my *Heretics: The Other Side of Christianity* (Louisville, KY: Westminster John Knox Press, 1996), p. 279n350.

2. Kurt von Fritz, ed., *Pseudepigrapha* (Bern: A. Francke, 1972).

3. Wolfgang Speyer, *Die literarische Fälschung im Altertum. Ein Versuch ihrer Deutung* (Munich: Beck, 1971).

4. Norbert Brox, *Falsche Verfasserangaben. Zur Erklärung der frühchristlichen Pseudepigraphie* (Stuttgart: Katholisches Bibelwerk, 1975); Brox, ed., *Pseudepigraphie in der heidnischen und jüdischen Antike* (Darmstadt: Wissenschaftliche Buchgesellschaft, 1977).

5. Martina Janssen, *Unter falschem Namen. Eine kritische Forschungsbilanz frühchristlicher Pseudepigraphie* (Frankfurt: Peter Lang, 2003), pp. 128–51 (on Brox).

6. Compare with this the statement in Annette Merz's thorough study, *Die fiktive Selbstauslegung des Paulus. Intertextuelle Studien zur Intention und Rezeption der Paulusbriefe* (Göttingen: Vandenhoeck & Ruprecht, 2004), p. 198: "An acceptance of pseudepigraphy can be found in antiquity only and sporadically among physicians and philosophers (e.g., Pythagoreans and Epicureans) who justify writings of pupils in the name of the master. Yet, I would stress more that this is according to the sources already a reaction to the results of investigations of authenticity which in turn reinforces the general reservations to writing with a false name."

7. Translation following P. N. Singer, *Galen: Selected Works: Translated with an Introduction and Notes* (Oxford: Oxford University Press, 1997), p. 3.

8. Ibid.

9. Translation based on R. D. Hicks, Loeb Classical Library, *Diogenes Laertius I* (London: William Heinemann, 1925), p. 547.

10. Translation based on R. D. Hicks, Loeb Classical Library, *Diogenes Laertius II* (London: William Heinemann, 1925), p. 145.

11. The most obvious example of editing a prophetic book can be seen in the multistaged additions made to Isaiah 1–39 by later theological schools and commonly referred to as Deutero Isaiah (Isa. 40–55) and Trito Isaiah (Isa. 56–66). Meanwhile the original document was expanded by such additions as the "small apocalypse" of chapters 24–27 and the legendary material in chapters 36–37 (cf. 2 Kings 18:13–19:37). For further details see Reinhard G. Kratz, *Die Propheten Israels* (Munich: C. H. Beck, 2002), pp. 41–51.

12. See Reinhard Gregor Kratz, *The Composition of the Narrative Books of the Old Testament* (London: T & T Clark, 2005), pp. 153–215.

13. Cf. ibid., pp. 7–93.

14. "It must be allowed that the Chronicles owes its origin, not to the arbitrary caprice of an individual, but to a general tendency of its period. It is the inevitable product of the conviction that the Mosaic law is the starting-point of Israel's history, and that in it there is operative a play of sacred forces such as finds no other analogy; this conviction could not but lead to a complete transformation of the ancient tradition" (Julius Wellhausen, *Prolegomena to the History of Ancient Israel* [New York: Meridian Books, 1957], p. 224).

15. On the hypothesis of the existence of Ur-Deuteronomy see above, p. 32.

16. For the details of Deuteronomy's discovery under Josiah in 622 BCE and parallel discovery-accounts of other sacred books from antiquity to modern times (e.g., the book of Mormon), see my *The Unholy in Holy Scripture: The Dark Side of the Bible* (Louisville, KY: Westminster John Knox Press, 1997), pp. 59–73. In recent times some scholars tend to ascribe the composition of 2 Kings 22–23 (on the basis of Deuteronomy [!]) to exilic or postexilic circles who wanted to connect King Josiah with a radical reform of the cult in Jerusalem (see Kratz, *Propheten Israels*, p. 73). See further my *Altes Testament und christliche Kirche: Versuch der Aufklärung* (Springe: zu Klampen, 2006), pp. 59–124.

17. For the Old Testament see Prov. 30:6 (cf. Eccles. 3:14; Sir. 18:6; 42:21).

18. Udo Schnelle, *Einleitung in das Neue Testament*, 3rd ed. (Göttingen: Vandenhoeck & Ruprecht, 1999).

19. Udo Schnelle, *The History and Theology of the New Testament Writings* (Minneapolis, MN: Fortress Press, 1998), p. 279.

20. Schnelle, ibid., p. 279, shows an awareness of this problem when he writes, "[W]e may surmise from 2 Thess. 2.2 that opponents of what came to be mainstream Christianity were claiming Paul's authority in pseudepigraphical writings."

21. Ibid., p. 280.

22. See above, pp. 213–28.

23. Schnelle, *The History and Theology of the New Testament Writings*, p. 326.

24. Against Schnelle see also Marco Frenschkowski, "Pseudepigraphie und Paulusschule: Gedanken zur Verfasserschaft der Deuteropaulinen, insbesondere der Pastoralbriefe," in *Das Ende des Paulus: Historische, theologische und literaturgeschichtliche Aspekte*, ed. Friedrich Wilhelm Horn (Berlin: Walter de Gruyter, 2001), pp. 241–42.

Appendix 4

THE THIRD LETTER TO THE CORINTHIANS: TRANSLATION AND COMMENTARY

1. THE STATE OF RESEARCH

For a long time 3 Corinthians was regarded as an original ingredient of the Acts of Paul, a document that has come down to us in fragments. Indeed, that was the opinion of Walter Bauer, who had early recognized the importance of this letter for the problem of orthodoxy and heresy.[1] But now the publication of a Greek papyrus from the beginning of the third century[2] has confirmed the Greek origin of 3 Corinthians and also shown that a letter of the Corinthians to Paul and the answering letter, 3 Corinthians, were originally independent of the Acts of Paul.[3] In the time of the Syrian church fathers Aphrahat (d. after 345 CE) and Ephraem (306–373) both letters belonged to the Syrian Bible, the Armenian Bible, and to some Latin versions.

2. INTRODUCTION TO 3 CORINTHIANS

In chapter 5 (pp. 109–67) it became clear how aggressively the author of the Pastorals defended himself against Gnostic and Marcionite appropriations of Paul by fabricating letters that he all too effectively passed off as part of Paul's legacy. In 3 Corinthians the pseudepigraphic author solves the same problem of defending against Gnostic and Mar-

243

cionite heresies by picturing Paul pausing in the midst of his missionary work to assail the false teachers.[4] Thereby our author takes up the fight to be found in 1 and 2 Corinthians, and in this way he seeks to put both himself and the second-century Catholic Church in the best possible light. After all, he is defending its creed.

The content of the "Letter of the Corinthians to Paul"[5] must always be drawn upon to interpret 3 Corinthians and the situation that prompted its composition. Indeed, its introduction sets the scene and outlines the agenda for both letters: the heretics Simon and Cleobius[6] had arrived in Corinth saying, (10) "We must not . . . appeal to the prophets, (11) and that God is not almighty, (12) and that there is no resurrection of the flesh, (13) and that the creation of man is not God's (work), (14) and that the Lord has not come in the flesh, nor was he born of Mary, (15) and that the world is not of God, but of the angels."[7] Moreover, the letter ends with an urgent call upon Paul: (16) "Wherefore, brother, make all speed to come hither, that the church of the Corinthians may remain without offense, and the foolishness of these men be made manifest."[8]

The doctrinal issues taken up in the "Letter of the Corinthians to Paul" seems to reflect Marcionite and Gnostic teachings. (On the latter see appendix 1, pp. 213–28.) Bishop Irenaeus, basing himself on reliable sources, provides some information on Marcionite doctrines.

Against All Heresies 1.27.2–3[9]

(2) Marcion of Pontus succeeded Cerdon and amplified his doctrine. He uttered the impudent blasphemy that the God who was proclaimed by the law and the prophets was the author of evil, and desirous of war. He was inconsistent in his teaching and contradicted himself. Jesus, however, who has his origin in the Father who is above the God who made this world, came to Judea at the time when Pontius Pilate presided as procurator of Tiberius Caesar. He was manifested in the form of a man to those who were in Judea. He abolished the prophets and the law and all the works of the God who made this world, whom he also styled as the World-Ruler. Besides all this, he mutilated the Gospel according to Luke, discarding all that is written about the birth of the Lord, and discarding also many of the Lord's discourses containing teaching in which it is most clearly written that the Lord confessed His Father as the Maker of the universe. Marcion persuaded his disciples that he was more truthful than the apostles

who handed down the Gospel, though he gave them not the Gospel, but only a portion of the Gospel. In like manner, he mutilated the Letters of Paul, removing whatever was clearly said by the Apostle about the God who made the world inasmuch as he is the Father of Our Lord Jesus Christ; for the Apostle taught by quoting from the Prophetical Writings that foretold the Lord's coming.

(3) Only those souls that learned his doctrines would attain salvation. The body, on the contrary, since it was taken from earth, is incapable of sharing in salvation. Besides the blasphemy against God, he added this one (thus truly speaking with the devil's mouth and uttering all things contrary to the truth): Cain and those like him, the Sodomites and the Egyptians and those like them, and all the pagans who walked in every mess of wickedness were all saved by the Lord when he descended into the netherworld and they met him, and he took them into his kingdom. But Abel, Enoch, Noah, and the rest of the righteous and the patriarchs who came from Abraham, together with all the prophets and those who pleased God, did not share in salvation, as the Serpent that was in Marcion proclaimed. For, he says, since these people know that their God always tempted them, they had a suspicion that he was tempting them at that time, and they did not go to meet Jesus, nor did they believe in his preaching. As a result their souls remained in the netherworld.

COMMENT

Concerning the reference to Marcionite teachings in the Letter of the Corinthians to Paul: (a) As cited in the letter of the Corinthians, the prohibition against referring to the prophets is directed against the custom of proving the coming of Christ by reference to passages from the prophets, and goes back to Marcion and his disciples. (b) The statement that God is not almighty refers to the God of the Old Testament, who is said to be imperfect and accordingly must be distinguished from the God of love preached by Jesus. For this reason, human beings are said to be not of God's making, but rather creatures of the creator of the world. These doctrines, too, recall Marcion, so that the partly anti-Marcionite thrust of the letter becomes abundantly understandable.

Concerning the reference to Gnostic teachings in the Letter of the Corinthians to Paul: (a) The two items just adduced as referring to Marcionite teaching could as well derive from Gnostics. (b) The denial that Jesus came in the flesh is a typical element of Gnostic doctrine.

In reply to all this, "Paul" composes a letter (3 Corinthians) that has two interrelated goals: it both defends the doctrines of the nascent church catholic and presents Paul, to whom the heretics have laid claim, as a thoroughly orthodox teacher in order to secure him for the church.

3. TRANSLATION AND EXEGESIS OF 3 CORINTHIANS[10]

Verse 1: Prescript

(1) Paul, the prisoner of Jesus Christ in (the midst of) many enmities, to the brothers in Corinth—greeting.

COMMENT

Verse 1: The prescript differs from all the authentic letters of Paul by using the one-part Greek form, but an apparent imitation of Eph. 3:1 and Philemon 1 occurs in the designation "prisoner of Jesus Christ." The reference to the many enmities recalls 2 Cor. 2:4 and Gal. 1:6.

Verses 2–3: Proem

(2) I do not wonder that the teachings of the Evil One are so quickly gaining ground. (3) For my Lord Jesus Christ will quickly come, since those who falsify his words reject him.

COMMENT

Verse 2: The author's lack of surprise that the teachings of the Evil One are so rapidly gaining ground seems at first glance to echo Gal. 1:6; but in fact it expresses the opposite of the historical Paul's astonishment at the Galatians' desertion, for this "Paul" is *not* amazed by what is happening. In the next verse he reports that people who falsify Jesus' words spread the teachings of the Evil One.[11] In the same vein note Polycarp

Phil. 7:1: "Whoever perverts the words[12] of the Lord to suit one's own desires, saying that there is neither resurrection nor judgment, this one is the first-born of Satan." Thus even at the beginning of the letter the author may be referring to a sort of Antichrist (see further below, pp. 249–50).

Verse 3: In almost all of his authentic letters the apostle Paul writes about the imminent coming[13] of the Lord.[14] In this verse the author connects Jesus' swift coming with the appearance of false teachers.[15] Like Polycarp, "Paul" probably has Marcionites and Gnostics in mind.

Verses 4–8: The confession of faith and its interpretation

(4) I passed on to you in the beginning what I also received from the apostles who were before me, who at all times were together with Jesus Christ,

(5) that our Lord Jesus Christ was born of Mary of the seed of David, when the Holy Spirit was sent down from heaven by the Father into her,

(6) **in order that he** come into this world and redeem all *flesh* through his own *flesh*, and **in order that he** raise up from the dead us who are *fleshly*, even as he has shown himself as our example.

(7) And since the man was created by his Father, (8) for this reason he was also sought when he went to his corruption, **in order that he** be made alive by sonship.

COMMENT

Verse 4: The author combines the introductory formula 1 Cor. 15:3a[16] with Acts 1:21, and following Gal. 1:17 sees the origin of the tradition in the apostles—at least those who meet Luke's criterion of having followed Jesus during his lifetime. Needless to say, this item cannot be harmonized with the historical Paul's understanding of the apostolate.

Verse 5: On Jesus' origin from the seed of David see Rom. 1:3. On Mary see later verse 13. As a parallel for the whole verse compare with Aristide *Apology* 15:1: Christ "descended in the Holy Spirit from heaven and became flesh from the virgin."

Verse 6: Jesus' coming into this world has as its goal the redemption of human beings by his flesh (cf. verse 16), thus fulfilling their resurrection hope. "Flesh" here does not designate the perishability of human beings but their individual bodies and the resurrected body of Jesus. On the theological background of this, consider the following excerpt from Bishop Irenaeus on the faith that the church has received from the apostles and their pupils:

Against All Heresies 1.10.1[17]

The Church, though disseminated throughout the world, even to the ends of the earth, received from the apostles and their disciples the faith

in one God the Father Almighty, the Creator of heaven and earth, and the seas and all things that are in them; and

in the one Christ Jesus, the Son of God, who was enfleshed for our salvation; and

in the Holy Spirit, who through the prophets preached
- [1] the Economies,
- [2] the coming,
- [3] the birth from a Virgin,
- [4] the passion,
- [5] the resurrection from the dead, and
- [6] the bodily ascension into heaven of the beloved Son, Christ Jesus our Lord, and
- [7] His coming from heaven in the glory of the Father

"to recapitulate all things,"[18] and to raise up all flesh of the whole human race.

The last part of the last sentence corresponds to the formulation in verse 6 that Jesus Christ will perform the fleshly resurrection. But while 3 Corinthians thinks of the fleshly resurrection of believers, Irenaeus envisions the fleshly resurrection of the whole human race.

Verses 7–8: As humanity is a creation of the Father, the latter has sought all people, made them alive again, and adopted them as his children. Redemption results from creation. This explanation serves as a connecting link with the earlier quoted confession and also as an introduction to what follows.

Verses 9–11: The pre-Christian order of grace

(9) For the GOD who is almighty over all things, who made heaven and earth, first sent the **prophets** to the Jews, that they might be snatched away from their sins; (10) for he had determined to save the house of Israel. Now he sent a portion of the spirit of Christ into the **prophets**, who at many times proclaimed the inerrant worship of GOD. (11) But since the prince who was unrighteous wished himself to be GOD, he influenced them and so fettered all human flesh to desire.

COMMENT

Verse 9: On God almighty who has created heaven and earth see Acts 4:24; 14:15; Ps. 146:6; Exod. 20:11; and the passage from Irenaeus just quoted. Like Irenaeus, the author has a positive view of the prophets, and therefore attacks the false teachers who had supposedly given instruction not to appeal to the prophets.[19] On the role of the prophets, note Theophilus of Antioch *To Autolycus*:

> 2.9: "The men of God, who were possessed by a holy Spirit and became prophets and were inspired and instructed by God himself, were taught by God, and became holy and righteous."[20] Ibid., 3.11: "Now when the people transgressed the law which God had given them, because God is good and merciful and did not want to destroy them he not only gave the law but later sent *prophets from among their brothers* [Deut. 18:15] to *teach and remind* them [John 14:26] of the content of the law and to convert them to repentance so that they would no longer sin."[21]

See also Irenaeus *Apostolic Preaching* 30:

> Hither God sent the prophets through the Holy Spirit. They instructed the people and turned them to the God of their fathers, the Almighty; and they became messengers of the revelation of our Lord Jesus Christ the Son of God.

Verse 10: This view of Christ—that God sends a part of Christ's Spirit into the prophets—is found nowhere else in the Acts of Paul and is no doubt to be attributed to a primitive tradition.

Verse 11: The phrase "the prince... wished himself to be God"[22] is an allusion to the fall of the archangel[23] who thereupon led the prophets astray and thus enslaved all human flesh to lust. Earlier in verse 2 the author had mentioned the pernicious teachings of the Evil One. Later in verse 15 the author describes the fallen angel as the evil figure who falsely claims to be God and who for that reason must be defeated. Thus he is the end-time opponent, like the Antichrist in 2 John 7.

Verses 12–15: The birth of Mary and the sending of the Holy Spirit

(12) GOD the almighty, who is righteous, and did not want to repudiate his own creation, (13) sent the Holy Spirit through fire into Mary the Galilean, (14)[24] (15) in order that through the same flesh by the corruption of which he held sway, the Evil One be conquered, and convinced that he was not GOD.

COMMENT

Verse 12: The almighty God—note the repeated stress on "almighty"—receives the predicate "righteous" in contrast to the prince, whom the author in verse 11 had described as "unrighteous."

Verse 13: On the connection of the Spirit with fire see Acts 2:3; 1 Thess. 5:19. God sends into Mary the Spirit that earlier the prophets had received. The expression "Mary, the Galilean" is unique in early Christianity. Note that the prophets had received only a part of the Spirit while Mary receives it all.

Verse 15: Jesus' appearance undoes the damage described in verse 11 (see further verses 16–18 on this). The last words of the verse ("that he [the Evil One] was not God") point back to verses 2 and 11.

Verses 16–18: The salvation of the flesh by the body of Christ

(16) For by his own **body** Jesus Christ has saved all flesh (17) representing a temple of righteousness in his **body**, (18) through whom we are freed.

COMMENT

Verse 16: Christ's flesh (his body) has saved all human flesh. Through his own resurrection the savior is an example of the resurrection of the dead.

Verse 17: Cf. 1 Cor. 6:19; 2 Cor. 6:16; 2 Clem. 14:2–3.

Verse 18: The liberation undoes the enslavement of all human flesh to desire (verse 11).

Verses 19–21: Polemic against those who deny God the Father to have been the maker of heaven and earth

(19) They are thus not children of righteousness but children of wrath, who reject the providence of God, saying that heaven and earth and all that is in them are not works of the Father, (20) for they have the accursed faith of the serpent. (21) From them turn away, and flee from their teaching![25]

COMMENT

Verse 19: The statement that the opponents are not children of righteousness picks up the remark about the temple of righteousness in verse 17, while the business about denying heaven and earth as the works of the Father points back to verse 9. The author implies that the blessing of God's providence devolves from his having created the earth.

As parallels cf. Theophilus of Antioch *To Autolycus* 1.5:[26] "God cannot be seen by human eyes but is seen and apprehended through his providence and his works." Ibid., 3.9:[27] "We confess a god, but only one, the Founder and Maker and Demiurge of this whole universe. We know that everything is governed by providence, but by him alone."

Verse 20: See Genesis 3 and Irenaeus's excerpt about the Ophites.[28] The serpent, which the author curses, was held in high esteem by Gnostics because it supposedly imparted knowledge. Indeed, the Ophites and the Naassenes[29] named themselves after the serpent.

Verse 21: For the first time the author personally directs his words to the community, urging its members to stay away from the false teachers and their teachings. (In the next verse we will learn that the deniers of the resurrection have addressed their teaching to the congregation ["those who tell you"]). The command to maintain strict separation from the false teachers corresponds to the praxis of the proto-orthodox church of the second century.

Verses 24–25: Polemic against the deniers of the resurrection

(24) As for those who tell you that there is no **resurrection** of the flesh, for them there will be no **resurrection**, (25) who do not believe in him who is thus **risen**.

COMMENT

Verse 24: Cf. 1 Cor. 15:12b. Note, however, that in connection with the resurrection the historical Paul never speaks of "flesh."

Verse 25: The author defines faith as belief in the fleshly Risen One.

Verses 26–27: The comparison with the grain of wheat

(26) For indeed, you Corinthians, they do not know about the sowing of wheat or the other seeds, that they are cast naked into the ground and when they have perished below are raised again by the will of God as a body and clothed, (27) so that the body which was cast off (into the earth) is not only raised up, but also abundantly blessed.

COMMENT

Verse 26: Cf. 1 Cor. 15:36–38; 2 Cor. 5:3. See also 1 Clem. 23–24.

Verse 27: In this verse the author displays a greater freedom in construing Paul's statements in 1 Corinthians 15 than was evident in the previous verse. Now the dead and the risen body are not, as in 1 Cor. 15:35–49, radically different from one another. Rather, the risen body finds itself in a better state than the dead body. Indeed, the author seems to claim continuity between the earthly and the raised body. Two reasons account for this emendation of the historical Paul's statements: not only did the opponents flatly reject bodily resurrection, but the leaders of the church catholic felt it necessary to assert a binding authority that only the bodily resurrection, literally understood, could furnish.

Verses 28–31: The story of Jonah from the Old Testament as proof for the certainty of the resurrection

(28) If it is necessary that we derive the similitude not only from the seeds, but from nobler bodies, (29) know that Jonah the son of Amathios, when he would not preach in Niniveh, but fled, was swallowed by a whale, (30) and after three days and three nights God heard Jonah's prayer out of the deepest abyss, and no part of him was damaged, not even a hair or an eyelid. (31) How much more, O you of little faith, will he raise you up who have believed in Christ Jesus as he himself was raised up?

COMMENT

Verse 28: This comparison provides an even better explanation than the previous one.
   Verse 29: See Matt. 12:40.
   Verse 30: See Jonah 2:3.
   Verse 31: See Rom. 6:4.

Verse 32: The story of Elisha from the Old Testament as proof for the corporal integrity of the raised bodies

(32) And if, when a corpse was thrown by the children of Israel upon the bones of the prophet Elisha, the man's body rose up, so you also who have been cast upon the body and the Spirit of the Lord shall rise up on that day with your flesh sound.[30]

COMMENT

Verse 32: Cf. 2 Kings 13:21; Luke 24:39. On the adjective "sound"[31] note the following excerpt from Theophilus's *To Autolycus* 2.26: "[The human being] has virtually been shattered so that in the resurrection he may be found sound, I mean spotless and righteous and immortal."[32] The author of 3 Corinthians again interprets an Old Testament story from a Christological perspective. Christians are to be all but literally thrown upon the bones of Christ, and will rise in sound—that is undamaged—flesh.

Verses 34–40: Personal matters.
Conditional curse and wish of peace

(34) Now *if* you receive anything else, do not cause me trouble; (35) for I have these fetters on my hand that I may gain Christ, and his marks in my body that I may attain to the resurrection from the dead. (36) And *if* anyone abides by the rule which he received through the blessed prophets and the holy gospel, he shall receive a reward. (37) But *if* anyone turns aside from this, there is a fire for him and for those who go before him in the way, (38) since they are godless people, a generation of vipers; (39) from these turn away in the power of the Lord, (40) and peace will be with you. Amen.

COMMENT

Verse 34: The reference to Gal. 6:17a suggests the topicality of and the reason, indeed the necessity, for 3 Corinthians.

Verse 35: Cf. Phil. 3:8; Gal. 6:17b. On the resurrection of the dead as an object of hope see Phil. 3:11.

Verse 36: Cf. Gal. 6:16; 1 Cor. 3:14. Note the importance of the role of the Old Testament prophets—a theme that permeates 3 Corinthians. The rule alluded to is the confession of the resurrection of the flesh. Everyone abiding in it will be rewarded, that is, raised from the dead in the flesh.

Verses 37–38: For the motives see Matt. 3:7. These verses depict the future judgment that awaits those who repudiate the resurrection.

Verses 39–40: On the command of separation see verse 21. On the "power of the Lord" compare with 1 Cor. 5:4. On the wish of peace see 2 John 3. "Amen" at the end emphasizes the urgency of the letter. See similarly Gal. 6:18.

NOTES

1. Walter Bauer, *Orthodoxy and Heresy in Earliest Christianity* (Philadelphia: Fortress Press, 1971), pp. 39–40.

2. M. Testuz, *Papyrus Bodmer X–XII* (Cologne: Bibliotheca Bodmeriana, 1959), pp. 33–45. See also Willy Rordorf, *Lex Orandi—Lex Credendi* (Freiburg: Universitätsverlag, 1993), pp. 429–30.

3. "It is most probable that these letters were not invented by the author of the *Acts of Paul*, but are a document written earlier in the 2d century and later incorporated into the *Acts of Paul*" (Helmut Koester, *Introduction to the New Testament*, 2nd ed., 2 vols. [New York: Walter de Gruyter, 1995–2000], 2:302).

4. See Antti Marjanen and Petri Luomanen, eds., *A Companion to Second-Century Christian "Heretics"* (Leiden: Brill, 2005) and especially the contributions by Birger A. Pearson ("Basilides the Gnostic," ibid., pp. 1–31), Michael A. Williams ("Sethianism," ibid., pp. 32–63), Ismo Dunderberg ("The School of Valentinus," ibid., pp. 64–99), and Heikki Räisänen ("Marcion," ibid., pp. 100–24).

5. The pseudepigraphic author was inspired to compose a "Letter of the Corinthians to Paul" by the historical Paul's reference to a real letter from the Corinthians that he had taken pains to answer (see 1 Cor. 7:1: "Concerning what you wrote, . . ."). I leave open the question of whether 3 Corinthians ever circulated independently of the "Letter of the Corinthians to Paul," and use the latter heuristically for an explanation of 3 Corinthians.

6. Here, as in Justin *1 Apology* 26.3 and the Pseudo-Clementines, Simon appears as an arch-heretic. The author of the *Epistle of the Apostles*, which probably originated in Egypt, speaks of "Simon and Cerinthus" as a pair of heretics in the same way as Simon and Cleobius are introduced here. At any rate, the challenging of the heretics continues in the letter of the Corinthians, which in the second century derives Gnostics and Marcionites from Simon, the first heretic. On the *Epistle of the Apostles* see further my *The Resurrection of Christ: A Historical Inquiry* (Amherst, NY: Prometheus Books, 2004), pp. 134–37.

7. Translation based on *New Testament Apocrypha*, revised edition of the Collection initiated by Edgar Hennecke and ed. Wilhelm Schneemelcher, English translation ed. R. McL. Wilson, vol. 2, *Writings Related to the Apostles, Apocalypses, and Related Subjects* (Louisville, KY: Westminster John Knox Press, 1992), p. 254.

8. Ibid.

9. Translation after *St. Irenaeus of Lyons against the Heresies*, translated and annotated by Dominic J. Unger with further revisions by John J. Dillon, vol. 1, bk. 1 (New York: Paulist Press, 1992), pp. 91–92.

10. Translation based on my *Heretics: The Other Side of Early Christianity*

(Louisville, KY: Westminster John Knox Press, 1996), pp. 223–24, and *New Testament Apocrypha*, pp. 255–56. Emendations result from my own further analysis of the Greek text.

11. On the falsification of Jesus' words see also Bishop Dionysius of Corinth in Eusebius *Church History* 4.23.12. See above, p. 77.

12. In Greek, *logia*.

13. In Greek, *eleusis*. Cf. Acts 7:52.

14. See Rom. 13:11; 1 Cor. 15:51–52; Phil. 1:6; 1 Thess. 4:13–17.

15. On the connection of false teachers with the Second Coming of Jesus see Mark 13:21–22; 2 Thess. 2:1–3; 1 John 2:18; 1 Tim. 4:1; 2 Tim. 3:1; 4:3.

16. A similar introductory formula can be found in 1 Cor. 11:23a.

17. Translation after *St. Irenaeus of Lyons against the Heresies*, pp. 48–49.

18. Eph. 1:10. Since this is a favorite passage of Irenaeus (see further *St. Irenaeus of Lyons against the Heresies*, pp. 185–86n11) I assume that he added it to the tradition which consists of seven items.

19. See *Epistle of the Corinthians to Paul* 10 (above, p. 244).

20. Translation after *Theophilus of Antioch: Ad Autolycum*, text and translation by Robert M. Grant (Oxford: Clarendon Press, 1970), p. 39.

21. Ibid., p. 115.

22. My translation is based on the Latin version. "Prince" translates the Latin *princeps*.

23. 2 Enoch 29:4ff attributes the fall of the devil to his self-exaltation above God, for he has set his throne higher than the clouds.

24. Verse 14 ("who believed with all her heart, and she received the Holy Spirit in her body that Jesus might enter into the world) does not belong to the oldest text.

25. Verses 22–23 ("For you are not sons of disobedience but of the most dearly beloved church. Therefore the time of the resurrection is proclaimed") do not belong to the earliest text.

26. Translation after *Theophilus of Antioch: Ad Autolycum*, p. 7.

27. Ibid., pp. 111, 113.

28. From the Greek, *ophis* (serpent) in Irenaeus *Against all Heresies* 1.30. Cf. verse 9 with ibid., 1.30.11; verse 10 with ibid. 1.30.6; verse 11 with ibid., 1.30.13; verse 12 with ibid., 1.30.6

29. From the Hebrew, *nachasch* (serpent).

30. Verse 33 ("further Elijah, the prophet took the son of the widow in his arms and awoke him from the dead [1 Kings 17:17–24]; how much more will Jesus Christ wake you with an uncorrupted body on that day, just as he himself arose from the dead") is secondary.

31. In Greek, *hygiês*. Other scholars translate it by "whole," which seems a little too pale.

32. Translation after *Theophilus of Antioch: Ad Autolycum*, p. 69.

Appendix 5

THE INTOLERANT GOSPEL[1]

The Early Christian message announces that God has brought to pass a new epoch. It began with the coming of his son into this world, culminated provisionally in the latter's resurrection from the dead, and was supposed to reach its fulfillment in his imminent Second Coming. The gospel—its literal translation is "Good News"—has Jesus Christ as its center. The salvation or eternal damnation of individual human beings depends on whether they believe or do not believe in him. "Whoever believes and is baptized will be saved. But whoever does not believe will be condemned":[2] this is the clear message of the risen Jesus at the end of Mark's gospel, the first of the four canonical accounts to be written.

But how soon the Good News developed into Threatening News— that is, if the offer of salvation was turned down! Church leaders soon equated right belief with obedience. They projected onto the screen of heaven a social fabric based on subordination and increasingly shaped by a culture of suppression. The canonical status of the New Testament writings—henceforth an eternal norm for the church—has radically blurred the vision of its followers, inhibiting their ability to recognize that all these texts emerged from controversies whose marks they still show.

The Christian church benefited from the destruction of Jerusalem by the Romans in 70 CE, and until the end of the first century it spread rapidly within the Roman Empire. Indeed, so rapid was its continued growth that a little more than two and a half centuries later this new and formerly outlawed faith became the official religion of the empire. Judaism laid the groundwork for Christianity's enormous success by

From *Free Inquiry* (February–March 2006): 49–50. Reprinted with permission.

endowing the church with the high ethical standards of the Old Testament. What an irony of history that the Christian religion showed so little gratitude to her Jewish mother as to relegate her along with other "enemies" of the Gospel to the realm of darkness. Yet in so doing she did no more than certify her inheritance, for the legacy of Israel included the doctrine of election and with it the exclusive monotheism that judged all other kinds of worship as service to idols.

As an integral part of their missionary efforts these enthusiastic Christians introduced First Commandment intolerance ("I am Yahweh, your God, you shall have no other gods besides me") into the Greco-Roman world. Oddly enough, it was their own religious tolerance and inclusiveness that afforded the competing Hellenistic religions but little chance of asserting themselves against the Christians. Acquiescence, far from being an antidote against the Christian claim of exclusive revelation, allowed the church to take advantage of Rome's laissez-faire politics in religious matters and thus to expand relentlessly.

In this context it is worth noting that the generally exaggerated accounts of Roman persecutions of Christians were limited in scope and severity. Lusting after martyrdom, many Christians in effect condemned themselves, and many a Roman governor failed to do them the favor of execution. And once they had begun participating in the political power structure, Christian bishops guided the governmental sword against pagans, heretics, and Jews to an extent that far exceeded the intensity of previous persecutions against their coreligionists. This intolerance remained in force until modern times.

Contrary to the popular thesis that Luther's understanding of freedom included tolerance, there can be no doubt about the great reformer's intolerance toward Catholics, Jews, Turks, Gentiles, and Protestant heretics. Rather, Humanists and Christian minorities first raised the call for tolerance. And despite the initial lack of success these groups achieved, they finally succeeded *against* the will of both the Roman and Reformed churches. To be sure, the church's resistance against tolerance was, historically speaking, a necessity. For the overall thrust of Holy Scripture, both the Old and New Testaments, is to promote God and his reign and to silence all dissenting voices.

And while "peace" is a central theme in Holy Scripture, the aggressive side of Christian faith is all but certainly responsible for the many bloody wars started in and from Christian Europe. A key issue, of course, is how that peace is to be achieved. Here the New Testament message is as crystal clear as it is—at least by modern standards—indefensible: Jesus Christ himself will return to carry out God's will, and by force, empowered by the authority of his resurrection, will establish his father's kingdom of peace on Earth. On the basis of this promise, believers in Jesus Christ have at all times claimed access to that power and used it with a good conscience against those they perceive to be enemies of the Gospel.

Indeed, intolerance seems to an inherent, even necessary ingredient of the Christian religion. The noted theologian Karl Barth says it quite openly: "No sentence is more dangerous or revolutionary than that God is One and there is no other like Him. Let this sentence be uttered in such a way that it is heard and grasped, and at once 450 prophets of Baal are always in fear of their lives. There is no more room now for what the recent past called toleration. Beside God there are only His creatures or false gods, and beside faith in Him there are religions only as religions of superstition, error, and finally irreligion." Clearly it would be misleading to think that freedom in general and freedom of religion specifically are the consequences of the Christian message. Indeed, the religious tradition that claims as its founder the Prince of Peace has through the centuries shown an inability to endure other religious viewpoints. And this is as true today as ever, despite the protestations of church leaders who would like to have it appear otherwise in order to retain their welcome within the institutions of power that comprise the secular state.

In reality, neither Christian theology nor the church can champion freedom of religion without betraying a considerable degree of hypocrisy. For tolerance requires an unconditional acknowledgment of the freedom and dignity of human beings without recourse to God. Yet the jealous Yahweh of the Bible who demands unconditional obedience can never approve of such liberal affirmations.

NOTES

1. This essay was first published in German under the title "Intolerantes Evangelium" in *Die Welt am Sonntag* (December 5, 2004). My thanks go to Alan Posener of *Die Welt am Sonntag* for allowing me to publish it in English.

2. Mark 16:16.

SELECT BIBLIOGRAPHY

Baier, Thomas. *Werk und Wirkung Varros im Spiegel seiner Zeitgenossen: Von Cicero bis Ovid.* Stuttgart: F. Steiner, 1997.

Bainton, Roland H., ed. *Concerning Heretics: Whether They Are to Be Persecuted and How They Are to Be Treated: A Collection of the Opinions of Learned Men Both Ancient and Modern: An Anonymous Work Attributed to Sebastian Castellio.* New York: Columbia University Press, 1935.

Barbers, Meinulf. *Toleranz bei Sebastian Franck.* Bonn: Ludwig Röhrscheid Verlag, 1964.

Barclay, John M. G. *Jews in the Mediterranean Diaspora from Alexander to Trajan (323 BCE–177 CE).* Edinburgh: T & T Clark, 1996.

Barrow, R. H. *Prefect and Emperor: The Relationes of Symmachus A.D. 384.* Oxford: Clarendon Press, 1973.

Bassler, Jouette M. *1 Timothy, 2 Timothy, Titus.* Nashville, TN: Abingdon Press, 1996.

Bauckham, Richard J. *Jude, 2 Peter.* Waco, TX: Word Books, 1983.

———. *Jude and the Relatives of Jesus in the Early Church.* Edinburgh: T & T Clark, 1990.

———. *Jude, 2 Peter.* Dallas: Word Publishing, 1990.

Bauer, Walter. *Orthodoxy and Heresy in Earliest Christianity.* Philadelphia: Fortress Press, 1971.

Bauer, Walter, William F. Arndt, and F. Wilbur Gingrich. *A Greek-English Lexicon of the New Testament and Other Early Christian Literature.* 2nd ed. Chicago: University of Chicago Press, 1979.

Bettenson, Henry. *St. Augustine Concerning the City of God against the Pagans.* New York: Penguin Books, Pelican Books, 1972.

Bickerman, Elias. *The God of the Maccabees: Studies on the Meaning and Origin of the Maccabean Revolt.* Leiden: Brill, 1979.

Bleicken, Jochen. *Verfassungs- und Sozialgeschichte des Römischen Kaiserreiches.* Vol. 2, 2nd ed. Paderborn: Schöningh, 1981.

Bowersock, G. W. *Martyrdom and Rome.* Cambridge: Cambridge University Press, 1995.

Brown, Peter. *Authority and the Sacred: Aspects of the Christianisation of the Roman World.* Cambridge: University Press, 1995.

Brox, Norbert. *Die Pastoralbriefe.* Regensburg: Friedrich Pustet, 1969.

———. *Falsche Verfasserangaben. Zur Erklärung der frühchristlichen Pseudepigraphie.* Stuttgart: Katholisches Bibelwerk, 1975.

———, ed. *Pseudepigraphie in der heidnischen und jüdischen Antike.* Darmstadt: Wissenschaftliche Buchgesellschaft, 1977.

261

Bultmann, Rudolf. *Theology of the New Testament*. 2 vols. New York: Charles Scribner's Sons, 1951, 1955.

———. *Primitive Christianity: In Its Contemporary Setting*. New York: Meridian Books, Living Age Books, 1956.

———. *Existence and Faith*. New York: Meridian Books, Living Age Books, 1960.

———. *Faith and Understanding I*. Edited with an introduction by Robert W. Funk. New York: Harper & Row, 1969.

———. *The Gospel of John: A Commentary*. Oxford: Basil Blackwell, 1971.

———. *The New Testament and Mythology and Other Basic Writings*. Selected, edited, and translated by Schubert M. Ogden. Philadelphia: Fortress Press, 1984.

Burckhardt, Jacob. *Reflections on History*. London: George Allen & Unwin, 1943.

Butterweck, Christel. "Martyriumssucht." In *Der Alten Kirche?* Tübingen: J. C. B. Mohr/Paul Siebeck, 1995.

Campenhausen, Hans von. *Polycarp von Smyrna und die Pastoralbriefe*. Heidelberg: Carl Winter Universitätsverlag, 1951.

———. *Tradition and Life in the Church: Essays and Lectures in Church History*. London: Collins, 1968.

———. *Ecclesiastical Authority and Spiritual Power in the Church of the First Three Centuries*. Stanford, CA: Stanford University Press, 1969.

———. *The Formation of the Christian Bible*. Philadelphia: Fortress Press, 1972.

Chadwick, Henry. *Lessing's Theological Writings: Selections in Translation with an Introductory Essay*. Stanford, CA: Stanford University Press, 1957.

———, ed. Origen. *Contra Celsum*. Translated with an introduction and notes, reprinted with corrections. Cambridge: University Press, 1965.

Charlesworth, James H., ed. *The Old Testament Pseudepigrapha*. Vol. 2, *Expansions of the "Old Testament" and Legends, Wisdom and Philosophical Literature, Prayers, Psalms, and Odes, Fragments of Lost Judeo-Hellenistic Works*. New York: Doubleday, 1985.

Collins, John J. *Between Athens and Jerusalem: Jewish Identity in the Hellenistic Diaspora*. 2nd ed. Grand Rapids, MI: W. B. Eerdmans, 2000.

Collins, Raymond F. *1 & 2 Timothy and Titus: A Commentary*. Louisville, KY: Westminster John Knox Press, 2002.

Colpe, Carsten. *Die religionsgeschichtliche Schule. Darstellung und Kritik ihres Bildes vom gnostischen Erlösermythos*. Göttingen: Vandenhoeck & Ruprecht, 1961.

Conzelmann, Hans. *Theologie als Schriftauslegung*. Munich: Christian Kaiser, 1974.

Dibelius, Martin, and Hans Conzelmann. *The Pastoral Epistles: A Commentary on the Pastoral Epistles*. Philadelphia: Fortress Press, 1972.

Easton, Burton Scott. *The Pastoral Epistles: Introduction, Translation, Commentary and Word Studies*. New York: Charles Scribner's Sons, 1947.

Ehrman, Bart. *The New Testament: A Historical Introduction to the Early Christian Writings*. 3rd ed. New York: Oxford University Press, 2004.

Feldmeier, Reinhard. *Der erste Brief des Petrus*. Leipzig: Evangelische Verlagsanstalt, 2005.

Feuerbach, Ludwig. *The Essence of Christianity*. Amherst, NY: Prometheus Books, 1989.

Frend, W. H. C. *Martyrdom and Persecution in the Early Church: A Study of a Conflict from the Maccabees to Donatus*. Garden City, NY: Doubleday, Anchor Books, 1967.

Fritz, Kurt von., ed. *Pseudepigrapha*. Bern: A. Francke, 1972.

Gibbon, Edward. *On Christianity*. Amherst, NY: Prometheus Books, 1991.

Harrington, Daniel J. "Jude and 2 Peter." In Donald P. Senior and Daniel J. Harrington, *1 Peter, Jude, and 2 Peter*, 159–299. Collegeville, MN: Liturgical Press, 2003.

Hedrick, Charles W., ed. *Nag Hammadi Codices XI, XII, XIII*. Leiden: Brill, 1990.

Hengel, Martin. *Judaism and Hellenism: Studies in Their Encounter in Palestine during the Early Hellenistic Period*. 2 vols. Philadelphia: Fortress Press, 1974.

———. *Crucifixion in the Ancient World*. Philadelphia: Fortress Press, 1977.

———. *Jews, Greeks and Barbarians: Aspects of the Hellenization of Judaism in the Pre-Christian Period*. Philadelphia: Fortress Press, 1980.

———. *The Johannine Question*. Philadelphia: Trinity Press International, 1989.

Hughes, Frank Witt. *Early Christian Rhetoric and 2 Thessalonians*. Sheffield: Sheffield Academic Press, 1989.

Hurd, John C. *The Earlier Letters of Paul—and Other Studies*. Frankfurt: Peter Lang, 1998.

Janssen, Martina. *Unter falschem Namen: Eine kritische Forschungsbilanz urchristlicher Pseudepigraphie*. Frankfurt: Peter Lang, 2003.

Jaspers, Karl. *Der philosophische Glaube*. Munich: R. Piper & Co. Verlag, 1948.

Jewett, Robert. *Christian Tolerance: Paul's Message to the Modern Church*. Philadelphia: Westminster Press, 1982.

———. *The Thessalonian Correspondence: Pauline Rhetoric and Millenarian Piety*. Philadelphia: Fortress Press, 1986.

Kaufmann, Walter. *The Portable Nietzsche*. New York: Viking Press, 1954.

King, Karen L. *The Gospel of Mary of Magdala*. Santa Rosa, CA: Polebridge Press, 2003.

———. *What Is Gnosticism?* Cambridge, MA: Harvard University Press, 2003.

Klein, Richard. *Der Streit um den Victoriaaltar. Die dritte Relatio des Symmachus und die Briefe 17, 18 und 57 des Mailänder Bischofs Ambrosius*. Darmstadt: Wissenschaftliche Buchgesellschaft, 1972.

———. *Symmachus. Eine tragische Gestalt des ausgehenden Heidentums*. Darmstadt: Wissenschaftliche Buchgesellschaft, 1986.

Koester, Helmut. *Introduction to the New Testament*. 2 vols. 2nd ed. New York: Walter de Gruyter, 1995, 2000.

Koschorke, Klaus. *Die Polemik der Gnostiker gegen das kirchliche Christentum*. Leiden: Brill, 1978.

Kötting, Bernhard. *Religionsfreiheit und Toleranz im Altertum*. Opladen: Westdeutscher Verlag, 1977.

Kratz, Reinhard Gregor. *Die Propheten Israels*. Munich: C. H. Beck, 2002.

———. *The Composition of the Narrative Books of the Old Testament*. London: T & T Clark, 2005.

Lang, Bernhard. *Monotheism and the Prophetic Minority: An Essay in Biblical History and Sociology*. Sheffield: Almond Press, 1983.

———. "Segregation and Intolerance." In *What the Bible Really Says*, edited by Morton Smith and R. Joseph Hoffmann, 115–35. Amherst, NY: Prometheus Books, 1989.

Layton, Bentley, ed. *Nag Hammadi Codex II, 2–7*. 2 vols. Leiden: Brill, 1989.

Lindemann, Andreas. "Zum Abfassungszweck des Zweiten Thessalonicherbriefes." *Zeitschrift für die neutestamentliche Wissenschaft* 68 (1977): 35–47.

———. *Paulus im ältesten Christentum: Das Bild des Apostels und die Rezeption paulinischer Theologie in der frühchristlichen Literatur bis Marcion*. Tübingen: J. C. B. Mohr/Paul Siebeck, 1979.

———. *Apostel und Lehrer der Kirche: Studien zu Paulus und zum frühen Paulusverständnis*. Tübingen: J. C. B. Mohr/Paul Siebeck, 1999.

Lüdemann, Gerd. *Opposition to Paul in Early Christianity*. Minneapolis, MN: Fortress Press, 1989.

———. *Heretics: The Other Side of Early Christianity*. Louisville, KY: Westminster John Knox Press, 1996.

———. *The Unholy in Holy Scripture: The Dark Side of the Bible*. Louisville, KY: Westminster John Knox Press, 1997.

———. *Paul: The Founder of Christianity*. Amherst, NY: Prometheus Books, 2002.

———. *Primitive Christianity: A Survey of Recent Studies and Some New Proposals*. London: T & T Clark, 2003.

———. *The Resurrection of Christ: A Historical Inquiry*. Amherst, NY: Prometheus Books, 2004.

———. *The Acts of the Apostles: What Really Happened in the Earliest Days of the Church*. Amherst, NY: Prometheus Books, 2005.

Lüdemann, Gerd, and Martina Janssen. *Suppressed Prayers: Gnostic Spirituality in Early Christianity*. Harrisburg, PA: Trinity Press International, 1998.

Malherbe, Abraham J. "The Inhospitality of Diotrephes." In *God's Christ and His People: Studies in Honour of Nils Alstrup Dahl*, edited by Jacob Jervell and Wayne A. Meeks, 222–32. Oslo: Universitetsforl, 1977.

———. *The Letters to the Thessalonians: A New Translation with Introduction and Commentary*. New York: Doubleday, 2000.

Marjanen, Antti, ed. *Was There a Gnostic Religion?* Helsinki: Finnish Exegetical Society, 2005.

Marjanen, Antti, and Petri Luomanen, eds. *A Companion to Second-Century Christian "Heretics."* Leiden: Brill, 2005.

Markschies, Christoph. *Gnosis: An Introduction*. London: T & T Clark, 2003.

Marrou, Henri-Irénéé. *A History of Education in Antiquity*. New York: New American Library, Mentor Books, 1964.

Menken, Maarten J. J. *2 Thessalonians*. London: Routledge, 1994.

Merz, Annette. *Die fiktive Selbstauslegung des Paulus. Intertextuelle Studien zur Intention und Rezeption der Paulusbriefe*. Göttingen: Vandenhoeck & Ruprecht, 2004.

Meyer, Eduard. *Ursprung und Anfänge des Christentums*. Vol. 2, *Die Entwicklung des Judentums und Jesus von Nazareth*. Stuttgart: Klett-Cotta, 1922.

Müller, Ulrich B. *Zur frühchristlichen Theologiegeschichte*. Gütersloh: Gerd Mohn, 1975.

Parrott, Douglas M., ed. *Nag Hammadi Codices V, 2–5 and VI with Papyrus Berolinensis 8502, 1 and 4*. Leiden: Brill, 1979.

Paulsen, Henning. *Der Zweite Petrusbrief und der Judasbrief*. Göttingen: Vandenhoeck & Ruprecht, 1992.

Pearson, Birger A., ed. *Nag Hammadi Codices IX and X*. Leiden: Brill, 1981.

———. *Nag Hammadi Codex VII*. Leiden: Brill, 1996.

———. *The Emergence of the Christian Religion: Essays on Early Christianity*. Harrisburg, PA: Trinity Press International, 1997.

Richard, Earl J. *First and Second Thessalonians*. Collegeville, MN: Liturgical Press, Michael Glazier Books, 1995.

Robinson, James M., ed. *The Beginnings of Dialectical Theology*. Vol. 1. Richmond, VA: John Knox Press, 1968.

———, gen. ed. *The Nag Hammadi Library in English*. 3rd ed., completely revised. Leiden: Brill, 1988.

Rordorf, Willy. *Lex Orandi—Lex Credendi*. Freiburg and Schweiz: Universitätsverlag, 1993.

Rudolph, Kurt. *Gnosis: The Nature and History of Gnosticism*. San Francisco: Harper & Row, 1983.

Sanders, E. P. *Paul and Palestinian Judaism: A Comparison of Patterns of Religion*. Philadelphia: Fortress Press, 1977.

Schnackenburg, Rudolf. *The Johannine Epistles: Translation and Commentary*. New York: Crossroad, 1992.

Schneemelcher, Wilhelm, ed. *New Testament Apocrypha*. Revised edition. English translation edited by R. McL. Wilson. *I: Gospels and Related Writings. II: Writings Related to the Apostles, Apocalypses and Related Subjects*. Louisville, KY: Westminster John Knox Press, 1991, 1992.

Schnelle, Udo. *Antidocetic Christology in John: An Investigation of the Place of the Fourth Gospel in the Johannine School*. Minneapolis, MN: Fortress Press, 1992.

———. *The History and Theology of the New Testament Writings*. Minneapolis, MN: Fortress Press, 1998.

Schoedel, William R. *Ignatius of Antioch: A Commentary on the Letters of Ignatius of Antioch*. Philadelphia: Fortress Press, 1985.

Schopenhauer, Arthur. *Parerga and Paralipomena: Short Philosophical Essays.* Vol. 2. Oxford: Oxford University Press, 1974.

Schürer, Emil. *The History of the Jewish People in the Age of Jesus Christ (175 B.C.–A.D. 135).* 3 vols. Revised and edited by Geza Vermes, Fergus Millar, and Matthew Black. Edinburgh: T & T Clark, 1973–87.

Sheils, W. J., ed. *Persecution and Toleration: Papers Read at the Twenty-second Summer Meeting and the Twenty-third Winter Meeting of the Ecclesiastical History Society.* Oxford: Basil Blackwell, 1984.

Sherwin-White, A. N. *The Letters of Pliny: A Historical and Social Commentary.* Oxford: Clarendon Press, 1966.

Söding, Thomas, ed. *Ist der Glaube Feind der Freiheit? Die neue Debatte um den Monotheismus.* Freiburg: Herder, 2003.

Speyer, Wolfgang. *Die literarische Fälschung im Altertum. Ein Versuch ihrer Deutung.* Munich: Beck, 1971.

Stanton, Graham N., and Guy G. Stroumsa, eds. *Tolerance and Intolerance in Early Judaism and Christianity.* Cambridge: Cambridge University Press, 1998.

Stowers, Stanley K. "Greeks Who Sacrifice and Those Who Do Not: Toward an Anthropology of Greek Religion." In *The Social World of the First Christians: Essays in Honor of Wayne A. Meeks,* edited by L. Michael White and O. Larry Yarbrough, 293–333. Philadelphia: Fortress Press, 1995.

Strecker, Georg. *The Johannine Letters: A Commentary on 1, 2, and 3 John.* Minneapolis, MN: Fortress Press, 1996.

————. *Theology of the New Testament.* New York: Walter de Gruyter, 2000.

Testuz, M. *Papyrus Bodmer X–XII.* Cologne: Bibliotheca Bodmeriana, 1959.

Theissen, Gerd. *Fortress Introduction to the New Testament.* Minneapolis, MN: Fortress Press, 2003.

Trilling, Wolfgang. *Der zweite Brief an die Thessalonicher.* Neukirchen-Vluyn: Neukirchener Verlag, 1980.

Veijola, Timo. "Wahrheit und Intoleranz nach Deuteronomium 13." *Zeitschrift für Theologie und Kirche* 92 (1995): 287–314.

Vielhauer, Philipp. *Geschichte der urchristlichen Literatur: Einleitung in das Neue Testament, die Apokryphen und die Apostolischen Väter.* Berlin: Walter de Gruyter, 1975.

Vögtle, Anton. *Der Judasbrief / Der 2. Petrusbrief.* Freiburg: Herder, 1994.

Watson, Duane Frederick. *Invention, Arrangement, and Style: Rhetorical Criticism of Jude and 2 Peter.* Atlanta, GA: Scholars Press, 1988.

Weder, Hans. "Gesetz und Sünde. Gedanken zu einem qualitativen Sprung im Denken des Paulus." *New Testament Studies* 31 (1985): 357–76.

Wehnert, Jürgen. *Die Reinheit des "christlichen Gottesvolkes" aus Juden und Heiden: Studien zum historischen und theologischen Hintergrund des sogenannten Aposteldekrets.* Göttingen: Vandenhoeck & Ruprecht, 1997.

Wellhausen, Julius. *Prolegomena to the History of Ancient Israel.* New York: Meridian Books, 1957.

Wilken, Robert L. *The Christians as the Romans Saw Them*. New Haven, CT: Yale University Press, 1984.

Williams, Michael Allen. *Rethinking "Gnosticism": An Argument for Dismantling a Dubious Category*. Princeton, NJ: Princeton University Press, 1996.

Wrede, William. *Die Echtheit des zweiten Thessalonicherbriefs untersucht*. Leipzig: J. C. Hinrich'sche Buchhandlung, 1903.

———. *Paul*. Boston: American Unitarian Association, 1908.

Young, Frances M. *The Theology of the Pastoral Letters*. Cambridge: Cambridge University Press, 1994.

Index of Biblical Passages
Old Testament

Index of Modern Authors